Disaster Risk Reduction for Economic Growth and Livelihood

T0300454

The prevalence of natural disasters in recent years has highlighted the importance of preparing adequately for disasters and dealing efficiently with their consequences.

This book addresses how countries can enhance their resilience against natural disasters and move towards economic growth and sustainable development. Covering a wide range of issues, it shows how well-thought-out measures can be applied to minimize the impacts of disasters in a variety of situations. Starting with the need for coping with a rapidly changing global environment, the book goes on to demonstrate ways to strengthen awareness of the effectiveness of preventive measures, including in the reconstruction phase. The book also covers the roles played by different actors as well as tools and technologies for improved disaster risk reduction. It focuses on a variety of case studies from across Asia, Africa and Latin America, drawing out lessons that can be applied internationally.

This book will be of great interest to professionals in disaster management, including national governments, donors, communities/citizens, NGOs and the private sector. It will also be a highly valuable resource for students and researchers in disaster management and policy, development studies and economics.

Ian Davis, an architect, is a Visiting Professor in Disaster Risk Management in Copenhagen, Kyoto, Lund and Oxford Brookes Universities. He works in Disaster Risk Reduction and Recovery. In 1996 he received the UN Sasakawa Award for his contribution to Disaster Prevention.

Kae Yanagisawa is Vice President of Japan International Cooperation Agency (JICA). She has a long-term career in international development at JICA and the United Nations Development Programme (UNDP). She gained knowledge and experience in disaster risk reduction while she was leading the disaster relief operations of JICA. She is a Visiting Professor in development cooperation at Meiji University, Japan.

Kristalina Georgieva is Vice President of the European Commission. From 2010 to 2014, she was the European Commissioner for International Cooperation, Humanitarian Aid and Crisis Response. Before joining the European Commission, she held various positions at the World Bank, including Director for Sustainable Development and Vice President and Corporate Secretary.

Routledge explorations in environmental studies

Disaster Risk Reduction for Economic Growth and Livelihood

Investing in resilience and development

Edited by Ian Davis, Kae Yanagisawa and Kristalina Georgieva

Routledge
Taylor & Francis Group

LONDON AND NEW YORK

First published 2015
by Routledge
2 Park Square, Milton Park, Abingdon, Oxfordshire OX14 4RN

and by Routledge
711 Third Avenue, New York, NY 10017

First issued in paperback 2016

Routledge is an imprint of the Taylor & Francis Group, an informa business

British Library Cataloguing-in-Publication Data
A catalogue record for this book is available from the British Library.

Library of Congress Cataloging-in-Publication Data
Disaster risk reduction for economic growth and livelihood : investing in resilience and development / edited by Ian Davis, Kae Yanagisawa and Kristalina Georgieva.
pages cm
1. Disasters--Economic aspects. 2. Hazardous geographic environments--Economic aspects. 3. Natural disasters--Planning. 4. Emergency management--Planning. 5. Sustainable development.
I. Davis, Ian, 1960- II. Yanagisawa, Kae. III. Georgieva, Kristalina.
HC79.D45D57 2015
363.34'6--dc 3
2014041634

ISBN: 978-1-138-70030-7 (pbk)
ISBN: 978-1-138-82548-2 (hbk)

Typeset in Goudy
by Servis Filmsetting Ltd, Stockport, Cheshire

"We cannot eliminate extreme poverty and boost shared prosperity without building resilience to climate change and natural disasters. This book combines an excellent overview of lessons learnt and sound analysis that provide a valuable contribution to the global discussions around the post-Hyogo Framework for Action to reduce the devastating impact of disasters on countries and communities."

Jim Yong Kim, President, World Bank Group

"The International Federation of Red Cross and Red Crescent Societies strongly supports the Hyogo Framework for Action 2 (HFA2) and will set ambitious targets to improve community resilience programming. This book will add great value to discussions around the implementation of the HFA2, particularly actions that address underlying risks and vulnerabilities and underpin sustainable development efforts."

Tadateru Konoé, President, International Federation of Red Cross and Red Crescent Societies

"This publication offers innovative solutions to building resilience to disaster, focusing on three essential components: protecting development through risk informed decision-making; managing uncertainties linked to unsustainable growth patterns and climate change; and strengthening the enabling environment through advanced risk governance processes. It is a worthwhile contribution to the discussions on the post-2015 frameworks for disaster risk reduction and development."

Helen Clark, Administrator, United Nations Development Programme

Contents

Contributors

Yusuke Amano is Director of the International Affairs Office, Water and Disaster Management Bureau, Ministry of Land, Infrastructure, Transport and Tourism, Japan. His experience is in the field of water resources management and disaster risk reduction, particularly policymaking, project programming, project planning, project implementation, facility operation and maintenance, emergency response, and rehabilitation and reconstruction following disasters.

Hitoshi Baba is Senior Advisor of JICA and a specialist in flood control, hydrological modelling and disaster management. He has over 30 years' extensive national and international experience in technical and administrative management in disaster and water resource areas in the Ministry of Land, Infrastructure and Transport (MLIT) of the Government of Japan, and in technical cooperation with developing countries to strengthen national capacity for disaster risk reduction, response and reconstruction.

Henrike Brecht is Senior Infrastructure Specialist at the World Bank, leading disaster risk management projects in South-East Asia. Her research focuses on water resource management and hydro-meteorological services. Before joining the World Bank in 2007, she worked for the Louisiana Hurricane Center after Hurricane Katrina and for the United Nations High Commissioner of Refugees (UNHCR). She holds an MSc degree in environmental science and a PhD in disaster risk management.

Ian Davis, an architect, is a Visiting Professor in Disaster Risk Management in Copenhagen, Kyoto, Lund and Oxford Brookes Universities. He works in Disaster Risk Reduction and Recovery. In 1996 he received the UN Sasakawa Award for his contribution to Disaster Prevention. He has been on the board of four NGOs, advised governments/UN Agencies and is author or editor of 17 books. He edited *Disaster Risk Management in Asia and the Pacific* (2014) for the ADBI.

Jan Eijkenaar is ECHO's Technical Assistant in charge of supporting the AGIR Alliance and the resilience file in the West Africa and Sahel Region, based in Dakar. From 2006 to 2012 he coordinated ECHO's programs in response to the food and nutritional crisis in the Sahel preceded by assignments in other regions, mainly on the African continent. An engineer by training and experience (Manchester, UK, and Tilburg, NL), he worked in humanitarian emergency aid from the late 1980s, including with MSF and other NGOs, as well as UN organizations. He continues to be involved in the planning, implementation, monitoring and evaluation of projects as well as strategy and policy work.

Kristalina Georgieva is Vice President of the European Commission. From 2010 to 2014, she was the European Commissioner for International Cooperation, Humanitarian Aid and Crisis Response. Before joining the European Commission, she held various positions at the World Bank, including Director for Sustainable Development and Vice President and Corporate Secretary. In October 2014, she was recognized as a Champion of Disaster Risk Reduction by the secretariat of International Strategy for Disaster Reduction.

Junichi Hirano is Deputy Director, Disaster Management Team 2, Water Resources and Disaster Management Group, Global Environment Department, JICA, and is in charge of formulation and coordination of DRR projects, mainly in South-East Asia and the Southern America region. He received a Master's degree in Disaster Management at the University of Copenhagen, Denmark, and also conducted a research study named "A study on culture of safety and resilience to natural disaster in the Republic of the Union of Myanmar" based on the experience in DRR Projects related to the cyclone "NARGIS" in 2008 at JICA's Myanmar Office.

Yukinari Hosokawa, Deputy Director, Disaster Management Team 2, Water Resources and Disaster Management Group, Global Environment Department of JICA. He gained his experience in DRR at JICA's El Salvador Office and Hyogo International Center (currently the Kansan International Center) of JICA. He has been responsible for planning, monitoring, and implementing various programs on DRR, particularly on DRR culture, making use of the knowledge and experience from the Great Hanshin Awaji earthquake.

Sylvie Montembault Jamal is an engineer in agronomy with more than 15 years' overseas experience within the UN, NGO and formal education sectors. She has worked in a range of emergency and development contexts across Africa and Asia, and assisted in disaster preparedness planning in collaboration with both national and international partners. Currently, she is ECHO's DRR regional expert based in Nairobi. She has overseen the final phase of the ECHO regional drought preparedness program in the Horn of Africa, promoting drought preparedness, mitigation measures and the links between relief and development.

Abhas Jha is the Practice Manager for Urban and Disaster Risk Management for East Asia and the Pacific at the World Bank. He has been with the World Bank since 2001, leading the World Bank's urban, housing and disaster risk management work in Turkey, Mexico, Jamaica and Peru. He earlier served for 12 years in the Indian Administrative Service in the Government of India in the Federal Ministry of Finance and in the state of Bihar. His interests focus on urban resilience, integrated urban flood risk management and using open data for improved service delivery.

Kuntoro Mangkusubroto was Minister/Head of the post-tsunami Aceh-Nias Rehabilitation and Reconstruction Agency from 2005 to 2009. Since late 2009 he has been Minister/Head of the presidential Delivery Unit for the Development of Monitoring and Oversight. He has built a career as a dynamic and creative reformer in the public sector of Indonesia. He is also a leading thinker and practitioner in the area of decision science.

Ryo Matsumaru is a Professor in the Faculty of Regional Development Studies, Toyo University, Japan. His research and publications concentrate on disaster risk reduction and management, including disaster recovery in both developing countries and Japan.

Taichi Minamitani is Representative of JICA's Turkey Office. During his career with JICA since 2007, he was responsible for projects relating to the Chile earthquake in 2010, the Van earthquake in 2010, and the Chao Phraya flood in 2011, among others. In addition, he was a study member of JICA which proposed "three principles" through lessons from recent mega-disasters, including the Great East Japan earthquake. His academic background is soil mechanics and landslides.

Masafumi Nagaishi is a Professer of the Office for the Planning and Coordination of International Affairs at Kyushu University, Japan. Previously he was managing overall DRR issues in the Global Environment Department, JICA, while he served as senior Advisor of the department as well as Director of the Disaster management team. He is also Visiting Professor of the Graduate School of Environmental Studies at Nagoya University.

Noriaki Nagatomo is Deputy Director General of the Rural Development Department, JICA. Previously he was in charge of DRR in JICA while he served as Senior Advisor to the Director General of the Global Environmental Department for 4 years (2009–2013). He also led JICA's knowledge management network for DRR during his tenure and played a key role in promoting DRR projects in line with HFA.

Satoru Nishikawa, PhD, is Vice-President of the Japan Water Agency. He has had a long career dealing with disasters, including senior relief coordination officer at UN Geneva and executive director of ADRC. He was director of international cooperation for disaster reduction at the Cabinet Office Japan where he coordinated the Japanese technical assistance to the Indian Ocean tsunami-affected countries and hosted the 2005 UN World Conference on Disaster Reduction.

Hidetomi Oi is an expert on water resources development and disaster management. He has worked for the Japanese government (1962–1990) and JICA (1990–2009). His long-term assignments abroad include projects for international organizations and JICA in Manila, Geneva, Kathmandu and Barbados, each for 3 years. He is currently President of the International Sabo Association, Japan.

Wataru Ono is Assistant Director, Program Division 2/Disaster Reduction Learning Center (DRLC), Kansai International Center, Japan International Cooperation Agency (JICA). He has a Master's degree in science and his research focused on Indonesian rainfall variation affected by climate change. He also worked as project coordinator of the Project of Capacity Development for Climate Change Strategies in Indonesia, after he gained experience in managing DRR projects in the Disaster Management Division, JICA.

Yuichi Ono is a Professor and Assistant Director of the International Research Institute of Disaster Science at Tohoku University, Japan. His research and publications concentrate on international policy on disaster risk reduction, early warning systems and wind-related disasters.

Eiji Otsuki is Senior Advisor to the Director General of the Global Environment Department, Japan International Cooperation Agency (JICA). He advises on disaster risk reduction (DRR) issues in JICA, and has considerable experience with water-related disaster risk reduction and climate change adaptation in the Ministry of Land, Infrastructure, Transport and Tourism (MLIT) of the Government of Japan.

Angelika Planitz is Disaster and Climate Risk Governance Advisor at the UNDP Bureau for Policy and Programme Support (BPPS) in New York. She has over 18 years' professional experience in disaster and climate risk management at national, regional and global levels in Africa, Asia and the Pacific. Her academic background is in public administration and development studies.

Muhammad Saidur Rahman is the Founder and Director of Bangladesh Disaster Preparedness Centre (BDPC), an organization of professionals in disaster risk management. He has held positions such as the first director of the widely acclaimed Cyclone Preparedness Programme (CPP) and was the Country Representative of Oxfam UK in Bangladesh. He is the only Bangladeshi to have received the Certificate of Distinction under the UN Sasakawa Award by United Nations secretariat of the International Strategy for Disaster Reduction in 2002.

Ryosuke Shibasaki is a Professor of the Center for Spatial Information Science, the University of Tokyo, Japan. He is a pioneer of applying large location data derived from cell phone logs and so on to estimate population distribution and movement for social benefit services such as disaster response support and transportation planning, and public health. His most current research is on applying cell phone data for disaster risk management in Bangladesh.

Toshiyuki Shimano has 10 years' experience in development cooperation in the Japan International Cooperation Agency (JICA). He was involved in over ten Asian Countries' disaster management projects while he was an assistant director of the Disaster Management Division. Since 2013, he has been based in Colombo as a representative of JICA Sri Lanka, and is responsible for disaster management cooperation in Sri Lanka as well as in the Maldives.

Zuzana Stanton-Geddes is an Operations Analyst in the Urban and Disaster Risk Management team in East Asia and the Pacific at the World Bank, working on projects focusing on urban resilience, flood risk management and integrating gender concerns into disaster risk management programs. She has co-edited and contributed to the World Bank publications *Strong, Safe, and Resilient: A Strategic Policy Guide for Disaster Risk Management in East Asia and the Pacific*; and *Building Urban Resilience: Principles, Tools and Practice*.

Sho Takano is Assistant Resident Representative of JICA's Bhutan Office. He has worked on the formulation and use of geospatial information in developing countries. His current research on geospatial information is related to JICA's Project Study on the Future Direction of the Cooperation using Geospatial Information Technology.

Kimio Takeya is a Visiting Senior Advisor of the Japan International Cooperation Agency. He has significant experience in disaster recovery and reconstruction plans, and was involved in most of the recent mega-disasters' post-disaster needs assessment surveys which were conducted in cooperation with WB, ADB, JICA and others. He is an advisory group member of "Assessing and Measuring Resilience", a research study for the OECD.

Kae Yanagisawa is Vice President of Japan International Cooperation Agency (JICA). She has a long-term career in international development at JICA and the United Nations Development Programme (UNDP). She gained knowledge and experience in disaster risk reduction while she was leading the disaster relief operations of JICA. She authored and edited a book on international cooperation in disaster management, published in Japanese language in 2013. She is a Visiting Professor in development cooperation at Meiji University, Japan.

Foreword

Sustainable development is an overarching goal that the international community has agreed to pursue in the "post-2015" period. It requires an environment in which social and economic progress is not interrupted. In reality, however, growth and development are often disrupted or slowed down by a number of factors. Disasters comprise one major downside risk to development, affecting people's livelihoods, well-being and property. Human security is also threatened as a result of severe disasters.

As the magnitude of natural hazards as well as vulnerability of societies to such hazards continues to increase, robust, innovative and flexible approaches to risk reduction are necessary at each stage of the disaster risk management process. In particular, pre-disaster investment is the key factor in sustaining growth and development, and more needs to be done to put this concept into action. Moreover, the post-disaster recovery process should be seen as an opportunity to increase resilience to future disasters. "Build back better" is indeed a concept that connects the post-disaster stage to the subsequent step of pre-disaster investment.

Disasters actually affect a wide range of social and economic activities, and thus they should not be treated as separate factors, isolated from development. Disaster risk reduction should therefore be mainstreamed within development policies, both at national and local levels, and across all sectors, in such a way that a wide range of actors are involved, including governments, communities, academic and research institutions, and the private sector as well as civil society. Above all, the strong leadership of governments is essential in promoting this mainstreaming.

This book was planned in the hope that it will provide a useful addition to the existing literature and assist countries in their endeavors to enhance resilience to disasters. To this end, professionals specializing in DRR were invited both from Japan and around the world to share their rich knowledge and experiences. JICA is grateful for the precious time and efforts devoted by the authors and hopes that this book will contribute to the deepening of discussions within the international community on the post-Hyogo Framework for Action and Sustainable Development Goals.

Akihiko Tanaka
President
Japan International Cooperation Agency

Foreword

This book is an admirable contribution to highlighting the economic impact of disasters upon our daily lives and across many sectors in this increasingly interconnected world. It also brings to the fore many positive measures than can be taken to avoid the creation of new risk and to reduce exposure to existing risk.

Disasters can affect everyone, and are therefore everybody's business. Disaster risk reduction should be part of everyday decision making: from how people educate their children to how they plan their cities. Each decision can make us either more vulnerable, or more resilient. This simple truth applies particularly to the private sector which is responsible for 70 to 85 percent of investment in the world we are building around us.

The UN Secretary-General, Ban Ki-moon, has warned that "economic losses from disasters are out of control." Losses to date this century are in the range of US$2.5 trillion, at least 50 percent higher than previous estimates.

When it expires in 2015, the current global blueprint for disaster risk reduction, the Hyogo Framework for Action, will be able to take some credit for reducing mortality linked to disasters and spreading a culture of resilience around the world.

However, as we prepare for the Third World Conference on Disaster Risk Reduction in Sendai, Japan in March 2015, there is raised awareness that much still needs to be done to address the underlying drivers of risk such as rapid urbanization, climate change, population growth, environmental degradation, poor land use and deficient building codes.

As this book makes clear, the world cannot afford to perpetuate a disconnect between disaster risk reduction, sustainable development and climate change. The post-2015 framework for disaster risk reduction which will be adopted in Sendai must be a pillar of the post-2015 development agenda, with clear links to the Sustainable Development Goals and the new climate change agreement. This volume is a very worthwhile contribution to the debate as we prepare for the World Conference.

Margareta Wahlström
Special Representative of the Secretary-General of the United Nations
for Disaster Risk Reduction

Preface

Kristalina Georgieva

We are living in an increasingly fragile world. Climate change, urbanization, population growth and environmental degradation mean that the frequency and intensity of disasters and their impact have been steadily rising. Over the past three decades the average annual losses caused by natural disasters have quadrupled – from US$50 billion in the 1980s to some US$200 billion today. The book in your hands sheds disturbing light on this trend and how it manifests itself in different parts of the world. It tells us that we must get used to a "new normal," where we face multiple challenges with finite resources.

Disasters know no borders. Rich and poor countries may be hit at any time. Still, the poorest suffer the most, as their cities, economies and people are more fragile, less prepared and unable to absorb either the losses or the costs to rebuild ruined infrastructure and lives. Consider, for instance, Haiti, which suffered tragically in 2010 when an earthquake killed 230,000 people in a matter of seconds. Its economy, already weak, was devastated. Years of development gains and investments evaporated overnight.

The rich also pay their price. Remember "Katrina" and the tragic days and nights in New Orleans? Or "Sandy" which hit the east coast of the United States in 2012, killing 285 and causing US$72 billion in losses? Or the 2011 Great East Japan earthquake? Europe is also not spared – it lost over 100,000 lives during the past decade and suffered damage of over US$180 billion. The 2014 floods in Eastern Europe alone (Serbia, Bosnia and Herzegovina, Croatia and Bulgaria) caused combined losses of over US$3.5 billion.

Yet, the difference between disaster impact upon the rich and upon the poor is significant. Haiti is still struggling to recover, while the developed world is able to rebuild better and faster, and to invest more in preparedness and prevention activities.

Disaster trends of the past decades have opened our eyes to the fact that effective disaster management is at the heart of poverty reduction and economic and social prosperity. This book gives us numerous practical examples and case studies proving that in today's more fragile world no national or regional economy can grow unless prevention, risk reduction and resilience are "embedded" in its planning and budgetary systems. Medicine invented immunization to strengthen human resistance to diseases: the same logic applies to economic health. Prevention, risk reduction and resilience are the "immunization" of the economy and people's well-being against disasters. The contributors in this publication offer us real solutions – tried and tested by policymakers and communities in different parts of the world.

And they convey a hopeful message: that our policies and practices are changing for the better. We no longer debate whether it makes sense to be prepared or to manage risk. The issue is how quickly we are doing it and how much we are willing to invest in risk reduction and resilience.

The outcomes of initiatives such as the Rio+20 Summit, the UNFCCC and the extensive international support for the resilience agenda make it clear that risk management policies are not only saving lives, but are also essential to ensure sustainable development and economic growth in developed countries, emerging economies and the developing world. Investments in disaster risk management bring extended economic benefits: they strengthen the resilience to increasing global shocks and threats and also act as a strong driver of innovation, growth and job creation. This can open new markets and business opportunities and help ensure structural sustainability of public and private finances in times when economic and financial downturn continues to put pressure on national budgets.

Against this background, a renewed international framework for disaster risk reduction (DRR) offers the opportunity to shift the paradigm of our approach in dealing with risks in today's increasingly complex and fragile world. This is the key conclusion of this book, dedicated to the Third World Conference on Disaster Risk Reduction in Sendai (Japan) on March 14 to 18, 2015. The Conference will adopt the successor of the Hyogo Framework for Action as a blueprint for societies and countries to better manage risks to achieve resilience in the decades to come. It should also prove that the lessons we learned after Hyogo will be implemented into actions after Sendai.

Building on successes and lessons learned, it is my hope that the arguments and evidence will now lead to a firm political commitment to forge an ambitious renewed international framework. The European Union has been a strong advocate for it: including in formulating a common EU position on the post-2015 Hyogo Framework for Action building on the achievements of a range of EU policies that may be shared and underpin the new framework.

A few key messages stemming from this common position can help us make our *Investing in Resilience and Development* a reality, leading to concrete risk management steps and tangible reduction of vulnerabilities.

First, saving lives and economic losses starts with changing minds. We need a mindset change when it comes to making disaster risk management (DRM) and resilience part of our daily lives. This requires a constant, non-stop all-generations and all-society sectors effort to adapt our cities, our economies and our lives to the new realities. Japan's example can inspire us all on this: it is one of the world leaders in this field, integrating disaster management into its education, public debate and policy at all levels. The chapters in this book that outline the Japanese experience and practices in disaster risk reduction should inform the thinking of policymakers and practitioners elsewhere. Transparency, good governance and result-oriented actions can only add value to this concept. The best and the brightest of the scientific minds must be engaged, helping us to create new measures for success and new horizons to reach.

Second, while we think globally, we must act locally. Local communities are the first and the last defensive wall against all disasters. If we help them to manage better the upcoming challenges and build resilience; if we empower local leaders, minorities, women, professionals and volunteers alike, we will win most of the battles ahead.

Third, we must invest properly in disaster risk management and resilience. We need to engage fully the private sector, the insurance companies and the scientific centers to combine the power of money with the power of intellect. Innovative ideas, best practices and knowledge sharing supported with proper funding can prevent or reduce the negative impact of most of the trouble Mother Nature has in store for us.

So let us start building our new defense lines against disasters and make the lives of our children safer and more predictable. We must never forget that they will judge us by our deeds, not by our intentions.

Kristalina Georgieva
European Commission Vice Present and former EU Commissioner for
International Cooperation, Humanitarian Aid and Crisis Response

Introduction

Ian Davis and Kae Yanagisawa

Aim

This book was planned with a view to contributing to the Third United Nations World Conference on Disaster Risk Reduction, to be held in Sendai, Japan, in March 2015, at which the next phase of the Hyogo Framework for Action will be discussed and agreed. The themes of the chapters were selected to relate to the outcomes of the Fourth Global Platform for Disaster Risk Reduction, held in May 2013, and subsequent preparatory discussions for the Sendai Conference. The themes are mostly in line with the possible elements of the post-2015 disaster risk reduction framework and are intended to add value to the forthcoming framework.

Scope

The chapters cover a broad range of subjects, with an overarching message that goes "beyond saving lives." This idea is based on the belief that sustainable development will not be achieved without preserving the livelihood and economic activities of communities and societies, even in disaster situations. Thanks to the efforts of the international community driven by the Hyogo Framework for Action, progress was made in building early warning systems and risk awareness of the population, resulting in a reduction in human losses. However, economic losses are increasing, especially in advanced and middle-income countries, while less developed countries are often trapped in the vicious circle of poverty and cyclical disasters. In order to reverse these tendencies, extra efforts are required, but complexity is increasing because we are living in an era of climate change and rapid urbanization. Taking these factors into consideration, this book attempts to present various approaches, methods, actors and tools to make society safer and more resilient.

Examples

Most chapters include case study examples, which is one of the strengths of the book. In addition, Japanese case studies are extensively covered. As one of the most disaster-prone countries in the world, Japan's experience is expected to provide valuable lessons to the international community.

Authors

The authors of each chapter were selected to provide readers with a broad perspective on this subject. They are drawn from varied countries (Bangladesh and Indonesia), international organizations (the European Union, the United Nations Development Programme and the World Bank), a donor organization (the Japan International Cooperation Agency) and ministries and universities in Japan. All authors are professionals in disaster risk reduction, with long-term experience in governments, international organizations, donor organizations and NGOs. With the experienced authors and editors coming from a rich background, chapters cover global and national perspectives as well as a community-based approach.

Content

The book looks at the complex subject of disaster risk reduction through a number of lenses:

> In Part 1, chapters 1 to 3 consider the need for resilience as a way to create sustainable development within a rapidly changing global environment. Three critical pressures are examined: urbanization, climate change and chronic patterns of vulnerability.
>
> In Part 2, chapters 4 to 6 explore how planning, economic analysis and the sharing of risk reduction experiences can strengthen an awareness of disaster threats and their management and reduction.
>
> In Part 3, chapters 7 and 8 look at ways to build safety into sustainable disaster recovery, by adopting Build Back Better.
>
> In Part 4, chapters 9 to 11 review ways to increase the roles of key stakeholders: local communities, the private sector and the various players who create effective governance.
>
> In Part 5, chapters 12 and 13 describe a pair of essential tools needed for risk reduction: data management and the use of geospatial technology.

Recommendations

Chapter authors have made recommendations in the conclusions of their chapters with a suggested audience for their advice. The summary draws together the recommendations from each chapter and highlights the implications for the future role of donors and international organizations in disaster risk reduction. This is followed by a general reflection on a key message that emerges from the book as it seeks to support the renewed emphasis on risk reduction promoted in the Third World Conference on Disaster Reduction.

Terminology

The adverse impacts of hazards often cannot be prevented fully, but their scale or severity can be substantially lessened by various structural, non-structural and environmental strategies and actions. The collective term for these approaches is *"Disaster Risk Reduction"* (DRR) and this overlaps with another expression *"Climate Change Adaptation"* (CCA) that is used within the climate change community. Sometimes the word *"mitigation"* is used to describe measures that encompass engineering techniques and hazard-resistant construction as well as improved environmental policies and public awareness. However, it should be noted that in climate change policy, *"mitigation"* is defined differently, being the term used for the reduction of greenhouse gas emissions that are the source of climate change.

Throughout the book the authors have refrained from using the highly optimistic and unrealistic term *"Disaster Prevention,"* since hazards have no upper limits of severity, and there are always financial limits on the resources that even the wealthiest of governments can deploy to reduce risks. Therefore more realistic terms are used: *"preventive," "preventive measures"* or *"preventive culture."*

Part I

Resilience for sustainable development in a changing environment

1 Building resilience to disasters and climate change in the age of urbanization

Abhas Jha, Henrike Brecht and
Zuzana Stanton-Geddes

Managing risks responsibly and effectively has the potential to bring about
security and a means of progress for people in developing countries and beyond.

World Development Report 2014

Introduction

Around the world, unplanned urban growth is expanding slums and degrading
ecosystems, leaving millions exposed to disaster and climate risks. Disaster and
climate risks pose a serious challenge for urban dwellers and systems. Over the
past decades, economic losses have been increasing due to the rising concentration of people and assets in hazardous areas, turning many of today's cities into
disaster hotspots. This trend is set to continue unless disaster and climate risk
management becomes part of urban planning and governance.

This chapter argues that rapid urbanization, if properly managed, can be an
opportunity to strengthen urban resilience. To reach this goal, key principles
need to be followed, including using risk assessments for better decisions in
urban planning, integrating structural and non-structural risk management measures, prioritizing adaptive and multi-purpose approaches, enabling the sharing of
risk information, engaging with different stakeholders, and using recovery as an
opportunity to forge stronger and safer communities.

The first section describes current trends in urbanization, and how poorly
planned urbanization can translate into increased exposure and vulnerability of cities. The second section highlights some of the key implications, and
provides recommendations and examples of innovative ways of reducing and
managing disaster risk, encouraging readers to view disasters both as a risk and
an opportunity. The final section summarizes the discussion and ways forward.

Cities as disaster hotspots: the imperatives for action

Rapid urbanization requires a new paradigm. A century ago, one out of every ten people in the world lived in urban areas. Now, the majority of people live in cities. By 2050, the United Nations projects that almost three-quarters of the world's population will be urban dwellers. In the next two decades, the world will witness unprecedented urban infrastructure expansion – in developing countries the expansion is equivalent to building a city of one million people every five days (Muller 2013).[1] Research on urban growth in the East Asia and the Pacific region, which used satellite imagery to analyze built-up areas for the entire region in the years 2000 and 2010, suggests that in this time frame, the total amount of built-up land in the region increased by 34,000 sq. km (World Bank 2015). A dominant trend is that urban areas in the region grew simultaneously larger and denser while becoming administratively fragmented, which poses a challenge for integrated urban planning, service delivery and infrastructure development (World Bank 2015).

Much of the urbanization is taking place in slums and hazardous areas. Globally, about one billion people live in slums, and this number is expected to shoot up to three billion by 2050 if rapid urbanization is not addressed (United Nations 2013). In urban areas in developing countries, slum dwellers already account for more than 50 percent of the population (UN Habitat n.d.). In sub-Saharan Africa, some 72 percent of urban dwellers live in slums, up from 62 percent 10 years ago (UN Human Settlements Programme 2006). Typically settling in informal areas, often at risk from disasters and with limited or no access to services such as water and sanitation, the urban poor are disproportionately affected by disaster impacts (World Bank 2012b). For example, it is estimated that in Metro Manila some 800,000 people, mostly informal settlers, live in high-risk areas. In Jakarta, spatial analysis of slum settlements and flood risk areas shows strong correlation between informal and high-risk areas (World Bank 2013).

The substantial growth of population and assets in at-risk areas is among the main reasons for the increase of disaster losses in recent years. Historically, many cities propagated around sites with agricultural advantages or importance, in areas with fertile volcanic soils, for example, or along major trade and transportation routes, such as coasts and river systems naturally prone to flooding and erosion (Dilley *et al.* 2005). In the past few decades, coastal areas have become even more densely populated:[2] between 1970 and 2010, while global population growth was 87 percent, populations living in flood plains grew by 114 percent and in cyclone-prone coastlines by 192 percent (United Nations secretariat of the ISDR 2013). Globally, between 2010 and 2015, the number of people living in large cities exposed to tropical cyclones and earthquakes have doubled – with 680 million people exposed to tropical hazards, and 870 million to earthquakes (Brecht *et al.* 2013).

The potential for losses is particularly high in urban areas. While, over the past decades, the human loss due to the impact of natural hazards has decreased significantly, thanks to improvements in hazard monitoring and early warning systems among others, economic losses have been increasing (see Figure 1.1). The concentrations of population, industry, infrastructure and economic activities in cities contribute to increased exposure and susceptibility to natural hazards: 1.5 percent of the world's land is estimated to produce 50 percent of worldwide gross domestic product (GDP). The same area accommodates about one-sixth of the world's population (World Bank 2009). A recent study quantifying the present and future flood losses in the 136 largest coastal cities estimates that by 2050, these cities will experience flood losses in the amount of US$52 billion (Hallegatte *et al.* 2013). In 2005, these 136 cities encountered flood losses of approximately US$6 billion per year (Hallegatte *et al.* 2013). Another study reports that more than 80 percent of all losses resulting from disasters reported in Latin America were in urban areas (Hardoy 2013).

In the global context, even local events can have consequences reaching beyond a country or region. The 2011 Thai floods affected industrial production, cutting down manufacturing for export, and affecting commodity-related manufacturing in the whole region (World Bank 2012c). Making a quarter of the world's hard drives, and serving as the South-East Asian production hub for Japanese car makers, the halt in production created supply chain disruptions for the automobile and electric industries, including Apple, Toyota, Honda, Nissan, Nikon, Sony, Canon and Toshiba, among others (Yang 2011).

Disasters are among the greatest threats to poverty reduction and shared prosperity: they can roll back years of development gains and plunge millions of people into poverty. In the Philippines, due to the recent Typhoon Haiyan, it is estimated that an additional 2.3 million people have been pushed into poverty, raising the poverty rate from 41 percent to about 56 percent in the worst affected

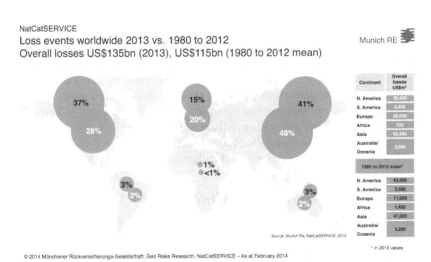

© 2014 Münchener Rückversicherungs-Gesellschaft, Geo Risks Research, NatCatSERVICE – As at February 2014

Figure 1.1 Loss events worldwide: 2013 vs. 1980–2012 in US dollars

Source: Natural Catastrophes in 2013. Loss Events by Continent. Globally, disasters in 2013 brought some US$125 billion in losses (Munich Re 2014).

areas. In Myanmar, 2 years after Cyclone Nargis, the average maximum debt of laborers and fishermen more than doubled, and that of small farmers was almost twice as high (World Bank 2013d). Research suggests that the impacts of climate change upon poverty will be regressive, "affecting most significantly the urban poor and highly vulnerable countries in sub-Saharan Africa and South Asia, where the number of exposed poor may reach 325 million by 2030."[3]

The growing recognition of development partners that disasters threaten the global goal of poverty reduction helped place disaster and climate resilience firmly in the global development agenda. The World Bank Group (WBG) is committed to reducing poverty and increasing shared prosperity. As part of this goal, disaster and climate risk management are now at the core of the new WBG strategy approved at the 2013 Annual Meeting. The growing commitment of the World Bank to urban resilience and disaster risk management is reflected in many ways. Seventy percent of the World Bank's Country Assistance and Partnership Strategies now include disaster and climate risk in their approach to development. The Bank has also doubled its investments in disaster risk management, investing, on average, US$2.3 billion per year in disaster prevention, preparedness and post-disaster construction, with two-thirds of new lending focusing on prevention and preparedness.

In the East Asia and the Pacific region, the World Bank supports urban planning and investments that take into account disaster and climate risks. For example, in the Philippines, the bank supported the development of the Master Plan for Metro Manila – a set of actions and priorities for sustainable flood risk management of Metro Manila and surrounding areas until 2035. The plan includes structural measures, land use management and resettlement, improvements in the urban drainage system, establishment of an integrated flood risk management institutional system, flood forecasting and early warning systems, along with community-based flood risk management. In Vietnam, the Bank supports climate-resilient development in a number of cities, including Ho Chi Minh City and Can Tho, among others. In Indonesia, the National Community Empowerment Program in urban areas (PNPM) supports community-driven development that also includes disaster adaptation (e.g. flood prevention, water retention and storage facilities, slope stabilization and emergency evacuation routes). In Lao PDR, the Bank contributed to integrating resilience aspects into the five-year National Socio-Economic Development Plan (2011–2015), enabling, for the first time in Lao PDR, the allocation of the national budget for risk reduction investments.

Ten principles for developing a resilient city of the future

In the face of these challenges, there are many opportunities for cities to make a change. Poorly planned urban development, degraded ecosystems, poverty and climate change are all factors that contribute to the rising exposure and vulnerabilities of cities. However, these processes do not have to translate into increased risk if preventive measures are embedded into the design of cities. The following outlines ten tools that cities can use to increase resilience.

1 Use risk assessments for better-informed decisions

Reliable risk information at different levels helps assess and communicate the impacts of disasters, formulate effective risk management strategies and guide development planning. Risk assessments, prepared at various scales, serve as tools for quantifying the probable impacts of disasters in terms of the spatial distribution of damage and loss. Risk assessment results may be visualized through risk maps and integrated into a cost–benefit analysis for any given measure, which are useful for both making decisions and communicating the risks to stakeholders (World Bank 2013e). For example, in Dhaka, Bangladesh, a risk assessment and resulting risk map of the city were used to review the Dhaka City Master Plan to evaluate the adequacy of existing measures for flood mitigation. Similarly, in Istanbul, a risk assessment informed a strategic plan for the development of the Earthquake Mitigation Plan consisting of a city contingency plan and local action plans for high-risk areas.

Risk assessments can have many policy applications. They may be used, for instance, for territorial planning to identify flood plains, assessment of expected damage to infrastructure from specific hazard scenarios, cost–benefit analysis for mitigation planning, preparedness for support of emergency and contingency planning for different crisis scenarios, as well as insurance premium calculations that require accurate information about annual expected losses and probable maximum losses for a specific area (World Bank 2013e). In Latin America, a number of countries use the Probabilistic Risk Assessment (CAPRA) Program – an open-source risk calculation platform – which evaluates risk in terms of physical damage and direct economic and human losses using standard risk metrics (annual average loss and probable maximum loss). The platform can also visualize hazards and risk through geographical information systems (GIS).

2 Mainstream resilience into development planning and investments

Authorities need to integrate resilience strategies into their daily decisions about urban development. This, however, poses many challenges, as discussions about disasters have traditionally taken place in the emergency relief arena, resulting in an institutional division between disaster and development departments. Forward-looking cities are working to overcome this gap. For example, as part of the "Stronger, More Resilient New York" initiative, New York City is working with utilities to strengthen existing infrastructure resilience to flood and heat hazards, reconfigure networks for greater redundancy, and review with regulators the current system designs to include extreme weather conditions when evaluating performance. In Lao PDR, the government is taking steps to mainstream disaster and climate resilience into the strategic policies of the transport, irrigation, and urban sectors to disaster-proof new infrastructure. The following steps may be taken to mainstream resilience into sectors and line ministries.[4] First, sectoral risk assessments need to be developed. For example, in the transport sector, this would translate to mapping vulnerable road stretches. Second, technical guidelines should be specified to address the identified vulnerabilities, including options such as the relocation of roads to higher ground, larger culverts and bioengineering solutions for slope stabilization. Third, awareness raising and training should be provided for all levels of government as well as for the road engineers, supervisors and construction workers.

Mainstreaming resilience needs to be coordinated by a high-level ministry to enforce and monitor implementation. Following the 1999 Marmara earthquakes, Turkey established a high-level DRM agency under the Prime Minister's Office. This high-level agency has the mandate and authority to mainstream DRM into different sectors. It has overseen a number of significant initiatives that have positioned Turkey as a more resilient country, including a national catastrophic risk pool, risk reduction strategies through the Decree on Building Construction on the enforcement of earthquake-resistant building codes, the National Earthquake Strategy and Action Plan (NESAP), the Istanbul Seismic Risk Mitigation and Emergency Preparedness (ISMEP), the Integrated Urban Development Strategy Action Plan, and the regulation of building construction in earthquake micro-zoning (World Bank and Government of Mexico 2012).

3 Combine gray, green and soft measures

In the face of the uncertainties discussed above, cities cannot rely solely on hard-engineered measures, but rather take an integrated and flexible approach with the right balance between structural (engineered) and non-structural (non-engineered) measures. Risk-informed land use planning and zoning is an efficient way to increase urban resilience in combination with gray and green protection infrastructure. Risk-based land use planning is a non-structural approach that identifies the safest locations to guide development out of/within hazard-prone zones, by informing the location, type, design, quality and timing of development. Zoning enables the demarcation of safer areas, regulating land use, setting regulations on location, bulk, height, shape and use of structures in each zone, and identifying building codes by design type and purpose of structure (World Bank 2013e). In Indonesia, following the 2006 Java earthquake and the Mount Merapi eruption in 2010, the World Bank supported risk-sensitive land use planning and resettlements (see BNPB 2011). Detailed analysis identified zones and groups of vulnerable populations to guide resettlement and resilient reconstruction. For example, development, including housing construction, was not allowed in some zones; in other zones, partial resettlement was permitted; and in yet other areas, efforts focused on strengthening the preparedness of population. Reconstruction and resettlement were implemented through community-driven participatory processes, where community settlement plans were part of regional risk-sensitive land use planning.

Flood-prone cities need to adopt an integrated, multi-functional and cross-sectoral approach to risk management (World Bank 2012a). Measures may include improvements in early warning, multi-purpose flood control infrastructure, restoration of and building sewers in areas with limited drainage, installation of multi-purpose storm sewers, and expansion of green infrastructure, using natural and permeable materials. The Netherlands exemplifies the paradigm shift from flood control to an adaptive management approach, along the lines of "live and build with nature," which integrates natural forces and human interventions. The principle both gives more space to natural forces and tries to leave minimum footprints. At the same time, it signifies to the population that a residual level of risk is inevitable. The Delta Programme 2.0 (also called Room for the River) pilots over 40 projects that consider risk at different scales, deep uncertainties, climate change, multi-level governance, effective public participation, and importantly, integrates the long-term perspective with the short-term benefits, adding societal value through investment synergies. For example, a beach area close to Rotterdam is used as a multi-functional system combining both flood management and recreation benefits. The "Amsterdam Water Resilient City" plan also considers partial flooding, and building lower street levels to protect houses. The Stormwater Management And Road Tunnel (SMART) in Kuala Lumpur is both a motorway and a stormwater tunnel helping the city manage peak-hour traffic as well as stormwater during floods. To avoid a collapse of the water systems, cities should build in redundancy in and flexibility of the water supply network, and rethink parks and open spaces to serve as buffers for nearby neighborhoods. After floods in 2012, New York City is putting in place green infrastructure to better absorb and use floodwater. The city's MillionTreesNYC initiative is a citywide program with the goal to plant and care for one million new trees across the city. In some cities in India, rainwater harvesting is mandatory. In Japan, the Ryogoku Kokugikan Sumo-Wrestling Arena, the Sumida City Hall and other public buildings use rainwater for non-potable purposes; in the Mukojima district, local residents use roof rainwater collection for gardening, firefighting and drinking water in emergencies (UN Environment Programme 2002).

4 Prepare for "graceful" failure, prioritizing adaptive and low-regret solutions

With the growing size of cities and complex product and supply networks, there is deep uncertainty over the possibility of cascading disasters and spillover impacts across national and regional borders. Traditionally, complex infrastructure systems have been designed to resist external shocks – whether interrelated or occurring as a series – along with internal failures. However, with the growing complexity of the systems involved, the potential for failure increases, and the effects of even partial or secondary events can spread or cascade through the system or its subsystems. This is particularly true for complex interdependent systems, such as transportation, electric power and telecommunications systems, but also international trade patterns, as witnessed, for example, during the 2011 floods in Thailand, which affected industrial production throughout the whole region (Little 2010). Catastrophic disasters are a reminder that cities have to make sure the design of important systems takes into account risks of failure, and makes provisions to "fail gracefully"; that is, without affecting other parts of the system, and causing the least damage.

Because the risks of disasters cannot be entirely eliminated, cities need to adopt robust approaches to uncertainty and unknown risks that incorporate a greater degree of flexibility into the mitigation designs measures. Uncertainty over future disaster and weather patterns adds complexity to decision making over policies and investments. Cities need to be careful to avoid being "locked into" financing large-scale investments that might prove obsolete with changed circumstances. As a city develops, large-scale flood protection schemes often face new challenges even before they are completed, as, for example, in Ho Chi Minh City, where the 2001 Master Plan to mitigate flooding through improved drainage had to contend with higher than expected increases in peak rainfall. Rather than relying entirely on solely engineered solutions or on a single protection solution (such as a dyke), cities can adopt adaptive approaches in decision making and in actual design that enable them to make risk management a gradual and iterative process. Robust Decision Making (RDM), developed by RAND Corporation in the US, is a framework that supports decisions when there are no reliable predictions available. The framework helps identify solutions that can perform well over a wide range of conditions, balance many competing interests, draw on a range of planning options and that are adaptive in nature. The approach has been applied, for example, in Ho Chi Minh City as a way of assessing different adaptive options such as groundwater management, elevation, rainwater storage, and relocation of affected populations. The analysis demonstrated that adaptation and retreat measures can improve the set of futures under which policies succeed in promoting the city's objectives to make equitable decisions, so that all segments of the society benefit from public infrastructure and services, as well as sustainable investments in flood protection.

By managing residual risk, cities can focus on low-regret risk management investments, which bring benefits under a range of future scenarios. Hydromet networks provide vital information for the advance warnings that save lives and reduce damage to property. Apart from the incalculable benefit to human well-being, every dollar invested in meteorological and hydrological services produces an economic return many times greater, even in the context of uncertain future risks. A recent study shows that a dollar invested in improving hydro-meteorological information and early warning systems could bring benefits of between US$4 and US$36 per year through the optimization of economic production in weather-sensitive sectors, such as agriculture or energy (Hallegatte 2012).

5 Use urban revitalization to build resilience and address underlying problems

Upgrading and retrofitting offer opportunities for cities to build resilience into public and private infrastructure. Risk assessments and risk-based land use planning can inform the retrofitting, upgrading or complete rebuilding of a given area following a disaster.[5] Retrofitting efforts often focus on critical infrastructure such as hospitals, emergency structures, schools and vital transportation lines. In Japan, fiscal incentives have been used to promote the retrofitting of buildings in heavily urbanized areas (World Bank, GFDRR and Government of Japan 2012b). Urban upgrading programs prioritize investments in infrastructure, housing, livelihoods and social networks for the vulnerable urban poor (The World Bank Institute 2009). In the city of Bogota, Colombia, the World Bank supported the retrofitting of more than 200 schools and six hospitals as well as the resettlement of more than 5,000 families living in hazardous areas (World Bank, GFDRR and Government of Japan 2012a). In Turkey, under the Istanbul Seismic Risk Mitigation and Emergency Preparedness Project (ISMEP) supported by the World Bank, 510 primary and high schools, eight hospitals, ten infirmaries, 16 governmental buildings and 14 dormitories were retrofitted (strengthened and modernized), and 102 primary and high schools, one health care facility and two social buildings were reconstructed. Retrofitting of a further 47 schools and 38 health care facilities, along with the reconstruction of 48 schools, one dormitory, two health care facilities and three social buildings, is ongoing (Azili 2012).

Post-disaster, cities can combine reconstruction with socioeconomic revitalization and building resilient features. In New York, in the aftermath of Hurricane Sandy, as part of efforts to upgrade buildings, the city signed some 17 new laws to improve building resilience and incentivize people to build back smarter. To support social and economic resilience, the city has sought to incorporate citywide resiliency initiatives (rebuilding programs for homes, businesses and infrastructure), and to work through programs targeting specific localities, such as the "Neighborhood Game Changer Competition," "NY Rising Community Reconstruction Program" or "Rebuild by Design." These initiatives not only serve the purpose of post-Sandy recovery but are intended to revitalize local communities, and to create livable, enjoyable and safe places to live in.[6] Recovery efforts in the aftermath of Hurricane Sandy demonstrate new approaches not to simply rebuild but improve the overall quality of life. Sandy disrupted many of New York City's core systems, incapacitating urban life for months or even years. In the health sector, six hospitals had to close, ten other hospitals lost primary power and/or other critical building systems, and overall hospital bed capacity dropped 8 percent (New York City 2013). The "Special Initiative for Rebuilding and Resilience" (SIRR), set up in the aftermath of the disaster, analyzed five key affected areas, including Brooklyn/Queens Waterfront, East and South Shore Staten Island, South Queens, Southern Brooklyn and Southern Manhattan. The initiative conducted a system-by-system analysis of citywide infrastructure and environment (coastal protection, insurance, energy, utilities, liquid fuels, health care, telecommunications, transportation, water and wastewater, solid waste, food supply, parks). The resulting plan, "A Stronger, More Resilient New York," informs neighborhood authorities and residents on how to rebuild with more resilience, and strengthen citywide infrastructure systems, as well as private housing. It comprises 257 initiatives to reduce extreme weather and climate change risks, with funding needs and an implementation schedule outlined for the next 10 years. The initiatives are aimed at strengthening community networks and improving overall quality of life.

Cities can address underlying social problems through resilient revitalization. While disasters affect everyone, the poor and vulnerable are disproportionately affected, particularly if living in informal settlements and lacking access to public services. In developing countries, the poor and vulnerable are often concentrated in hazardous areas. This is also the case in many developed countries, where the historically poorest areas of the city are often also the most exposed to hazards. In the aftermath of a disaster, choosing whether and how to rebuild these areas has profound social justice and public safety consequences. In New Orleans, a number of initiatives dealt with rebuilding areas that were poor and heavily impacted by Hurricane Katrina. The Faubourg Lafitte Redevelopment initiative seeks to turn a once derelict public housing project into an actual neighborhood. Built through collaboration among private sector, non-profit and public entities, new, affordable housing has replaced previous housing units, with first priority offered to Lafitte housing development's former residents. In the areas of the city's Upper Ninth Ward, which was one of the areas most heavily impacted by Katrina, Habitat for Humanity, an international non-governmental organization, is striving not to just rebuild housing, but to leverage the city's musical heritage. The Musicians' Village set a good example of how flood-resilient new building designs have been adopted in some reconstruction programs. However, these higher standards are yet to be adopted citywide.

6 Engage partners from different sectors

The public sector can greatly benefit by learning from the preparedness and disaster mitigation planning of the private sector. The role of the private sector in humanitarian and emergency response has traditionally been strong, in some cases even outperforming the public sector. For example, Google Earth was launched in June 2005 two months before Hurricane Katrina struck the US. The tool was quickly used by search and rescue teams to access the coordinates of houses from street addresses and to locate those who had become displaced, saving over 4,000 people.[7] At the onset of Hurricane Katrina, private companies such as Wal-Mart or Home Depot started planning ahead of the disaster, increasing their supply of articles needed in emergencies, and making plans for the rapid reopening of their stores.[8] When Typhoon Haiyan (Yolanda) struck the Philippines, Federal Express arranged for the expedited shipment of critical aid and relief supplies from New York to the port of Cebu for the Philippines Red Cross (Lift 2013).

However, with increasing exposure, businesses also need to develop forward-looking preparedness and mitigation arrangements. In the Philippines, Deutsche Post DHL and the United Nations Development Programme provided training for the Mactan Cebu International Airport Authority to prepare for a natural disaster situation (DHL 2013). In Colombia, the International Finance Corporation is working with a private port facility to assess its vulnerability to long-term sea-level rise. The port has already increased its planned investments to anticipate these risks, and will make improvements to all eight ports that it owns and manages (Miller 2014). However, it is not only large companies that invest in research applicable to disaster risk management. In Sierra Leone, small and medium-sized enterprises offer affordable water harvesting, storage and distribution systems that help communities weather projected changes in rainfall patterns and intensity. In the area of private catastrophe insurance, Munich Re, a global reinsurance company, invests in in-depth analysis and management of the impacts of natural hazards, and works with clients not only to transfer and spread financial risks but also to make them more resilient and to reduce losses through specific conditions or incentives. This both improves the company's profitability and helps clients avoid business interruption (Miller 2014).

Partnership with civil society and academia can help target local problems, strengthen community capacity and increase the accountability of public programs. Communities have in-depth knowledge about local problems. Modern crowdsourcing initiatives such as the Digital Humanitarian Initiative and OpenStreetMap – a global mapping effort – bring together professionals and volunteers from developed and developing countries to analyze local problems and find solutions. Linking academics, students and practitioners strengthens capacity and awareness. Participatory mapping tools offer a practical approach to address this challenge by linking local authorities with communities and experts, and increasing the capacity of the involved stakeholders. The OpenStreetMap Humanitarian team supported recovery efforts in the Philippines after the Ketsana typhoon in 2009, post-earthquake efforts in Haiti and others. Within 22 days of Typhoon Haiyan striking the Philippines in 2013, over 1,500 OpenStreetMap volunteers from 82 countries added data inputs onto local maps of the affected area, mapping 448,797 buildings, 34,713 roads, 7,857 residential areas and 4,060 rivers, shared for free online to support disaster response and reconstruction. Engaging civil society can also increase the accountability and responsiveness of government. Recovery programs in Indonesia following the Aceh and Yogyakarta earthquakes used monitoring and evaluation systems where communities could track the progress of financed projects, as well as provide feedback through different means of communication (Multi Donor Fund for Aceh and Nias and the Java Reconstruction Fund 2012). In New York, Rutgers University made the Encyclopedia of Social Work Online available to seven agencies dealing with recovery, and teamed up with field agencies to support the training and application of research. Students, in exchange, gained valuable hands-on experience from recovery planning and implementation (OUP Blog 2014).

7 Create resilience through open data

Geographic information system (GIS) software and tools are instrumental in creating and analyzing geospatial data to support monitoring, forecasting and communicating risks (World Bank 2013e). Connecting global and local knowledge, innovative applications of GIS in the field of disaster risk management can provide low-cost high-tech solutions for the collection, cataloging, analysis and sharing of risk information. Launched in 2011 by the World Bank's Global Facility for Disaster Reduction and Recovery (GFDRR), the Open Data for

Resilience Initiative (OpenDRI) supports more than 20 countries around the world through the mapping of tens of thousands of buildings as well as urban infrastructure, by providing more than 1,000 geospatial datasets to the public, and in developing innovative application tools.

Non-proprietary open-source platforms and tools enable the pooling, sorting, analysis and sharing of risk data that may be used for disaster response, preparedness or planning. The Indonesia Scenario Assessment for Emergencies (InaSAFE) is an open, easy-to-use visualizing and analytical tool for creating impact assessments to inform targeted risk reduction measures. The assessments are based on how a hazard – such as a tsunami, flood or earthquake – affects populations or buildings. Users can create maps and input information back through GeoNode – an open-source platform. InaSAFE was put to the test in contingency planning for the 2012 flood season in Jakarta, and its success provoked a rapid national rollout, along with widespread interest from the international community. Apart from making vertical connections between authorities and communities, tools like InaSAFE can link different groups with the government, namely disaster risk management and planning/development authorities. The tool enables the use of different types of information, including data from OpenStreetMap.

8 Strengthening resilience using big data

Improvements in Information and Communication Technology (ICT) can help collect and create more accurate local data to inform risk management and resilience efforts. Big data can contribute to providing the big picture, while offering at the same time granular, real-time information at the local level. In the US, there are a number of initiatives linking big data and sustainability. At the federal level, the government has recently launched an initiative making climate change-related data from different agencies, including the National Oceanic and Atmospheric Administration (NOAA), the Department of Commerce and the Federal Geographic Data Committee, publicly available (Rozenberg 2014). The website www.data.gov/climate provides datasets, for example, on coastal flooding, geophysical data, severe weather inventories, as well as listing tools, such as the NOAA Digital Coast Tool, that individuals, businesses and local governments can use. In the US, at the state level, due to its exposure to multiple hazards, California has been at the forefront of using innovative web tools. Cal Adapt is a web-based toolkit that can access climate change data and provides tools to show impacts for Californian public and private stakeholders.[9] Smart phone-collected big data has the potential to transform the way in which weather systems are predicted. Recent smart phone models contain barometers, hygrometers, ambient thermometers and even light meters – all of which produce important data for meteorologists that could form part of a granular network of millions of interconnected weather stations. South Korea has recently invested in upgrading its national weather information system to better understand and predict weather patterns and the impact of specific events. The upgrade relies on the installation of big data-processing technology, which in combination with a system of sensors and satellites has dramatically improved the accuracy of forecasts, potentially saving thousands of lives and damage to assets (Hamm 2013).

Using social media stimulates research and actions, and is also increasingly used in the response to disasters. In the private sector, some utilities companies and service providers of critical systems, such as transport and energy, already integrate Twitter feeds into their monitoring and contingency management systems to quickly spot an emergency or see whether a problem has been resolved. They try to detect, for example, where localized damage occurred to better plan equipment and labor needs. In the public sector, the United States Geological Survey (USGS) is currently developing an earthquake detection system that uses Twitter streams in real time. In Japan, mobile phone data was used to track population displacement following the 2011 Great Eastern Earthquake and Tsunami, and was subsequently used for decision making in infrastructure planning and disaster management. In Haiti, following the 2010 earthquake, the Haiti Ushahidi platform, which crowdsourced information largely in the form of SMS texts, but also email, Twitter and the web, was used to estimate the structural damage in Port-au-Prince and showed surprisingly high accuracy.

9 Protecting assets through disaster risk financing and insurance solutions

While financial protection against natural hazards has traditionally focused on sovereign and private risk insurance markets, the scope for solutions in cities is broadening. Disaster risk instruments for cities and municipalities face a number of challenges, linked to the localized nature of hazards in cities, limited scale for efficient risk pooling, the high vulnerability of the urban environment, as well as limited public finances and the availability of localized risk information (World Bank 2013e, 119). While there are not many instruments developed for cities and municipalities, there are a number of initiatives. Following the 1985 earthquake that occurred in Mexico City, the government set up a Natural Disaster Fund (FONDEN) as part of their efforts to better manage catastrophic risk. Thirty-two subnational FONDEN Trusts in each state government serve as vehicles to receive funds from the national trust, governed by the FONDEN rules that regulate the sharing of losses between national and subnational budgets for a defined list of infrastructure types. There are incentives in place to encourage Mexican states to participate in the national program.

In most developed countries, urban dwellers have the option to protect their assets from hazards through private insurance. Some countries, like the US or the UK, also offer national government-driven flood risk insurance schemes for their citizens, especially in areas where private insurance companies do not offer flood insurance on the grounds that it would not be profitable. These public schemes are a controversial means to financially protect private assets, since they can lead to encouraging building in flood-prone areas and lead to large tax-financed payouts. In the US, for example, the value of property covered by the National Flood Insurance Program (NFIP) has increased nine times in real terms since

1978, posing a problem for the long-term sustainability of the program. In 2012, the US government passed reforms that decreased federal subsidies for NFIP. However, in 2014, a bill has been approved levying a 'surcharge on all the NFIP's residential policies to continue to subsidize premiums in high-risk areas' (*The Economist* 2014).

Public companies and private corporations are also taking steps to manage fiscal impacts. Like sovereigns and households, companies often struggle to obtain insurance coverage in the aftermath of a disaster, due to high premiums or dried-up market supply. Hurricane Sandy caused damage to the amount of US$4.8 billion to the Metropolitan Transportation Authority (MTA) in New York City, destroying sensitive electronic and physical infrastructure. In July 2013, to better protect itself from impacts of storm surges over the next 3 years, the MTA assembled US$200 million through a first-known storm surge catastrophe bond for a transport authority (Burne and Mann 2013). The bonds were enabled by a special-purpose insurer called MetroCat Re Ltd, which issued the securities, and yield 4.5 percent over three months. Investors would lose their investment if storm surges exceeded the calculated thresholds, which trigger payout to the MTA's First Mutual Transportation Assurance Co. (Mead 2013).

10 Plan for rapid recovery through institutional preparedness and social cohesion

Cities at risk from natural hazards need to go beyond emergency planning and focus on recovery with clear coordination arrangements. Both the cost and duration of post-disaster recovery and reconstruction tend to increase due to delays in funding and lack of adequate institutional arrangements. In Japan, identification of priority infrastructure, legislation of financial arrangements for rehabilitation and the establishment of pre-disaster plans have enabled prompt emergency response operations and facilitated a quick rehabilitation in the aftermath of the Great East Japan Earthquake and Tsunami (World Bank, GFDRR and Government of Japan 2012b). Learning from the 1995 earthquake, the government issued basic guidelines and a law on reconstruction within 3.5 months of the disaster (World Bank, GFDRR and Government of Japan 2012b). The guidelines set in place innovative policies, positioning municipalities and residents at the center of the reconstruction; promoting the concept of multiple defenses and people-oriented measures in disaster reduction (departing from past over-reliance on defensive structures); and encouraging land use planning as a way to balance safety considerations with the need to preserve links between communities and infrastructure (World Bank, GFDRR and Government of Japan 2012b). The guidelines also set up a special zone for reconstruction containing financial and regulatory incentives, and a central one-stop reconstruction agency to respond to, and help coordinate, the needs of local governments (World Bank, GFDRR and Government of Japan 2012b). Specific responsibilities and planning procedures were established at the prefecture and municipal levels (see Figure 1.2). Participatory methods were used to ensure integration of the views of experts as well as the affected people.

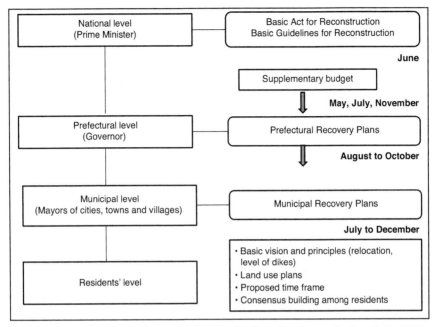

Figure 1.2 Prefecture-level planning following the Great East Japan Earthquake

Source: Re-created by the authors from Knowledge Notes Cluster 4: Recovery Planning in World Bank, Global Facility for Disaster Reduction and Recovery, Government of Japan (2012, 7). Learning from Megadisasters. The Great East Japan Earthquake. Knowledge Notes.

Social capital built up before a disaster plays a central role in how quickly communities can recover. For example, in New Orleans, the Vietnamese community, with robust social networks, was better able to coordinate recovery following Hurricane Katrina than neighborhoods with fewer social ties. Apart from rapidly disseminating information and financial and physical assistance, the Vietnamese community was able to implement recovery faster and minimize the migration of people and resources (Aldrich 2012). Similar observations were made during the 1995 Chicago heatwave, when the Hispanics accounted for only 2 percent of the heat-related deaths but represented 23 percent of the city's population. The Hispanic multi-generational family networks and vital neighborhoods contributed to their increased resilience. Social capital and community empowerment are not only important for disaster recovery but also for strengthening public awareness of disasters, thereby preventing communities from forgetting about past disasters and keeping the memory as well as lessons learned alive.[10]

Conclusion

The world has embarked upon the largest wave of urbanization in history. To illustrate the scale of this trend, over the next 20 years the world is going to build as much urban housing as was built during the past 6,000 years (Goethert 2010). For example, around 75 percent of the India of 2030 still needs to be built. To accommodate the skyrocketing urban growth in this country, urban space equivalent to the size of Chicago or twice the size of Mumbai will need to be constructed every year up until 2030 (McKinsey Global Institute 2010). Urbanization creates opportunities for poverty reduction but the urban context also introduces new risks, with natural hazards being one of them. Cities can benefit from innovative ways of seeking to better understand and communicate, reduce and manage disaster risks. There are a range of tools and examples available to inform local decisions to create strong, safe, resilient cities. Once the underlying risks in a city are known through risk assessments, urban planning can become an effective tool for risk reduction. The key drivers of risk may then be addressed through a range of policy options, for instance, through building codes, retrofitting, environmental rehabilitation and land use planning, concentrating new development away from hazards. Big data and social media tools are increasingly becoming better equipped to help collect and create accurate local data to inform risk management and resilience efforts. To address the residual risks, early warning systems constitute a valuable means of avoiding losses while disaster risk financing and insurance solutions can provide financial protection. Since the current lack of integration of urban planning and risk reduction increases vulnerabilities and the potential for future losses, a shift to proactive and preventive urban planning underpinned with the principle of diminishing risk is needed. The required increase in the role of urban planning as a tool for reducing the effects of disasters is the most important public policy recommendation from this chapter.

Going forward, there is a great opportunity for policymakers to include the principles of resilient development in urban planning and investments. This can be only realized if risk management is a shared responsibility between different economic and social systems, the public sphere and private sector, as well as communities, households and individuals. Based on this understanding, municipal decision makers have a responsibility to ensure that physical infrastructure and services benefit the city's residents, including the poor, that these have the smallest possible environmental impact and are resilient to disasters and climate change.

Recommendation

Cities can increase their resilience if they integrate preventive measures into their urban development processes. Fundamental principles to forge stronger and safer communities include openly sharing risk information for better decisions in urban planning, integrating risk management measures into all sectors, and prioritizing multi-purpose approaches. Balancing and integrating structural and non-structural solutions is a key priority, since improved institutional arrangements, land use planning and ecosystem management are as important as engineered infrastructure solutions.

Audiences of the recommendation: Communities/citizens, city governments, national governments, donors and international agencies.

Notes

1 For a comparison of urbanization in China and India, see Dobbs (2010).
2 The world's low-lying coastal elevation zone covers 2 percent of the world's land area but contains 10 percent of the world's population (McGranahan *et al.* 2007).
3 Shepherd *et al.* (2013) cited in World Bank (2013a).
4 These recommendations follow World Bank (2013d, 72).
5 For an in-depth discussion, see World Bank (2013e, 47).
6 The Rebuild by Design (www.rebuildbydesign.org) competition was launched by the Hurricane Sandy Rebuilding Task Force and United States Department of Housing and Urban Development (HUD) to encourage new thinking in the recovery of specific storm-affected areas. Currently, a final review of ten selected projects is under way.
7 Rebecca Moore, Engineering Manager at Google Earth Engine, speech at WH Open Climate Data Initiative.
8 See, e.g., Barbaro and Gillis (2005) or Speakeasy Forum (2005).
9 See http://cal-adapt.org/tools/.
10 Refer to Professor Bilham as mentioned by Revkin (2011).

References

Aldrich, Daniel. 2012. *Building Resilience: Social Capital in Post-Disaster Recovery*. Chicago, IL: University of Chicago Press.

Asian Development Bank. 2012. "Special Chapter: Green Urbanization in Asia." In *Key Indicators for Asia and the Pacific 2012*, 43rd edition. Manila: Asian Development Bank.

Azili, Fikret. 2012. "Istanbul Seismic Risk Mitigation and Emergency Preparedness Project." Presentation for Urban Risk Management Workshop, Arab States Community of Practice.

Badan Nasional Penanggulangan Bencana (BNPB). 2011. "Rehabilitation and Reconstruction of Post Disaster Areas of Mt. Merapi Eruption in the Provinces of Yogyakarta and Central Java 2011–2013," 169. Jakarta: BNPB.

Barbaro, Michael and Gillis, Justin. 2005. "Wal-Mart at Forefront of Hurricane Relief," *Washington Post*, September 6. www.washingtonpost.com/wp-dyn/content/article/2005/09/05/AR2005090501598.html.

Brecht, Henrike, Deichmann, Uwe and Wang, Hyoung Gun. 2013. *A Global Urban Risk Index*. Policy Research Working Paper No. 6506. Washington, DC: World Bank.

Burne, Katy and Mann, Ted. 2013. "MTA Sells Storm Bond. Agency Gets Creative in Disaster Planning as Usual Sources of Insurance Dry Up." *The Wall Street Journal*, July 21. http://online.wsj.com/news/articles/SB10001424127887323681904578640401075075198.

DHL. 2013. "Deutsche Post DHL and United Nations Development Programme Launch Second 'Get Airports Ready for Disaster' Workshop in the Philippines," Press Release, March 31. www.dhl.com/en/press/releases/releases_2014/group/dp_dhl_and_un_development_programme_launch_wordshop_get_ready_for_disaster.html#.U4YO46LW7X4.

Dilley, M., Chen, R.S., Deichmann, U., Lerner-Lam, A.L., Arnold, M. with J. Agwe, P. Buys, O. Kjekstad, B. Lyon and G. Yetman. 2005. "Natural Disaster Hotspots: A Global Risk Analysis." Synthesis Report, The World Bank and Columbia University, Washington, DC.

Dobbs, Richard. 2010. "Prime Numbers: Megacities. McKinsey Global Institute." *Foreign Policy*, September/October. www.mckinsey.com/insights/mgi/in_the_news/prime_numbers_megacities.

Economist, The. 2014. "Waves of Problems. New Proposals to Reform Subsidized Flood Insurance Do Little to Reduce Risk," March 8. www.economist.com/news/finance-and-economics/21598664-new-proposals-reform-subsidised-flood-insurance-do-too-little-reduce.

Goethert, Reinhard. 2010. "Incremental Housing. A Proactive Urban Strategy." Massachusetts Institute of Technology (MIT). *Monday Developments*, September. http://web.mit.edu/incrementalhousing/articlesPhotographs/pdfs/PagesMondayMag.pdf.

Hallegatte, Stéphane. 2012. "A Cost Effective Solution to Reduce Disaster Losses in Developing Countries: Hydro-meteorological Services, Early Warning, and Evacuation." Policy Research Working Paper No. 6058. Washington, DC: World Bank.

Hallegatte, Stéphane, Green, Colin, Nicholls, Robert J. and Corfee, Morlot, 2013. "Future Flood Losses in Major Coastal Cities." *Nature Climate Change* 3, 802–6. doi:10.1038/nclimate1979.

Hamm, Steve. 2013. "How Big Data Can Boost Weather Forecasting," *Wired*, February 27. www.wired.com/insights/2013/02/how-big-data-can-boost-weather-forecasting/.

Hardoy, Jorgelina. 2013. "Disaster Risk Reduction in Urban Areas. Evidence and Lessons from Latin America Undated," ELLA Policy Brief. http://ella.practicalaction.org/node/964.

Lift. 2013. Federal Express in cooperation with NCA, December 19. www.gotlift.org/news/12-19-2013-Federal-Express-with-NCA.

Little, Richard. 2010. "Managing the Risk of Cascading Failure in Complex Urban Infrastructure." In *Disrupted Cities: When Infrastructure Fails*, edited by Stephen Graham. New York: Routledge, 27–40.

McGranahan, Gordon, Balk, Deborah and Anderson, Bridget. 2007. "The Rising Tide: Assessing the Risks of Climate Change and Human Settlements in Low Elevation Coastal Zones." *Environment and Urbanization* 19(1): 17–37.

McKinsey Global Institute. 2010. "India's Urban Awakening: Building Inclusive Cities, Sustaining Economic Growth," www.mckinsey.com/insights/urbanization/urban_awakening_in_india.

Mead, Charles. 2013. "MTA Obtains $200 Million of Protection with Catastrophe Bond," *Bloomberg News*, July 31. www.bloomberg.com/news/2013-07-31/mta-obtains-200-million-of-protection-with-catastrophe-bonds.html.

Michel-Kerjan, Erwann and Slovic, Paul (eds). 2010. *The Irrational Economist.* New York: Public Affairs.

Miller, Alan. 2014. "Why We Must Engage the Private Sector in Climate Change Adaptation Efforts," Development in Climate Change Blog, September 1. http://blogs.worldbank.org/climatechange/why-we-must-engage-private-sector-climate-change-adaptation-efforts.

Muller, Scott. 2013. "The Next Generation of Infrastructure," *Scenario Journal: Rethinking Infrastructure* 3. http://scenariojournal.com/article/the-next-generation-of-infrastructure/.

Multi Donor Fund for Aceh and Nias and the Java Reconstruction Fund. 2012. *REKOMPAK. Rebuilding Indonesia's Communities After Disasters.* Jakarta: World Bank. www.multidonorfund.org/doc/pdf/20121029_rekompak_book.pdf.

New York City Special Initiative for Rebuilding and Resiliency. 2013. *A Stronger More Resilient New York.* www.nyc.gov/html/sirr/html/report/report.shtml.

OUP Blog. 2014. "Kathleen J. Pottick on Superstorm Sandy and Social Work Resources," Oxford University Press Blog, March 18. https://blog.oup.com/2014/03/superstorm-sandy-social-work-resources/.

Revkin, Andrew. 2011. "'Disaster Memory' and the Flooding of Fukushima," Dot Earth, April 4. http://dotearth.blogs.nytimes.com/2011/04/04/disaster-memory-and-the-flooding-of-fukushima/?_php=true&_type=blogs&_r=0.

Rozenberg, Norman. 2014. "Big Data Helps Solve Tough Problems," Tech Page One, March 27. http://techpageone.dell.com/technology/data-center/big-data-helping-solve-tough-problems/#.UzXLMdLXa18.

Shepherd, A., Mitchell, T., Lewis, K., Lenhardt, A., Jones, L., Scott, L. and Muir-Wood, R. 2013. *The Geography of Poverty, Disasters and Climate Extremes in 2030.* ODI, Met Office Hadley Center, RMS Publication, Exeter.

Speakeasy Forum. 2005. "In Katrina's Wake, Wal-Mart and Home Depot Came to the Rescue," CNet, September 10. http://forums.cnet.com/7723-6130_102-124746/in-katrina-s-wake-wal-mart-and-home-depot-came-to-the-rescu/Private%20FEMA%3Cbr%3EIn%20Katrina's%20wake,%20Wal-Mart%20and%20Home%20Depot%20came%20to%20the%20rescue.%20?tag=posts;msg1412669.

Tavaana. n.d. "Empowering Nairobi's Slums: The Map Kibera Project." https://tavaana.org/en/content/empowering-nairobis-slums-map-kibera-project.

United Nations. 2013. *World Economic and Social Survey 2013. Sustainable Development Challenges.* Department of Economic and Social Affairs. New York: United Nations.

United Nations Environment Programme. 2002. "Rainwater Harvesting and Utilization: An Environmentally Sound Approach for Sustainable Urban Water Management: An Introductory Guide for Decision-Makers." Brief. www.gdrc.org/uem/water/rainwater/rainwaterguide.pdf.

United Nations Habitat. n.d.. Website: www.unhabitat.org/.

United Nations Human Settlements Programme. 2006. *State of the World's Cities 2006/7.* London: Earthscan.

United Nations secretariat of the International Strategy for Disaster Reduction (ISDR). 2011. *Revealing Risk, Redefining Development: Global Assessment Report on Disaster Risk Reduction.* Geneva: United Nations.

—— 2013. *From Shared Risk to Shared Value. The Business Case for Disaster Risk Reduction. Global Assessment Report on Disaster Risk Reduction.* Geneva: United Nations.

World Bank. 2009. *World Development Report 2009. Reshaping Economic Geography.* Washington, DC: World Bank.

—— 2012a. *Cities and Flooding: A Guide to Integrated Flood Risk Management for the 21st Century,* edited by A. Jha, R. Bloch and J. Lamond. Washington, DC: World Bank.

—— 2012b. *Climate Change, Disaster Risk, and the Urban Poor: Cities Building Resilience for a Changing World,* edited by J. Baker. Washington, DC: World Bank.

—— 2012c. *East Asia and the Pacific Economic Update.* Volume 2, Remaining Resilient. Washington, DC: World Bank.

—— 2013a. *Building Resilience. Integrating Climate and Disaster Risk into Development. The World Bank Group Experience.* Washington, DC: The World Bank.

—— 2013b. *World Development Report 2014: Risk and Opportunity.* Washington, DC: World Bank.

—— 2013c. *Global Monitoring Report 2013: Rural–Urban Dynamics and the Millennium Development Goals*. Washington, DC: World Bank.

—— 2013d. *Strong, Safe, and Resilient: A Strategic Guide for Disaster Risk Management for Policy-Makers in East Asia and the Pacific*. Washington, DC: World Bank.

—— 2013e. *Building Urban Resilience. Principles, Tools and Practice*. Washington, DC: World Bank.

—— 2015. *East Asia's Changing Urban Landscape: Measuring a Decade of Spatial Growth*. Urban Development Series. Washington, DC: World Bank.

World Bank, Global Facility for Disaster Reduction and Recovery (GFDRR) and Government of Japan. 2012a. *The Sendai Report. Managing Disaster Risks for a Resilient Future*. Washington, DC: The World Bank.

—— 2012b. *Learning from Megadisasters. The Great East Japan Earthquake. Knowledge Notes*. Washington, DC: The World Bank.

World Bank and Global Facility for Disaster Reduction and Recovery (GFDRR). 2013. *Weather, Climate and Water Hazards and Climate Resilience: Effective Preparedness through National Meteorological and Hydrological Services*. Washington, DC: World Bank.

World Bank and Government of Mexico. 2012. "Disaster Risk Management in Turkey." In *Improving the Assessment of Disaster Risks to Strengthen Financial Resilience: A Special Joint G20 Publication by the Government of Mexico and the World Bank*. Washington, DC: World Bank.

World Bank Institute. 2009. *Approaches to Urban Slums: Adaptive and Proactive Strategies*. Washington, DC: World Bank.

World Bank and United Nations. 2010. *Natural Hazards, Unnatural Disasters: The Economics of Effective Prevention*. Washington, DC: World Bank.

Yang, Jun. 2011. "Worst Thai Floods in 50 Years Hit Apple, Toyota Supply Chains." *Bloomberg News*, October 21. www.bloomberg.com/news/2011-10-20/worst-thai-floods-in-50-years-hit-apple-toyota-supply-chains.html.

Further resources

Andrés, Luis, Biller, Dan and Herrera Dappe Mattías. 2013. *Reducing Poverty by Closing South Asia's Infrastructure Gap*. Washington, DC: World Bank.

Barthel, Fabian and Neumayer, Eric. 2011a. "A Trend Analysis of Normalized Insured Damage from Natural Disasters." *Climatic Change* 113, 215–237.

—— 2011b "Normalizing Economic Loss from Natural Disasters: A Global Analysis." *Global Environmental Change* 21(1), 13–24.

Douglass, M. 2013. *The Urban Transition of Environmental Disaster Governance in Asia*. Working Paper Series No. 210. Singapore: Asia Research Institute.

Gourio, François. 2012. "Disaster Risk and Business Cycles." *American Economic Review* 102(6), 2734–2766.

Hallegatte, S. 2011. *How Economic Growth and Rational Decisions Can Make Disaster Losses Grow Faster than Wealth*. Policy Research Working Paper No. 5617. Washington, DC: World Bank.

—— 2012. *An Exploration of the Link between Development, Economic Growth, and Natural Risk*. Policy Research Working Paper No. 6216. Washington, DC: World Bank.

Hallegatte, Stéphane, Ankur Shah, Robert Lempert, Casey Brown and Stuart Gill. 2012. *Investment Decision Making under Deep Uncertainty: Application to Climate Change*. Policy Research Working Paper No. 6193. Washington, DC: World Bank.

KC, Shyam. 2013. *Cost Benefit Studies on Disaster Risk Reduction in Developing Countries.* East Asia and the Pacific (EAP) Disaster Risk Management (DRM). Knowledge Notes Working Paper Series 27. Washington, DC: World Bank.

Klinenberg, Eric. 2002. *Heat Wave: A Social Autopsy of Disaster in Chicago.* Chicago, IL: University of Chicago Press.

Lall, Somik V. and Deichmann, Uwe. 2012. "Density and Disasters: Economics of Urban Hazard Risk." *World Bank Research Observer* 27(1), 74–105. Washington, DC: World Bank.

Meyer, Robert. 2010. "Why We Still Fail to Learn from Disasters." In *The Irrational Economist: Making Decisions in a Dangerous World*, edited by Erwann Michel-Kerjan and Paul Slovic. New York: Public Affairs, 124–131.

Michel-Kerjan, Erwann (2012) "How Resilient Is Your Country?" *Nature* 491(7452), 497.

Pielke, Roger A. Jr., Gratz, Joel, Landsea, Christopher W., Collins, Douglas, Saunders, Mark A. and Musulin, Rade. 2008. "Normalized Hurricane Damage in the United States: 1900–2005." *Natural Hazards Review* 9(1), 29–42.

Satterthwaite, D., Huq, S., Pelling, M. Reid, H. and Lankao, P. 2007. *Adapting to Climate Change in Urban Areas, the Possibilities and Constraints in Low- and Middle-Income Nations.* Human Settlements Discussion Paper Series No. 1. London: International Institute for Environment and Development.

Todo, Yasuyuki, Nakajima, Kentaro and Matous, Petr. 2013. *How Do Supply Chain Networks Affect the Resilience of Firms to Natural Disasters? Evidence from the Great East Japan Earthquake.* Discussion Paper Series 13-E-028. Tokyo: Research Institute of Economy, Trade and Industry.

Viguie, Vincent and Hallegatte, Stéphane. 2012. "Trade-offs and Synergies in Urban Climate Policies." *Nature Climate Change* 2(5), 334–337.

World Economic Forum. (2014). *Global Risks 2013.* 9th edition. Geneva: World Economic Forum.

Yan Aalst, Maarten, Kellett, Jan, Pichon, Florence and Mitchell, Tom. 2013. *Incentives in Disaster Risk Management and Humanitarian Response.* Background Paper for the World Development Report 2014. Washington, DC: World Bank.

2 Climate change and disaster risk reduction

Adaptation to uncertainties of changing climate

Hidetomi Oi and Wataru Ono

Introduction

A number of discussions have been held among experts on the growing intensity of climate change and its impacts upon disaster risk. For example, the Intergovernmental Panel on Climate Change (IPCC) recently affirmed that climate change is already causing impacts upon natural and human systems on all continents and the oceans (IPCC 2014a, A-1). It warned that the increasing magnitude of warming will lead to severe, pervasive and irreversible impacts that may exceed adaptation limits (IPCC 2014a, B-1, C-2).

Noting that climate change is already magnifying the disaster risks, especially for developing countries, a series of Global Platform Sessions of the International Strategy for Disaster Reduction (GPDRR 2009, 2011, 2013) has reiterated the need for mainstreaming climate change adaptation policies in national development plans, while at the same time providing support for poverty reduction strategies. With the IPCC projecting that the effects of climate change will continue to grow in the future, actions towards "mitigation" (through the reduction of greenhouse gas emissions) and "adaptation" (to resiliently adjust to the impacts of climate change) should be taken as early and as proactively as possible. Only by doing so can critical situations be avoided in the future and pathways towards sustainable development ensured.

To facilitate such actions, this chapter presents data on observed and predicted climate change, followed by a projection of the risks. This is important in order to understand the potential seriousness of climate change impacts and to recognize the urgency of actions required to address these impacts. The chapter then identifies and analyzes the essential features of climate change-related risks and considers options to address them through disaster risk reduction (DRR) measures. In doing so, the chapter also demonstrates how climate change-related DRR is different from "conventional" DRR. Finally, strategies employed by JICA to help developing countries build resilience to climate change impacts are presented, together with two short case studies of JICA-supported projects aimed at climate change adaptation: Sri Lanka and Thailand.

Among the two approaches of "adaptation" and "mitigation" for climate change risk management, this chapter focuses on adaptation rather than mitigation because the former is an issue to be addressed by all nations according to their respective disaster risk, while the latter is an issue to be addressed mainly by major GHG (greenhouse gas) emission countries. Furthermore, while there are a variety of climate change-related disasters, this chapter will consider those associated with heavy rainfall, cyclones and sea-level rise, and not drought, heatwave, glacial retreat, etc. which are not so widely studied in Japan and, accordingly, the relevant knowledge and information is not easily available. It is expected that this chapter will be helpful for international and national officials/experts in the preparation of the post-2015 DRR framework and subsequent action plans so that climate change adaptation may be considered and implemented as a key component of DRR in the coming decades.

Climate change and impacts upon disaster risk

Since its establishment in 1988, the IPCC has issued assessment reports in 1990, 1995, 2001, 2007 and 2014. The Fourth Assessment Report (AR4) in 2007 stated for the first time that warming of the climate system was unequivocal and that human influence on the climate system was clear (IPCC 2007), dispelling any lingering doubts about global warming predictions. AR5 in 2014, supporting these statements, provided updated information on global warming and forecast its resulting impacts. These are shown in Figure 2.1 and Table 2.1, based, first, on observations and subsequently by applying improved climate simulation models.

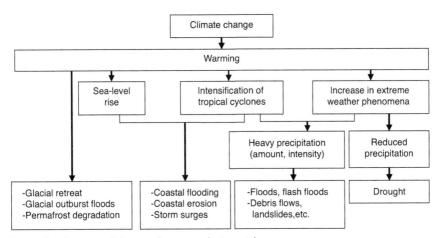

Figure 2.1 Impacts of climate change on disaster risk

Source: Developed by the author based on IPCC (2014) AR5 WGI, The Physical Science Basis, Summary for Policymakers.

Table 2.1 Climate change and impacts, observed, and projection for the end of the twenty-first century

Temperature	• Almost the entire globe has experienced surface warming. Each of the past three decades has been successively warmer than any preceding decade since 1850. Global surface temperatures change between the average of 1850 to 1900 (pre-industrial era) and 1986 to 2005 was 0.61°C. Warming is unequivocal.
	• Global surface temperatures will rise by 0.3 to 4.8°C during the twenty-first century. COP 16 agreed that increases in global temperature should be kept below 2°C to prevent dangerous anthropogenic interference with the climate system.
	• Risks with regard to extreme weather events are already "moderate," but will be "considerable" at 1 or 2°C above pre-industrial levels and "high" to "very high" at 4°C or more.
Precipitation	• Annual precipitation will increase in high latitudes, equatorial Pacific Ocean and mid-latitude wet regions, and will decrease in mid-latitude dry regions, with increasing contrast between wet and dry regions and between wet and dry seasons.
	• Extreme precipitation events will become more intense and frequent over most of the mid-latitude regions and wet tropical regions.
	• In some regions increases in heavy precipitation will occur despite projected decreases in total precipitation.
Monsoon	• Globally the area encompassed by monsoon systems will increase.
	• Monsoon winds will weaken but precipitation will intensify.
	• Onset dates will be earlier and retreat dates will be delayed, resulting in lengthening of the monsoon season.
Tropical cyclones	• Global frequency of tropical cyclones will either decrease or remain essentially unchanged.
	• However, wind speed will increase and heavy rainfall associated with tropical cyclones will increase.
Sea level	• Global mean sea level rose by 0.19m during 1901 to 2010 and will rise by 0.26 to 0.82m during the twenty-first century due to ocean warming and loss of mass of glaciers and ice sheets.
	• Sea-level rise coupled with increases in tropical cyclone maximum wind speed is a specific issue for tropical small island states.

Source: Developed by authors based on IPCC (2014) AR5 WGI The Physical Science Basis, Summary for Policymakers.

Climate-related disaster risk reduction (DRR)

Overview of DRR

Mitigation and adaptation

Climate-related disaster risk reduction (DRR) is pursued through "mitigation" and "adaptation" (Climate Change Adaptation: CCA) as the two wheels of a vehicle (see Figure 2.2). Mitigation refers to ways of reducing the rate and magnitude

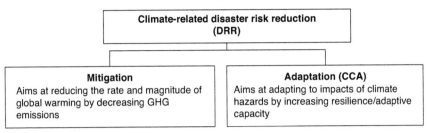

Figure 2.2 Components of climate-related disaster risk reduction

Source: Authors.

of warming by lowering GHG emissions, while adaptation means developing methods of adjusting to climate change impacts by decreasing vulnerability and exposure while increasing resilience and adaptive capacity.

Mitigation is an essential task, without which risks will increase exponentially. However, this is likely to require drastic actions and a significant amount of time before becoming effective. In order to attain the goal of "less than 2°C relative to pre-industrial levels" as agreed at COP (Conference of Parties) 15, global emissions should be 40 to 70 percent lower by 2050 than those recorded in 2010 and near zero or below in 2100, according to IPCC WGIII for AR5 (IPCC 2014b). The IPCC report states that it is still possible to meet this goal with more rapid improvements of energy efficiency, etc. However, it also warned that "delay in mitigation efforts will substantially increase the difficulty of the transition to low emissions levels and narrow the range of options consistent with maintaining temperature change below 2°C." This projection tells us that while emission countries are expected to accelerate mitigation measures, all countries will need to make extra efforts in adaptation measures to address increasing disaster risks associated with climate change. Adaptation being a common issue among countries across the world, this chapter focuses on this aspect of DRR.

Characteristics of climate-related disaster risks

From the analysis on climate change in section 1, *uncertainties* and *continuous increases in the level of risks* in the future are identified as characteristics of climate-related disaster risks which require particular attention in planning CCA.

Uncertainty is in terms of range of the climate-related disaster risks and is attributed to limitation of global warming modelling, effectiveness of mitigation policies, changes in socioeconomic conditions, etc. Uncertainty has been more or less involved even in the planning of DRM, as it deals with the natural hazards that are uncertain by nature; however, CCA has to consider larger ranges of uncertainty than DRM because of the additional uncertain factors as mentioned above.

Risks will increase in any scenario for the climate simulations for AR5 continuously for many centuries in the future, even if emissions of CO2 are stopped, due to the cumulative emissions of CO2 (IPCC 2013, 12.5). This grim reality of ever-increasing risks with uncertainties should be recognized and considered in the principle of CCA approaches.

Approaches for climate change adaptation (CCA)

Approaches for CCA considering the characteristics of climate-related disaster risks

Considering these characteristics of climate-related disaster risks, this chapter refers to two approaches for CCA: the *resilient approach*, which provides means of building resilience to address the uncertain magnitude of the risks, and *the phased approach*, by which the increasing risk with uncertainty may be addressed flexibly and effectively through an iterative process. While the names of these two approaches may not be widely known, the concepts and measures are similar to those involved in approaches suggested by IPCC and various organizations from different angles of adaptation, which include a scenario-based approach, robust approach, iterative approach, non- and low-regret approach, win–win (co-benefit) approach, synergy generation approach and so on.

1 RESILIENT APPROACH

The resilient approach aims at developing resilient responses to hazards in ways that will help avoid catastrophic situations, even if hazards exceed the assumed level, and to ensure early recovery. The multi-layer approach (MLIT 2008, 2010a, 2010b) and redundancy approach (JICA 2013a) are similar concepts to this approach.

In the case of flood DRR, a comprehensive approach in the combination of structural measures and non-structural measures may be an option, in that the structural measures are designed to cope with hazards by constructing embankments, dams and other structures as far as is feasible considering cost–benefit and other factors, while non-structural measures are to supplement structural measures by means of early warning, hazard mapping and other low-regret measures, and play an important role especially in the case of hazards which exceed the coping capacity of the structural measures.

Figure 2.3 illustrates this concept. When risks are not so high, they can be managed substantially by structural measures. As risks increase, non-structural measures become essential to supplement structural measures. As risks increase further even with mitigation by reducing GHG emissions, the gap between the risk and coping capacity of structural measures will expand and consequently the role of non-structural measures will increase. The structural measures are essential for protecting human lives as well as private and public physical assets but the effectiveness is limited to the design level, which is determined depending on financial and other conditions of each country.

The policy "Climate Change Adaptation Strategies to Cope with Water Related Disasters Due to Global Warming" is in line with this concept. It assumes

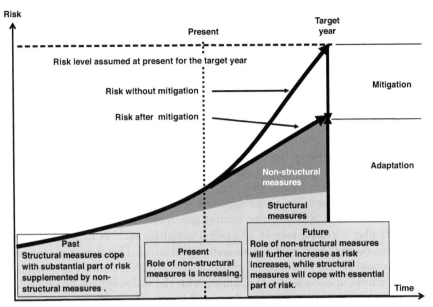

Figure 2.3 Approaches for coping with increasing levels of risk

Source: Authors.

that precipitation will increase 1.1 to 1.3 times over the next 100 years in Japan and subsequently the design safety level of flood mitigation will not be achieved as planned: for rivers where the design safety level has been set for 1/200 (once every 200 years), the safety level will be lowered to 1/90–1/145; likewise 1/100 will be lowered to 1/25–1/90. Against these severe drops in safety levels projected for the future, the strategies emphasized the basin approach with multi-layered measures to effectively cope with possible increases in excess floods in the future (MLIT 2008).

Following the strategies, the *Practical Guidelines on Strategic Climate Change Adaptation Planning* (MLIT 2010a) were prepared to provide planning procedures and options for adaptation measures. They targeted countries where socioeconomic development and urbanization are expected especially in alluvial plains, like the history of development in Japan, but effective flood mitigation measures are yet to be developed.

Meanwhile, JICA prepared the *Handbook on Climate Change Adaptation in the Water Sector* (JICA 2011a) which is in the same line as the strategies and guidelines of MLIT as mentioned above, emphasizing the need for radical amendments to the conventional planning of flood management and recommending approaches to cope with changing and uncertain climate in a resilient and sustainable manner (Box 2.1).

The basin approach as emphasized by these documents consists of flood mitigation works in rivers and various measures in river basins. As for flood mitigation works in rivers, they emphasize the merit of traditional methods such as "open levees" and "ring levees," instead of long, continuous levees, which allow inundation over riverine areas to reduce peak discharge of the river and protect downstream areas from flooding. Since riverine areas are largely non-residential and mostly rice fields, damage is limited.

Measures in river basins include (1) measures to reduce run-off into rivers, such as rainwater storage at playgrounds, parking areas, etc. in residential areas (Figures 2.4 and 2.5); and (2) measures to increase resilience and reduce damage in flood plains, such as land use control based on hazard maps, flood proofing of houses by raising floors, and early warning, evacuation, flood fighting and other measures employed at the time of emergency.

The basin approach requires the understanding and cooperation of stake-holders of different interests, between upstream areas and downstream areas, urban areas and rural areas, development sectors and DRR sectors, citizens, communities, local governments, central government, etc. In addition, communities play a crucial role in adaptation activities such as hazard mapping, awareness raising, early warning/evacuation and so on. Therefore a mechanism for the coordination of stakeholders is necessary. JICA recommends establishing a platform at early stages of planning with the following key functions: to build consensus on planning, to reflect local knowledge in planning, to clarify responsibilities of each agency, and to encourage voluntary activities (JICA 2011a).

2 PHASED APPROACH

The phased approach aims at responding flexibly to the changing climate based on the assumption that conditions will continue to change and technological advances occur over time. The "iterative approach," involving a process of monitoring, research, evaluation, learning and multiple feedback, is based on similar concepts.

Any approach will always be subject to consequences that were not anticipated. Climate change impacts are likely to have such consequences and should be monitored carefully to ensure that plans can be modified based on revised projections. Phased approaches should be considered in dealing with complex situations characterized by uncertainties, long time frames, the potential for learning, etc., and particularly for climate change DRR because of the changing climate with major uncertainties.

Figure 2.6 illustrates the concept of a phased approach. Adaptation plans should be developed using a long-term perspective. For practical purposes the target years of each phase will need to cover a period of 20 to 30 years. This is because differences in projections among global warming scenarios during this time span are small. The target level of risk will be determined based on the range of projections between a low-emissions scenario (RCP 2.6) and a high-emissions scenario (RCP 8.5). The plan will be reviewed and amended at appropriate intervals, taking into consideration the changes in climate-related disaster risks as well as the social and economic conditions

Figures 2.4 and 2.5 Examples of rainwater storage using urban facilities. Measures to temporarily store rainwater at the time of heavy rainfall using urban facilities to reduce the peak flood discharge of rivers

Source: Authors.

and consequences of the project being undertaken, and incorporating new knowledge learned from experience and the development of technology/science for adaptation.

This approach is a participatory process which requires inputs of the knowledge and experience of practitioners and stakeholders. However, deficits of knowledge of the actors about climate change and adaptation measures are among key factors which constrain the promotion of the wide range of iterative processes. Also constraining are social and cultural factors: religious beliefs leading to mis-perception of risks or non-motivation to act, gender issues due to cultural and institutional pressure unfavorable to women, and so on (IPCC 2014a, 16.3.2). In view of the increasingly pressing demands of CCA, the training of practitioners and stakeholders is necessary to overcome these constraints and to enhance the adaptive capacity for CCA, and, further, higher education and school education are necessary for broader human resources development and to create societies which will promote CCA on a long-term basis in the future.

With regard to the interval of the review, the National Land Resilience Basic Plan currently under preparation by the Japanese government will be reviewed at least every 5 years and the Action Plan being prepared in parallel with the Basic Plan will be reviewed every year. IPCC (2014a, Box 5.1, 5.5.3.1, 14.3.1.1) refers to sea-wall construction in the UK after the North Sea storm surge in 1953:

> The engineered alterations resulted in a new array of coastal instabilities including disturbance in sediment supply and damages to coastal eco-systems. As a result, many have promoted a "phased capacity expansion" strategy, which allows engineered projects to undertake design modification as conditions or knowledge change and facilitate incremental project con-struction to ease the burden of upfront financing. An example is the Thames Estuary 2100 Plan.

One area that needs greater attention for CCA is the predicted increase in extreme weather events resulting in flash floods, debris flows, slope fail-ures, landslides, etc. Inundation of urban areas and debris flowing down hillsides caused by concentrated rainfall are occurring more frequently and caus-ing greater damage. In order to deal with this type of disaster, it is necessary to detect heavy rainfall concentrated over narrow areas as early and precisely as possible to provide timely warnings and prepare for evacuation. However, the national meterological networks, especially in developing countries, are inadequate to monitor such rainfall. In Japan, risk management in this type of disaster is a priority area for climate change DRR. To monitor concentrated rainfall, rain gauges that incorporate radar have rapidly advanced to a point where they are able to measure rainfall in a 250m × 250m grid. This technology could be more widely applied in countries prone to this type of disaster. Cheaper and simpler equipment needs to be progressed for application in developing countries.

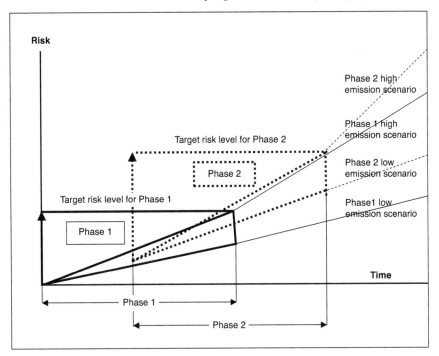

Figure 2.6 Concept of phased approach

Source: Developed by the authors.

Building resilience to climate change in developing countries: the experience of JICA

Vulnerability and exposure of developing countries

While the impacts of climate change are global concerns, disasters often have disproportionate impacts upon developing countries and poor communities. Developing countries are particularly vulnerable to climate change because of a variety of constraints, including inadequate adaptive capacity due to poor DRR infrastructure, and insufficient social/economic institutions capable of responding to climate change issues. Moreover, the lack of government capacity hinders the improvement of vulnerable circumstances and the fulfillment of even basic needs for social/economic development in addressing high poverty rates. People in developing countries are particularly exposed to climate change risks because, with a higher proportion of the population engaged in primary production, their livelihoods are much more dependent upon natural resources such as water resources, marine resources, ecosystems, etc. that are subject to climate change. Expansion of informal settlements of the poor in hazardous areas in and around major urban areas is a typical example of exposure to risks in developing countries.

Strategies

Disaster risk, poverty and climate change are closely interlinked. Therefore strategies to assist developing countries should focus on mainstreaming climate change adaptation measures within other development strategies with the goal of establishing a more resilient society and to achieve sustainable development. To incorporate a perspective of mainstreaming adaptation into development strategies, a "soft" institutional approach to reduce vulnerability and exposure is particularly important as part of an integrated approach in combination with "hard" structural approaches. Soft approaches include planning/implementing national adaptation plans (NAPs) and establishing legal institutions, regulations for operation at the sector level, etc. in order to make consistent progress in adaptation measures.

It is important to make predictions based on scientific analyses and to assess the impacts of climate change, as well as to understand the current adaptive capacity of a country or society in order to gauge vulnerability to climate change. Enhancement of the capacity for climate change adaptation at sectoral, regional or community level plays a key role in reducing vulnerability. Box 2.1 provides basic strategies and methodologies relating to climate change prediction and the use of scientific assessment on the impact of climate change.

Box 2.1 *Handbook on Climate Change Adaptation in the Water Sector* (JICA 2011a)

The *Handbook* emphasizes the need for radical amendments to the conventional planning of flood management and water resources development while recommending approaches to cope with a changing and uncertain climate in a resilient and sustainable manner. Historically, flood control and water resources management have been planned based on the premise that past precipitation patterns will not change over time (a principle referred to as stationarity). However, the concept of stationarity is no longer viable due to the effects of climate change. Approaches without considering climate change impacts could lead to under- or over-design.

Explaining the methodology of climate change prediction as well as the use of scientific assessments of climate change impacts, this book indicates that approaches to project formulation in the future should be fundamentally different from the conventional ones in the following ways:

1   Projects will need to deal with a changing climate.
2   Greater consideration will need to be given to projecting future impacts during project formulation and implementation.
3   Technologies available for projection and adaptation are developing, and water management systems will change or must change accordingly.

The book suggests five fundamental approaches in water management policy for disaster management, as indicated below.

1   Human security: Focusing on individuals, particularly the most vulnerable.
2   Engagement with society: Engaging with the whole of society, including policymakers, heads of governments (central and local) and community members, as a key to mainstreaming adaptation in development policies.
3   Building a sustainable adaptive society: Building a resilient society that can sustainably adapt to the changing and uncertain climate.
4   Disaster risk management: Managing disaster risks with a focus on the society's vulnerabilities and exposure, especially those associated with urbanization and climate change, and strengthening adaptive capacity.
5   A "zero victim" goal of flood control: Taking a three-tier adaptive approach: (a) protecting critical areas with suitable structures; (b) discouraging settlement in disaster-prone areas, and (c) coping with unavoidable inundation through community-based disaster management.

Climate change adaptation measures on disaster management, taken by countries in Asia with the support of JICA

Case 1: *Disaster Management Capacity Enhancement Project Adaptable to Climate Change in Sri Lanka*

The Government of Sri Lanka has been making efforts to strengthen its disaster management capacity, with activities such as the establishment of the Disaster Management Center (DMC). This is a focal organization designed to deal with disaster management issues, and was established after the tsunami disaster following the Indian Ocean Earthquake (2004). Furthermore, following the increased risks caused by the impacts of climate change, there is growing acknowledgment of the need to tackle climate change issues. In Sri Lanka, these risks include increases for torrential rainfall/drought and uncertainty related to the changes in timing of the rainy and dry seasons.

As a result of this situation, a technical cooperation project entitled "Disaster Management Capacity Enhancement Project Adaptable to Climate Change" commenced in March 2010 between the Government of Sri Lanka and Japan. The project was composed of five components: (1) strengthening the leadership and coordination capacity of DMC; (2) enhancement of the capacity of the Department of Meteorology (DOM) to monitor, analyze and provide basic weather forecasts; (3) enhancement of the capacity of the National Building Research Organization (NBRO) to provide disaster management for floods and landslides; (4) establishment of early warning systems, and (5) enhancement of community-based disaster management. While structural measures, which consider the impact of climate change upon floods, had been studied in a preceding project, this project focused on non-structural measures.

Thus, this project focused on non-structural measures that are important, especially in dealing with disasters of unexpected magnitude, as well as climate change impacts that involve high levels of uncertainty. Among non-structural measures, particular attention was given to the institutional strengthening of DMC, which included not only capacity building in the methodology of science-based analysis and research on climate change but also basic human resource development of DMC and related organizations. The project also aimed at systemic reformulation of existing designs/manuals/activities to adjust to societal and natural environment changes, including climate change. For example, capacity building to improve existing plans flexibly for officers who are responsible for formulating disaster management plans will enable them to rebuild and design or plan based on refined climate change predictions in the future.

Many countries have been making efforts to strengthen institutions in accordance with the Hyogo Framework for Action. This gives institutional strengthening the top priority among five priority actions, based on the experience of the Indian Ocean Tsunami disaster in 2004. JICA has been supporting several countries in making such efforts and this project is one such example. Institutional strengthening is regarded as the first requirement for disaster risk management, including climate change adaptation.

Case 2: Integrated Study on Hydro-Meteorological Prediction and Adaptation to Climate Change (IMPAC-T) in Thailand

In Thailand the issues relating to water, such as increasing damage from floods, as well as land subsidence due to overuse of groundwater, have become significant problems. At the same time, dependence on water resources is growing. In addition, the Government of Thailand needs to implement measures not only to deal with current issues but also to ensure that proper adaptation measures are in place to manage future climate change impacts. Under these circumstances, the "Integrated Study on Hydro-Meteorological Prediction and Adaptation to Climate Change" was initiated in 2009 in Thailand within the framework of the Science and Technology Research Partnership for Sustainable Development (SATREPS). The project was implemented jointly by universities in Thailand and Japan. The aim of the project was to develop capacity in research on the variations in water circulation affected by future climate change and the methodology to assess the influence of disasters in order to establish appropriate adaptation policies and measures.

Under the project, three components have been implemented to reduce the risks caused by climate change:

1 capacity enhancement of meteorological and hydrological observation in consideration of climate change;
2 development of a water circulation and water resource management model in consideration of human activities;
3 development of an integrated water circulation information system that recognizes human activities as well as climate change.

Through examination of data obtained by enhanced ground/satellite-based observations as well as climate change prediction information, the project ana-lyzed trends in climate change impacts upon river water flow and assessed the reliability of a model of water circulation produced in this project. It also looked at water resource management in consideration of climate change as well as human activities. Based on this information, the project identified the risks posed by climate change on water circulation. Finally, products that were established during the project, such as meteorological and hydrological data, a water circula-tion/water management model, and risk analysis were compiled to develop an integrated water circulation information system as a supporting tool to generate adaptation policies. This system will be used in various aspects of water resource management on both a short-term and long-term basis to consider the impacts of climate change. This is also useful for an early warning system for floods, using quasi-real-time monitoring developed by the project, and for making hazard maps incorporating risk analysis produced in the project into a GIS (geographic information system). This project was implemented for Thailand as the primary target area, with possible expansion in the future to the Mekong River basin of similar conditions, applying the methods developed by this project.

Conclusion

1   Climate change impacts have been increasing and will continue to inten-sify in the future. Recognizing this negative prognosis, pre-emptive and proactive activities to address climate change impacts should be taken in order to avoid critical situations arising in the future.
2   "*Uncertainties*" and "*continuous increase in risk*" have been identified as essen-tial features of climate-related disaster risks which require particular atten-tion in the planning and implementation of climate change adaptation (CCA).
3   Considering these essential features of climate-related disaster risks, CCA is to be pursued through a "*resilient approach*" and "*phased approach*." A resilient approach responds to hazards in ways that will minimize damage as far as possible, even if hazards exceed the assumed level of risk, and to ensure early recovery. A phased approach entails responding to the changing climate flexibly and effectively through an iterative process, modifying plans accord-ing to new projections of risks and applying technological advances.
4   For these approaches to be successful in each country, projections of climate change risk should be made continuously by the IPCC at appropriate inter-vals as in the past, and need to be interpreted preferably by international organizations for practical application to the national adaptation plan in each country by those concerned with disaster risk reduction and sustainable development.
5   Developing countries are particularly vulnerable and exposed to climate change impacts. In view of the close linkage between poverty, disaster risk and climate change, assistance is necessary for mainstreaming climate

change adaptation within national development policies. To this end, it is necessary to assist in institutional frameworks, including planning/implementation of national adaptation plans and other policy approaches. Enhancement of adaptive capacity and the provision of information on climate change are also necessary to ensure consistent progress in adaptation measures.

6   Extreme weather events causing flash floods, debris flows, landslides, etc. require greater attention in view of the increase in such disasters in recent years and the possible increase in the future due to climate change. To deal with these types of disasters, the monitoring of concentrated rainfall is essential. The technology to monitor such rainfall has been advancing and should be more widely applied in countries prone to this type of disaster. While promoting advancement of technologies for application at national level, cheaper and simpler equipment needs to be developed for community early warning.

7   Additional ways forward:

- The Fifth IPCC Synthesis Report (IPCC 2014) was issued in October 2014 integrating reports of Working Groups I, II and III. It contains an abundance of recommendations on principles, strategies and approaches for climate change adaptation. These should be incorporated into the post-2015 DRR Framework to be adopted at the Third World Conference on DRR in March 2015. This presents an opportunity to renew efforts for climate change adaptation over the coming decades, and in the subsequent national plans for post-2015 disaster risk reduction.

- In order to facilitate implemention of these recommendations at the national level, practical guidelines should be prepared by international organizations and others as they did for the Hyogo Framework of Action, such as "A Guide for Implementing the Hyogo Framework of Action by Local Stakeholders" (United Nations secretariat of the ISDR/Kyoto University). Guidelines prepared thus far, such as *Practical Guidelines on Strategic Climate Change Adaptation Planning* (MLIT 2010a) and *Handbook on Climate Change Adaptation in the Water Sector* (JICA 2011a) are expected to be reviewed and updated for wide distribution.

Recommendations

In an era of changing climate, adaptation should be pursued with new approaches to respond flexibly to growing and uncertain climate-related disaster risks. A resilient approach will minimize casualties and damage, and avoid catastrophic situations even when hazards exceed anticipated levels of severity. A phased approach will entail a flexible response by modifying plans according to new projections and other changes. To facilitate CCA, especially in developing countries, practical guidelines should be prepared by the international community.

Audiences of the recommendations: national governments, donors, international agencies and the United Nations secretariat of the ISDR.

References

ADBI. 2014. *Disaster Risk Management in Asia and the Pacific.* London: Routledge.

Cabinet Office. 2011. Report of the Committee for Technical Investigation on Countermeasures for Earthquake and Tsunamis Based on the Lessons Learned from the "2011 off the Pacific Coast of Tohoku Earthquake" 4. Principles for Future Tsunami Hazard Assumptions and Developing Tsunami Countermeasures, 28 September. Tokyo, Japan: Cabinet Office.

Civil Engineering Society, Japan. 2014. Round-table Talk on "Ijoukishou ni Mukiautameni Ima Dekirukoto, Subekikoto" [What we can do, should do, to prepare for extreme weather events]. *Civil Engineering* 99(4).

European Climate Adaptation Platform. CLIMATE ADAPT. http://climate-adapt.eea. europe.eu/uncertainty-guidance.

Global Climate Change Alliance Support Facility (GCCA). Training Materials Module 4, "Understanding and Planning Under Uncertainty." GCCA website: www.gcca.eu.

Global Facility for Disaster Risk Reduction (GFDRR). 2013. *Building Resilience: Integrating Climate and Disaster Risk into Development.* Washington, DC: The World Bank, World Bank Publication. worldbank.org/climate change.

Global Platform for Disaster Risk Reduction (GPDRR). 2007. Chair's Summary of the First Session. ISDR/GP/2007/6. Geneva: United Nations. www.preventionweb.net/ globalplatform/2007/first-session/docs/session_docs/ISDR_GP_2007_6.pdf.

—— 2009. Chair's Summary of the Second Session. Geneva: United Nations. www. preventionweb.net/files/10750_GP09ChairsSummary.pdf.

—— 2011. "Invest Today for Safer Tomorrow – Increase Investment in Local Action." Chair's Summary of the Third Session. Geneva: United Nations. www.preventionweb. net/files/20102_gp2011chairssummary.pdf.

—— 2013. "Resilient People, Resilient Planet." Chair's Summary of the Fourth Session. Geneva: United Nations. www.preventionweb.net/files/33306_finalchairssummaryof-fourthsessionof.pdf.

Intergovernmental Panel on Climate Change (IPCC). 1990. *Climate Change 1990: Synthesis Report. Contribution of Working Groups I, II and III to the First Assessment Report of the IPCC.* Geneva: IPCC.

—— 1995. *Climate Change 1995: Synthesis Report. Contribution of Working Groups I, II and III to the Second Assessment Report of the IPCC.* Geneva: IPCC.

—— 2001. *Climate Change 2001: Synthesis Report. Contribution of Working Groups I, II and III to the Third Assessment Report of the IPCC.* Geneva: IPCC.

—— 2007. *Climate Change 2007: Synthesis Report. Contribution of Working Groups I, II and III to the Fourth Assessment Report of the IPCC.* Geneva: IPCC.

—— 2011. *Managing the Risks of Extreme Events and Disasters to Advance Climate Change Adaptation.* Special Report of the Intergovernmental Panel on Climate Change. New York: Cambridge University Press.

—— 2013. *Report of Working Group I on the Physical Science Basis to the Fifth Assessment Report of the IPCC.* Geneva: IPCC.

—— 2014a. *Report of Working Group II on Impacts, Adaptation and Vulnerability to the Fifth Assessment Report of the IPCC.* Geneva: IPCC.

—— 2014b. *Report of Working Group III on Climate Mitigation to the Fifth Assessment Report of the IPCC.* Geneva: IPCC.

—— 2011. *Revealing Risk, Redefining Development.* Global Assessment Report. Geneva: United Nations.

Jha, A.K. and Stanton-Geddes, Z. 2013. "Managing Risks in East Asia and the Pacific: An Agenda for Action." In *Strong, Safe, and Resilient: A Strategic Policy Guide for Disaster Risk*, edited by Abhas K. Jha and Zuzana Stanton-Geddes. Washington, DC: The World Bank Press.

JICA. 2011a. *Handbook on Climate Change Adaptation in the Water Sector*. Tokyo: JICA.

——— 2011b. *Climate-FIT (Adaptation) Draft Ver. 1.0. Final Report for Study on Mainstreaming Climate Change Considerations into JICA Operation (Adaptation)*. Tokyo: JICA.

——— 2012. *Direction of Low Carbon and Resilient Development Cooperation by JICA*. Tokyo: JICA.

——— 2013a. *Linking Disaster Risk Reduction to Sustainable Development*. Tokyo: JICA.

——— 2013b. *Final Report of Disaster Management Capacity Enhancement Project Adaptable to Climate Change. 2013*. Tokyo: JICA.

——— 2014. Final Report of Integrated Study Project on Hydro-Meteorological Prediction and Adaptation to Climate Change in Thailand. 2014. Tokyo (draft version).

Martin, S. 2012. Homepage of ClimateXchange, "Example of 'No Regret', 'Low Regret' and 'Win–Win' Adaptation Actions." Scotland's center of expertise connecting climate change research and policy. www.climatexchange.org.uk.

MLIT. 2008. *Climate Change Adaptation Strategies to Cope with Water Related Disasters Due to Global Warming. Water and Disaster Management Bureau, Ministry of Land, Infrastructure, Transport and Tourism*. www.mlit.go.jp/river/kasen/index.html.

——— 2010a. *Practical Guidelines on Strategic Climate Change Adaptation Planning – Flood Disasters*. Tokyo: River Bureau, Ministry of Land, Infrastructure, Transport and Tourism.

——— 2010b. *Development of Practical Guidelines on Strategic Climate Change Adaptation Planning – Flood Disasters*. Water and Disaster Management Bureau.

UN Economic Commission for Europe. 2009. *Guidance on Water and Adaptation to Climate Change*. UN document No. ECE/MPWAT/30. Geneva: UN Publications.

United Nations secretariat of the International Strategy for Disaster Reduction Secretariat (ISDR). 2009. *Risk and Poverty in Changing Climate – Invest Today for Safer Tomorrow*. Global Assessment Report. Geneva: United Nations. www.preventionweb.net/english/hyogo/gar/report/documents/GAR_Cover.pdf.

World Bank. 2012. *The Great East Japan Earthquake, Learning from Mega Disasters – Knowledge Note*. Washington, DC: World Bank.

3   From drought to resilience

Sylvie Montembault Jamal and Jan Eijkenaar

Introduction

Drought-prone communities have fewer coping mechanisms and, when shock follows shock, more and more households fail to recover, making them more vulnerable to the next drought, or other shocks. This situation may be partly explained and compounded by rapid and profound change, the drivers of which include population growth, the move from rural to urban settlements, market fluctuations, and a growing reliance on cash-based incomes. Although there is little evidence that climate change has led to increased droughts, it is clear that vulnerability to recurrent drought has increased. Anticipated climate changes are likely to further compound an already fragile situation. This precarious situation is already untenable. Since the 2000 crisis the Horn of Africa has experienced four drought events[1] and the Sahel has suffered three large-scale drought-related food crises.[2]

This chapter examines the approaches taken by the European Commission's Humanitarian Aid and Civil Protection Office (ECHO)[3] towards drought response in the Horn of Africa and the Sahel since 2005. The two case studies presented in this chapter, from Niger and the Horn of Africa, point to the predictable nature of food and security crises, rooted in the state of poverty and fragile regional economies, with limited access and failing delivery of basic services for vulnerable populations. Although the contexts, needs and programs were different, ECHO's experiences in both regions led to similar conclusions and a shared commitment for change. They demonstrate that malnutrition and food insecurity are not necessarily a direct result of drought. "More precisely, drought is one of many factors that increase the vulnerability of certain sections of the population and might contribute to malnutrition and food insecurity" (Poulsen *et al.* 2007, 1). Attempts to reduce the impacts of drought and to put an end to cycles of suffering, poverty and destitution will only succeed if greater emphasis is placed on addressing vulnerability and not the hazard itself.

Case study 1: Experience from the West Africa Sahel region since 2005

Introduction: A variety of situation analyses, different risk perceptions, undetected and unmitigated risks

The 2005 food and nutrition crisis in Niger came as a total surprise for many. Suddenly, this country found itself in the midst of an emergency, confronted with very high levels of severe acute child malnutrition. Its health centers were overwhelmed and food prices skyrocketed, placing basic items well out of reach of a large part of the population. Different readings of warning signs, hesitation, procrastination and other delays all contributed to the surprise. Yet members of the food security network in Niger and the Sahel region had issued early warning signs of a possible 2005 food crisis in the autumn of 2004. Failing rains were expected to reduce pasture and water available for livestock, resulting in significant shortfalls in the primary sorghum and millet cereals harvests.

But warnings of a food crisis did not ring the major alarm bells reserved for massive famine, large population displacement, adult starvation or extensive livestock losses. The Government of Niger bears some responsibility for playing down the possibility of a "food crisis" for many months. As a result, government institutions and donors proceeded with a conventional response designed to meet "classic" food security needs, using established procedures such as the subsidized sale of cereals and "food for work" schemes. They planned for food deficits in a limited number of pocket areas in rural Niger and a significant but not excessive seasonal increase in the prices of staple foods. These measures were not at all sufficient to address rampant acute malnutrition and associated disease. In the second quarter of 2005[4] scores of emaciated and starving young children started to arrive at the health centers in rapidly increasing numbers. By this time, it was far too late to organize an appropriate emergency response. There was neither the time nor the specialized capacities to implement the necessary interventions on the required scale.

The traditional focus on rain and food production hid other underlying drivers of risk and vulnerability. The case of Maradi is illuminating. Maradi is Niger's main breadbasket and was considered to be entirely food secure for 2005 based on the early warning reports. Yet this region became the scene of shocking images of malnutrition and high child mortality, notably in Médecins Sans Frontières' (MSF) health centers and its nutrition interventions. Food prices rose fourfold suddenly and very rapidly in mid 2005. Following steep increases in the price of the main staple food of millet, the numbers of children under five admitted for severe acute malnutrition (SAM)[5] in Maradi rose quickly. This "paradox of Maradi" highlighted the existence of a large class of very poor landless laborers, working in the wealthy landowners' fields and producing food for meager wages, while depending on the market for their own food. Health care and other basic services were in short supply, of limited quality and not free. The crisis exposed the fragility of a society that included a large and growing number of households living under permanent duress and at the brink of subsistence, barely surviving.[6]

Another causal trigger of the crisis also came from outside Niger, notably from Nigeria. Nigeria's habitual flow of cereals to Niger came to a halt in 2005. Failing rains had hit parts of northern Nigeria as well, contributing to a domestic peak demand and high food price levels that made cereals in Niger more favorable for purchase. Nigeria started importing in 2005 and this had the effect of draining Niger's markets, already affected by production shortfalls, even further.[7]

With hindsight, it is clear that for many years prior to 2005, a structurally high and increasing malnutrition burden[8] in the West Africa Sahel region had not registered as a priority risk or urgent need for governments, foreign aid partners or the network of early warning actors and systems in the Sahel employed by them. Neither had the existence of a growing very poor and underserved population, with their vulnerability to food and nutrition insecurity insufficiently recognized.[9] Regional interdependencies and both the opportunities and risks that these bring had not been fully anticipated or grasped. In sum, urgent needs and vital risks were missing from the analysis or remained poorly understood, preventing them from being mitigated adequately or at all.

Anticipating risks "out of the box," exploring evidence-based progress and influencing policy

The 2005 crisis in Niger delivered a shock to existing food security conventions and triggered many questions in Niger, in the Sahel region and beyond, leading to demands for a new conceptual approach to food *and nutrition* security. It was essential that malnutrition be given far more central importance, being both a cause and a result of illness and mortality. A better understanding of its root causes was needed, along with its place in the food security concept and how it was related to vulnerable livelihoods and family practices. It was recognized that malnutrition treatments should be made available and integrated into the health care package, especially for those persons and households of the population most at risk and in need. The lack of access to these and other essential services and to adequate foods had to be explored and made the focus of interventions as well.

Conventional crisis early warning and response concepts, decision-making mechanisms and policies required a thorough review. The capacity to consider all food and nutrition security risks, in the countries and the region, was wanting. Early warnings had to be timelier, more transparent and also broader in scope, detecting immediate trends and recommending timely, more pertinent crisis mitigation and responses on an adequate scale. Moreover, greater analysis of the underlying structural and chronic aspects of crises and crisis risks and recommended durable preventive measures and policies would be necessary.[10]

The ECHO response

It was in this landscape that ECHO, itself a late responder to the 2005 crisis, decided to take a hard look at the circumstances in which such grave malnutrition had occurred, to question how it had been neglected and the high excess mortality that resulted. It was found that malnutrition (in its immediate life-threatening form, SAM) prevalence reported by all main Sahel countries permanently exceeded alert levels and often surpassed emergency levels,[11] while treatment was by and large unavailable and effective prevention was absent. The reflection raised a host of complex issues: should ECHO, a humanitarian emergency donor, contribute to the prevention of the next bad "surprise" in Niger and the larger West Africa Sahel region? Instead of addressing a "humanitarian problem," should ECHO be an advocate for change and prevention by governments and through structural measures? Could ECHO adopt a longer term vision and proactive strategies to be better positioned to anticipate future crises, which were sure to happen, and to be more effective in mitigating their effects?

ECHO's Sahel Plan, aim and objectives

In early 2007, ECHO commissioned a study by Poulsen and colleagues (2007) that confirmed the relevance of such a pre-emptive strategy for the Sahel region and a funding plan. Highlighting the slow-onset and almost predictable nature of food and nutrition security crises in the West Africa Sahel region, as well as the poverty and fragility of Sahel countries[12] and their failing basic service delivery instruments, the study pointed to an ever-increasing number of destitute households. The increase in the frequency of shocks made it apparent that more and more households were expected to never fully recover from one shock before the next one occurred.

ECHO's first so-called "Global Plan for the Sahel" was therefore adopted in March 2007.[13] Ongoing emergency response actions in Niger (following its response to the 2005 Niger crisis) were to be expanded to other main Sahel countries,[14] justified by reported high malnutrition prevalence, even if a crisis had not formally been declared. The aim was "to contribute to the reduction of acute malnutrition and mortality of the most vulnerable population and in particular of children under 5 years and lactating and pregnant women."

The proposal was framed around three axes of activity:

1   Improving the baseline knowledge within vulnerable communities to provide credible data for needs assessments and understanding the extent and causes of acute malnutrition. This includes support for more effective information gathering and management systems along with better analysis of the interlinkages between health, nutrition and livelihoods protection.
2   Promoting effective and innovative nutritional policies and treatment, improving access to basic services, and restoring the coping mechanisms of the most vulnerable population (attracting the bulk of the funding to maximize benefits for the beneficiaries).
3   Advocacy and public awareness building with partners and civil society in five priority countries of the Sahel (Burkina Faso, Chad, Mauritania, Mali, Niger) and to encourage the mainstreaming of humanitarian objectives into

long-term development planning in the Sahel (linking relief to rehabilitation and development, or LRRD).

Achievements and impact examples

A broad collective of ECHO partner implementing organizations,[15] working in close collaboration with national capacities up to community level, as well as with ECHO's field-based technical assistants, contributed to a range of achievements, progress and impact. The following overview proposes examples of several specific topics supported by ECHO.

1 Introduction and scale-up of community and integrated management of acute malnutrition (CMAM and IMAM) and associated pathologies

"Niger 2005" triggered a wide introduction – in Niger and progressively into the wider West Africa Sahel region – of effective ready-to-use therapeutic foods (RUTF, distributed in individual rations and requiring no water). Improved outpatient care methods were also developed, providing better care and more effective treatments for SAM on an adequate scale. At the community level, efforts were made to promote the community management of acute malnutrition (CMAM) with active screening and referral of acutely malnourished children for care and new, highly effective treatment methods and products to treat SAM. Neither of these new community-based detection approaches (developed in East and Central Africa in the late 1990s) had reached the region prior to 2005. The absence of CMAM programs also reflected a low availability of the basic medical care necessary to treat malnutrition.

Over the years, this situation changed entirely. Over a million children were admitted for the treatment for SAM in nine countries in the Sahel region in 2013,[16] reflecting around 70 percent coverage of an estimated actual burden number of 1.5 million SAM-affected children. It is also an indicator of the general severity of the problem. In comparison, around two million children under 5 were admitted for SAM treatment in the whole of Africa in 2012 and 2.6 million children with SAM in the entire world (UNICEF 2013).

2 Health services user fee exemption for children under five, and pregnant and breastfeeding women (PBWs)

Evidence suggests that the important efforts and mass campaigns in Niger contributed greatly to achieving rapid declines in child mortality (Amouzou *et al.* 2012). These included addressing child malnutrition in response to the nutritional crisis in 2005 and 2006. Children under five, as well as pregnant and breastfeeding women, were exempted from health services user fees. Nutrition care was reinforced by way of increasingly integrated emergency response interventions and an evolving network of nutrition treatment centers.

Nevertheless, an increase in the collaboration with other sectors and actors, beyond health care, is crucial to sustain this trend and the gains made (Ridde et al. 2013).

3 Promote more comprehensive, timely, transparent and functional national and regional early warning analysis and response processes, capturing food and nutrition security risks

Since 2007, ECHO has contributed to the proactive introduction of the Integrated Food Security Phase Classification methodology (IPC) into West Africa's own – albeit still theoretical at the time – Harmonized Framework (Cadre Harmonisé: CH) of Le Comité inter-États de lutte contre la sécheresse au Sahel (CILSS)/Economic Community of West African States (ECOWAS)). ECHO also supported the gradual development and rollout of the CH as the functional multi-actor and multi-sector analysis platform that it has since become (IPC 2013).

4 Contribute to a better understanding of nutrition in a livelihoods and food-security context and to determining a socioeconomic baseline

Since 2006, ECHO has supported the introduction and sustained the progressive rollout of the Household Economy Analysis (HEA) methodology in the West Africa Sahel region.[17] The analytical framework, and the particular qualitative regard and culture of approach to livelihoods that HEA proposes, has contributed to a more comprehensive understanding of food and nutrition security from a socioeconomic point of view. HEA is also able to help generate the qualitative information required for implementing the CH process, and provides an entry point to appropriate targeting of cash-transfer operations. Furthermore, it provides a procedure for better crisis severity forecasting ("outcome analysis") and other analytical work, such as calculating the cost of a minimum adequate diet.

Case study 2: Seeking optimal ways for mitigating effects of drought in Africa: the experience of ECHO in the Horn of Africa

Introduction

ECHO established its regional DRR program in the Horn of Africa in 2006, with the specific aim of strengthening the resilience of communities – in particular, those vulnerable to drought – through the piloting of community-based drought mitigation measures that could then be tested and scaled up. The ECHO Drought Risk Reduction Action Plans (DRRAP) focused on three types of activities:

1   **Community-based operations** to pilot solutions to develop and identify good practices, to support wider replication and evidence-based advocacy. Projects addressed gaps and shortfalls at the community level in the devel-

opment policies of respective countries, as well as cross-border issues. These were mainly implemented by NGOs due to their capacity to work with remote communities at a local level and in collaboration with the local authorities (where they existed).

2   **Technical support and technical coordination operations**, to enhance the technical quality of the solutions piloted at community level, as well as their coherence and coordination at national and local level.

3   **Advocacy and awareness-raising** for dissemination of the good practices and lessons learnt from the community-based activities. General stakeholders were targeted along with specific bodies (e.g. the Ministry for the Development of Northern Kenya and Other Arid Lands).

DRRAP was implemented by various international NGOs and UN agencies in the region together with some local organizations and in coordination with various national institutions. There was considerable cross-organization and cross-country exchanges and substantial scaling-up of good practice, laying a sound foundation for improved interventions in the dry lands of the Horn of Africa.

Major achievements: a coherent approach

1 The importance of regional and cross-border programming

The DRRAP adopted a regional approach to reducing the risk from drought and conflict in recognition of the regional nature of livelihood dynamics in the drylands of the Horn of Africa. The program helped with the drafting of practical guidance on livelihood programs, drought-cycle management and conflict-sensitive programming, and has contributed to documenting and strengthening good practice to enhance the evidence base and stimulate changes in policy and practice in cross-border areas.

These efforts aimed at forging relationships among program stakeholders, improving existing cross-border mechanisms, and restoring linkages and peaceful exchanges, particularly in contexts where they had been damaged by conflict or other hazards. The promotion of vaccination campaigns in border areas protected livestock assets and improved the livelihoods of these bordering communities. Furthermore, by involving relevant state authorities, these activities also contributed to laying the foundations for ongoing information exchange on disease control and surveillance across borders, and for potentially expanding regional collaboration to regulate, control and ultimately reduce the effects of negative externalities, such as trans-boundary animal diseases. These activities have helped improve the lives, livelihoods and resilience of bordering pastoralist communities.

2 The development and piloting of a number of community-based approaches

Under different funding allocations, ECHO DRRAP's partners have been sup-porting community-based actions, mainly related to the protection of livelihoods and assets, with a greater emphasis on disaster risk reduction. From 2011 onward, ECHO prioritized proposals that included community disaster management plans prior to the implementation of any small-scale mitigation measures. These community-based approaches focused on addressing underlying vulnerabilities (e.g. livelihoods) while protecting them with innovative DRR activities. As a result of the program, local-level disaster management plans started to repli-cate lessons learned from activities supported by ECHO to other communities through interventions in conjunction with district authorities. However, further expansion is needed and a greater focus is required on the needs of the most vulnerable populations.

3 Coordination and collaborative relationships

From program inception onward, ECHO created platforms to encourage differ-ent actors to work together instead of replicating past practices in which many aid agencies and actors focused on their own areas and specific problems. A core objective was to address information gaps among those working in the field and national and regional institutions with responsibilities for arid land development and policy formulation. Sharing of information and experiences among partners and national and international institutions was supported by DG ECHO at three levels: local, national and regional.

To aid coordination, FAO was tasked from the beginning of DRRAP to ensure that ECHO-funded NGOs and UN agencies would meet on a regular basis to share information about their programming and lessons learned as well as to discuss recent policy and institutional changes. The approach led to an increase in joint documentation of practices and evaluation – partners working on cross-border issues, for instance, were invited to jointly evaluate activities in the same technical category. Furthermore, key partners agreed to share messages and advocacy/communication strategies at the country level to influence national institutions and processes (Kenya, Uganda and Ethiopia).

One of these examples is cooperation with the Japan International Cooperation Agency (JICA) in Kenya. In its project titled "Enhancing Community Resilience against Drought in Northern Kenya," JICA took up most of the actions initiated by DG ECHO for long-term programming. The emphasis on community inclu-sion through the community-managed DRR approach practiced by ECHO in its DRR programming has been emphasized by JICA in development programming, thus positively encouraging the local authority to embrace it.

4 Knowledge management and learning

A central objective of ECHO DRR programming in the Horn of Africa has been "identifying and developing successful models in community-based DRR and disaster preparedness" that could be replicated elsewhere by national or subnational authorities, other EC funding instruments or other donors. Thus rigorous attention is placed on documenting experiences, analyzing effectiveness and building the evidence base for good practice. The regular publication of technical briefs based on NGO experiences has informed the broader community about concrete actions to be taken in the drylands. The vast library of good practices has been made available on the disasterriskreduction.net website managed by the FAO and is accessed regularly by aid actors from all continents.

5 Influence and impact upon development policies and implementation strategies

The most important result of the program – less tangible than the others – is the change of attitude created, the raised awareness and the improved response to drylands issues. Progress was made possible by the extensive community of practitioners as a result of their interaction with the affected communities for more than 6 years, as well as engagement with key UN and NGO actors in the capitals of the Horn of Africa. DRRAP partners firmly positioned marginalized areas and arid lands on the agenda, leading to the realization of the necessity to address the structural issues at stake and not to wait for the next drought to then react too late to unacceptable levels of destitution and malnutrition. ECHO believes this investment has, over time, created the momentum to end drought emergencies and an understanding of the need to do business differently.

Some of the challenges

1 Marginalization of the drylands

As clearly stated by Fitzgibbon and Crosskey,

> decades of political and economic marginalization in the drylands of the Horn of Africa have meant access to basic services such as health and education and infrastructure such as roads and electricity are way behind other parts of the same country. Consequently, drought-prone communities have few resources and a low asset base upon which to rely when droughts (or any other hazards) hit. Each successive drought further depletes assets, leaving households ever more vulnerable and less able to cope with circumstances.
> (Fitzgibbon and Crosskey 2013, 4)

Fundamentally, the opportunities and requirements for a linking relief, recovery and development approach are too often ignored. A non-consensual analysis of the root causes of the issues at stake, along with governments' constant promotion of economic growth over other development goals, work against any joint development and humanitarian strategy to address the needs of the most vulnerable. Development funding to the most drought-prone areas is usually insufficient. It also fails to support disproportionately weak government capacity in these areas or to address the fundamental gaps in government provision of basic services. For example, Kenya's most drought-prone districts would need at least a sixfold increase in schools and teachers to meet the national averages.

Drought is too often treated as an exogenous shock that sits in the risks column of the development program proposals and implementation plans. Instead, drought should be brought into the program design from the start, allowing sufficient flexibility to change plans when drought hits. For example, if a program is engaged in the training of teachers, it should also assess whether the school has sufficient water supplies or is capable of providing extra school meals during the hunger season or drought.

2 Escaping from our silos

To complicate matters further, donors generally do not recognize the broader picture and tend to fund projects/programs as separate entities (often referred to as a "silo mentality"), a practice that makes accounting easier but results in financing gaps and "stop–go" services that are inconsistent with comprehensive transitional models. Without strategic plans and frameworks, attempts to build household and community resilience are often undermined because there can be no guarantee that all actors and sectors are working to achieve the same goals. DRR itself is treated as a "stand-alone" activity rather than a cross-cutting issue that has to be mainstreamed into all sectors and all development planning. As a result, policymakers often fail to recognize that DRR also incorporates longer term resilience-building interventions required during and in between droughts in sectors not normally included in humanitarian response.

3 Country contexts

In a region where the development model for arid lands is unclear, where governments do not have clear policies, where donors have up until now been more reactive to crisis than proactive towards building resilience, space for replication is limited. Quality, community-based DRR plans do exist but are not set within wider sectoral and strategic planning frameworks. The fragility of dryland ecosystems and the mobile, isolated nature of pastoralism mean that individual communities often cannot make informed plans. Community-based DRR programs also offer a limited scale of coverage and are highly dependent upon NGOs or others for the majority of funding.

Despite these realities, ECHO and its partners have continued to be proactive for the inclusion of DRR in national policies, and with increasing effect. This has led to the Intergovernmental Authority on Development's (IGAD) Ending Drought Emergencies initiative. Under this initiative, IGAD created the Drought

Resilience Platform with the key objective of mobilizing resources, encouraging knowledge management; and formulating common regional goals and strategies.

Main lessons

A vision is needed for pastoralism in the drylands of the Horn of Africa

Drought resilience can only be enhanced through long-term development interventions. As concluded early on by Alinovi *et al.*, "if building the resilience of the vulnerable communities living in the drylands of Horn of Africa is the ultimate goal of donor-sponsored interventions, a more durable approach is imperative and resources need to be made available – with a long-term perspective" (Alinovi *et al.* 2010). These drylands and pastoralist communities must be higher on the national political agenda if political marginalization is to be addressed and pastoralist institutions strengthened.

As noted in the evaluation of the first phases of the DRRAP, "while a framework is needed both to guide planning and to provide a benchmark against which to measure achievements, there is no agreement on such a model." There has been some talk of "the end of pastoralism" resulting from too many people, insufficient livestock and a deterioration in the quantity and quality of natural resources. A different, and perhaps more widespread, view is that pastoralism can recover from its present crisis (as it has in the past) and can become (also as it has been in the past) a minority, specialized, quality production system with high labor and land productivity and good environmental management. Potentially, it could provide high-value outputs from inputs (extensive drylands and pastoral labor) which, otherwise, have low opportunity costs.

For this to happen, certain conditions must be met. Pastoral tenure rights to water and pasture must be secure, risk planning must be successful, prices must be appropriate, markets must be efficient and adequate credit must be available. Mobility must be maintained, despite the Government of Ethiopia's (announced but not implemented) policy of settling pastoralists where possible. Furthermore, minimum standards of education must be reached, and governance systems, necessarily through a mix of formal and customary structures, must be effective. Importantly for the future shape of interventions, pastoral populations should be lower than they are now if pastoralism is to meet its economic potential. Over time, the DRRAP has underlined the need for longer term, regional and cross-border perspectives in drylands programming: the problems underlying dryland livestock-based livelihoods cannot be solved by relief interventions alone; their solutions require long-term research and development strategies and programs that build on and strengthen rather than undermine local institutions, livelihood strategies and coping strategies.

Population growth and the continued and unplanned creation of settlements without access to permanent water continue to place a huge burden on humanitarian sources during periods of drought. While DRRAP has encouraged diversification of livelihoods and has promoted water development, it is critical to recognize that sustainability in pastoral production systems demands livestock mobility. Interventions that facilitate and/or maintain critical migratory movement and/or allow access to unused grazing areas will continue to serve as the most powerful way to mitigate livestock losses during droughts.

Governments have the primary responsibility of providing development visions and of ensuring their appropriate implementation as well as promoting community control and management of natural resources. The development and reduction of drought risks will only be achieved with government-led multi-sectoral planning processes over both the shorter and longer term. NGOs and civil society should support these plans and provide assistance in developing appropriate strategies as well as holding government and other stakeholders to account.

As reported in the review conducted by ODI and funded by ECHO in 2009 on the current trends of pastoralism, policies and practice in the Horn and East Africa,

> The current support system is not sufficient to get pastoralists onto the path of economic transformation, based on access to markets, opportunities for livelihood diversification and human resource and capacity development. Without adequate focus and strategies for comprehensive development in pastoral areas, humanitarian efforts to help pastoralists are akin to trying to clean up downstream pollution without addressing the root source upstream.
>
> (ODI/HPG 2009, 2 and 4)

> All the work on cross borders has also demonstrated the pivotal role of regional bodies, particularly in coordinating and ensuring that governments act together. The different incentives operating in Ethiopia and Kenya, and their diverging approaches to common veterinary issues arising from the cross-border livestock trade such as prevention and control measures for instance, the overall poor communication and coordination among state veterinarians of both countries undermine the potential for joint coordination and regional animal health management.
>
> (Pavanello 2010, 3)

Finally, it is critical for humanitarian and development organizations to recognize that many communities, and particularly pastoralist communities, are changing rapidly. And, as noted in the Lessons Paper of ALNAP on Humanitarian Action in Drought Related Emergencies, "consequently there is a great deal of livelihood diversification and urbanization in many drought-affected areas" (Hedlund and Knox Clarke 2011, 3). In order to remain relevant to changes in pastoralists' communities, international organizations must first understand the changes and the aspirations of the people and then diversify their work. This entails applying a single focus of, for instance, working exclusively on livestock interventions.

Conclusion

Both studies indicate that comprehensive development strategies are required that address root causes and dynamics of vulnerability if future – and predictable – humanitarian crises are to be avoided. This requires: (1) placing communities and their main duty bearers (local government) at the center of development and humanitarian efforts; (2) recognizing and responding to the different needs, capabilities and aspirations of different individuals, households and communities; (3) understanding and focusing on social and ecological systems rather than on individual components of those systems; (4) promoting integrated multi-sectoral approaches; and (5) increasing emphasis on longer term investments and addressing the underlying causes of vulnerability with the goal of strengthening the resilience of vulnerable communities and averting the unfortunate impact of drought in the Horn of Africa and the Sahel. These findings have contributed to extensive changes in EU humanitarian and development policies and practices, for example, increased commitments to disaster risk reduction (DRR): by 2013 DRR was integrated into 20 percent of ECHO projects. Further urgency was prompted by the 2010 food crises and EU response in the Horn of Africa in the Sahel.

In 2012 the EU issued the communication, "The EU Approach to Resilience: Learning from Food Crises" (European Commission 2012). This calls for the EU to place resilience to shocks and stresses as a central objective of all development and humanitarian assistance. Development and humanitarian programs must be focused on the areas and populations most at risk and work towards shared development objectives for the short and longer term. The communication, and subsequent Resilience Action Plan 2013, is organized around three key recommendations that stem directly from the lessons and experience of the two case studies (European Commission 2013).

First, development programs, and those of government, must be targeted at the most vulnerable, typically the poorest and those with least coping capacities to absorb, adapt or recover from shocks and stresses – whether these are from a natural hazard, social, economic or political origin. This is especially necessary in contexts where there are already humanitarian needs. Preventing future crises must be a priority. Basic needs must be met but more investments are required to unlock potential and to improve livelihoods – not just the provision of safety nets or the delivery of humanitarian assistance. Development programs that are targeted to improve the livelihoods of the most vulnerable must be risk-informed, integrating risk reduction strategies, crisis modifiers and contingency measures, so that assistance can be scaled up when and where it is needed most – when coping capacities are threatened or have been eroded. DRR is now mainstreamed into all ECHO actions with a strong emphasis on emergency preparedness and response. Humanitarian responses should be improved to respond earlier and more effectively. Wherever possible, a humanitarian response will establish the foundations for building resilience in the longer term – to avoid future recurrence. This means working differently: from a "stop–go" strategy (reacting to repetitive emerging crises) to building up the resilience and coping

capacities of the most vulnerable populations, especially in protracted and predictable crises.

This commitment to building resilience contributes to other policies, in particular food security, climate change adaptation and DRR. DRR will continue to
be an essential component of resilience, incorporating many facets of resilience
such as collaboration between humanitarian and development actors, integrating
risk reduction into normative planning processes and promoting multi-sectoral
approaches. However, resilience is a broader concept than DRR, covering a wider
variety of potential shocks and stresses to livelihoods and systems. The focus of
ECHO's DRR has been on natural hazards. This will continue but our DRR work
will be conducted within, and contribute to, holistic development strategies that
consider all risks and differing vulnerabilities and capacities to them.

The EU is applying the lessons learned from the experiences in the Horn
of Africa and the Sahel. In West Africa, the Global Alliance for Resilience
Initiative (AGIR 2014), led by the EU, is now established and the framework is
in place to coordinate government and donor support with the aim of improving
food security and nutrition over the longer term: zero hunger in 20 years. Under
the Supporting Horn of Africa Resilience (SHARE) initiative in the Horn of
Africa, Regional Resilience Programming Papers and Country Programming
Papers (four approved, four yet to be approved) are being developed.

Resilience approaches are also being applied to other contexts and hazards,
not just food insecurity and drought. Collaborative strategic assessments to determine resilience and DRR objectives are underway in a number of countries facing
risks from varied and multiple hazards, including fragility and conflict. Examples
of this include Nepal, Bangladesh, Haiti, Yemen, Mali and the Central African
Republic, with ECHO, Development and Cooperation – Europe Aid (DEVCO),
member states and others joining efforts. At a more general level, resilience
is now being systematically integrated into the European Development Fund
(EDF), Development Cooperation Instrument (DCI) programming as well as
into Humanitarian Implementation Plans.

In conclusion, the profound and rapid changes taking place in the drylands
of the Horn have yet to be researched in detail, but the trends are clear. While
the future is uncertain, it will certainly be very different from the traditional
pastoralist livelihoods that have dominated in the past. The shift from rural
and mobile communities to settlements and urban/peri-urban, commercialized animal rearing; more diversified and cash-based livelihood strategies, and
employment (formal/ informal), as well as emphasis on transition and educating
young people into more stable and lucrative livelihoods, raises a considerable
number of questions concerning the future objectives of DRR programs, and
indeed of humanitarian and development work in general.

Recommendation

ECHO recommends a "people-first" approach to address patterns of chronic vulnerability to avoid recurrent and predictable crisis situations. This calls for longer

term and comprehensive development strategies to build household capacities and livelihoods. A broad holistic approach is needed within hazard-prone and fragile contexts by incorporating disaster risk management with ways to reduce poverty and promote sustainable development. This requires:

- placing communities and their main duty bearers, such as local governments, at the center of development and humanitarian efforts;
- recognizing and responding to the different needs, capabilities and aspirations of different individuals, households and communities;
- understanding and focusing on social and ecological systems, rather than individual components of those systems;
- promoting integrated multi-sectoral approaches;
- placing emphasis on longer term investments to tackle the underlying causes of vulnerability.

Audiences of the recommendation: Communities/citizens, NGOs, national governments, donors, international agencies and the secretariat of the ISDR.

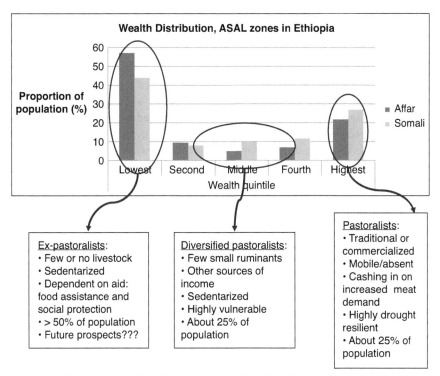

Figure 3.1 Changes in wealth differentiation and livelihood strategies

Source: Ethiopia Demographic and Health Survey (2011).

The vision for pastoralism in the drylands of the Horn of Africa

Pastoralism is not dead in the Horn of Africa, and livestock rearing remains the economic mainstay of the drylands. However, this is changing. The specifics have yet to be researched in detail, but the trends are clear: fewer people are engaging in traditional mobile pastoralism as a main livelihood strategy, while the wealthy are increasingly becoming commercialized.

The drivers of these changes are multiple. Perhaps the most important are the demographic changes in the context of limited natural resources: with the population doubling every 25 years (the drylands have high fertility rates of over 6 percent and improvements in health services have brought down infant and child mortality rates), the per capita livestock holdings have reduced as total livestock numbers remain steady over time (see Figure 3.1). However, this has not occurred uniformly over the pastoralist population. This leads us to the second driver: increased demand for meat both domestically within the Horn countries, and particularly in the Gulf States. Wealthy pastoralists especially have benefitted from this and have become more commercialized as a result, often being absent and preferring to employ others to herd their livestock.

The third driver is drought. There is little evidence that climate change has led to increased frequency or severity of droughts in the Horn, but it is clear that vulnerability to recurrent drought has indeed increased. The best way for a pastoralist family to enter a drought is with large numbers of livestock: along with other factors this increases the chance that a viable herd will emerge from the other side of a drought. As per capita livestock holdings have decreased, the chances of a poor- to middle-wealth-ranking family of retaining a viable herd during a severe drought diminishes, and recovery becomes more difficult. That is one major reason (along with factors such as reduced mobility) why so many pastoralists become destitute and settle around urban areas during and after droughts. The resulting trend is for middle-ranking pastoralist families to swell the proportion of the poor, who may own only a few or no small stock, while the wealthy generally maintain a resilient livelihood.

The fourth driver that is only recently becoming evident is the aspirations of pastoralist families themselves, and especially of young people. The "Changes in the Arid Lands" (Karimi et al. 2013) study suggests that, across the board, pastoralist families are seeking to educate their children in order to diversify sources of income through seeking professional or commercial work. The implication could be that the next generation may well be living elsewhere and adopting very different livelihoods than their parents. The study also examines the concept of an extended rangeland in which kinship groups have a wide variety of livelihood strategies from which to support each other, varying from traditional livestock keeping, to trading and professional employment.

Notes

1 Drought in the Horn of Africa: Preventing the Next Disaster (IFRC 2011).
2 Drought affects millions in the Sahel, World Food Programme (2012). www.wfp.org/stories/drought-returns-sahel.
3 The European Commission's Humanitarian Aid and Civil Protection Department (ECHO) aims to save and preserve life, prevent and alleviate human suffering, and safeguard the integrity and dignity of populations affected by natural disasters and man-made crises. Headquartered in Brussels with a global network of field offices, ECHO ensures the rapid and effective delivery of EU relief assistance through its two main instruments: humanitarian aid and civil protection.
4 This occurred at the start of the "hunger gap" in the agriculture calendar, between harvests of the main cereals and other crops in Niger (Save the Children 2009, 31: Fig. 11).
5 While estimates of the number of lives lost in 2005 are difficult to calculate, based solely on the mortality risk of untreated SAM (which is considered to reach up to 50 percent), the toll must have been severe.
6 In West and Central Africa, low levels of economic activity coupled with high population growth have led to negative or stagnant growth. Of the region's economic activity, 30 percent comes from agriculture while 60 percent of the economically active population is employed in agriculture. In many Sahelian countries, more than 30 percent of the population falls below the international poverty line of US$1 a day and over 30 percent of the population is undernourished (International Crop Research Institute for the Semi-Arid Tropics n.d).
7 Nigeria, however, did have the availability and capability to mobilize the quantities of relief food necessary for an adequate response to the crisis. But this "Nigeria factor" remained exclusively focused on domestic Nigerian needs, not on the situation in Niger, despite very strong ties between the (Hausa) people of the two countries and the close location of arguably Africa's largest cereals market Dawanau, next to Kano.
8 Although chronic malnutrition, a proxy indicator for acute malnutrition, dropped slightly by 5 percent to an average of 35 percent (well exceeding the 20 percent alert threshold) between 1990 and 2005, the total number of malnourished children under the age of five steadily increased. This burden (i.e. fueled by high demographic growth) is forecast to increase further by 2025 (WHO 2014).
9 "Much of poor households' total income is obtained through deploying their own labour, often locally on the farms of richer households and increasingly through seasonal migration to better-off areas both within and outside their own countries" and "the sheer size of the affordability gap between total income and the cost of a nutritious diet, particularly for the poorest households, suggests that a combination of strategies is needed in order to improve access to nutrients essential for the well-being of mothers and for the growth of children" (Boudreau 2013, 23–24).
10 All these topics and suggestions started to be discussed at different forums in Niamey as well as in several publications and papers in the specialist press in 2006, in the wake of the 2005 crisis. In 2010, Niger established a high food security authority to "harmonise emergency responses with long-term structural measures." Today, the national "3-N" initiative ("les Nigériens Nourrissent les Nigériens") has taken this a step further, aiming to promote multi-sector approaches to prevent and mitigate food and nutrition security needs and crises.
11 National nutrition and child survival surveys and in-depth reviews of child nutrition in Burkina Faso, Chad, Mali, Mauritania and Niger in 2006 and 2007 confirmed some of the world's highest under-five child mortality rates (222 per 1,000 live births, or 600,000 child deaths annually) and acute malnutrition rates (a regional average prevalence at the critical limit of 14.5 percent). Malnutrition was considered an

associated cause of 56 percent of child deaths, accounting for 300,000 child deaths annually, and rates of malnutrition in children remained above critical levels for at least a decade (UNICEF 2008).

12 Mauritania (155), Mali (182), Burkina Faso (183), Niger (186) and Chad (184) continue to be placed among the lowest ranked on the Human Development Index of all 187 countries listed (UNDP 2013).

13 This first strategy outline and funding plan for the Sahel by ECHO (Ref: ECHO/-WF/ BUD/2007/01000), with a value of 15 million euros and a duration of 20 months, marked the start of an uninterrupted approach and gradual scale-up (close to 350 million euros were eventually mobilized for these objectives by the end of 2012 (ECHO 2007). The strategy continues to be pursued.

14 The initial countries were Burkina Faso, Chad, Mauritania, Mali and Niger. This list eventually expanded to regularly or permanently include Togo, Côte d'Ivoire, Guinée Conakry, Nigeria, Cameroon, Senegal, The Gambia and Benin.

15 ECHO operates through three groups of humanitarian partner-implementing organizations: UN agencies, Red Cross organizations and INGOs (ECHO 2014).

16 Regional SAM admissions in nine West Africa Sahel countries from 2010 were: 480,000 (2010), 595,000 (2011), 914,000 (2012) and 1,034,000 (2013) (UNICEF 2014).

17 HEA is now actively used in at least seven Sahel countries with at least 50 profiles covering a multitude of livelihood zones currently available (HEA Sahel 2014).

References

AGIR. 2014. "Global Alliance for Resilience Initiative." The Food Crisis Prevention Network, OECD. www.oecd.org/site/rpca/agir/.

Alinovi, L., D'Errico, M., Mane, E. and Romano D. 2010. "Livelihoods Strategies and Household Resilience to Food Insecurity: An Empirical Analysis to Kenya," European Report on Development.

Amouzou, Agbessi, Habi, Oumarou and, Bensaïd, Khaled. 2012. "Reduction in Child Mortality in Niger: A Countdown to 2015 Country Case Study." The Lancet 380(9848), 1169–1178.

Boudreau, Tanya. 2014. Livelihoods at the Limit: Food Security in a Changing World. Evidence from the Consolidated Household Economy Analysis Database. London: Save the Children.

ECHO. 2007. "Humanitarian Aid for Vulnerable Populations at Risk in the Sahel Region of West Africa: Global Plan 2007." European Commission Decision on the Financing of a Global Plan for Humanitarian Operations from the General Budget of the European Communities in the Sahel Region of West Africa. ECHO/-WF/BUD/2007/01000. Brussels: ECHO.

——— 2014. "Humanitarian Partners." http://ec.europa.eu/echo/en/partnerships/ humanitarian-partners.

European Commission. 2012. "The EU Approach to Resilience: Learning from Food Crises." Communication from the Commission to the European Parliament and the Council. COM(2012) 586. Brussels: European Commission. http://ec.europa.eu/ europeaid/what/food-security/documents/20121003-comm_en.pdf.

——— 2013. "Action Plan for Resilience in Crisis Prone Countries 2013–2020." SWD(2013) 227 final. Commission Staff Working Document. Brussels: European Commission. http://ec.europa.eu/echo/files/policies/resilience/com_2013_227_ap_crisis_prone_ countries_en.pdf.

Fitzgibbon, C. and Crosskey, A. 2013. "Disaster Risk Reduction Management in the Drylands in the Horn of Africa." Brief prepared by a Technical Consortium hosted by CGIAR in partnership with the FAO Investment Centre. Technical Consortium Brief 4. Nairobi: International Livestock Research Institute.

Gitonga, Karimi, McDowell, Stephen, Bellali, Johara and Jeffrey, Davina. 2013. "Changes in the Arid Lands: The Expanding Rangeland – Regional Synthesis Report and Case Studies from Kenya, Ethiopia and Somaliland." IFRC, Oxfam and Save the Children.

HEA Sahel. 2014. "Analyse de l'Economie des Ménages" [Analysis of Household Economies]. www.hea-sahel.org/HEA-Sahel-The-Household-Economy-Analysis.

Hedlund, K. and Knox Clarke, P. 2011. "ALNAP Lessons Paper, Humanitarian Action in Drought-Related Emergencies."

IFRC. 2011. *Drought in the Horn of Africa: Preventing the Next Disaster.* Geneva: IFRC.

International Crops Research Institute for the Semi-Arid Tropics. n.d. Hyderabad: ICRISAT. http://exploreit.icrisat.org/page/west_and_central_africa/888.

IPC. 2013. "Integrated Food Security Phase Classification: IPC in West Africa." Rome: IPC Global Support Unit. www.ipcinfo.org/ipcinfo-countries/western-africa/en/.

McPeak, J.G. 2001. "Analysing and Addressing Localized Degradation in the Commons." *Land Economics* 79(4), 515–536.

ODI/HPG. 2009. "Pastoralism, Policies and Practice in the Horn and East Africa: A Review of Current Trends." *Synthesis Paper*, April, 2 and 4.

Pavanello, S. 2010. "Working Across Borders: Harnessing the Potential of Cross-Border Activities to Improve Livelihood Security in the Horn of Africa Drylands." *HPG Policy Brief* 41(July), 3.

Poulsen, L., Michael, M. and Pearson, N. 2007. 'Drought and Vulnerability: A Review of Context, Capacity and Appropriate Interventions with Respect to Drought and the Problem of Acute Malnutrition in the Sahel Region of West Africa'. Concept Paper. Agrisystems Consortium.

Ridde, V., Haddad, S. and Heinmüller, R. 2013. "Improving Equity by Removing Healthcare Fees for Children in Burkina Faso." *Journal of Epidemiology and Community Health* 0, 1–7. doi:10.1136/jech-2012-202080.

Save the Children. 2009. *Comprendre l'économie des Ménages Ruraux au Niger* [The Economy of Rural Households in Niger]. London: Save the Children.

UNDP. 2013. *Human Development Report 2013, The Rise of the South: Human Progress in a Diverse World.* New York: UNDP.

—— 2014. "Human Development Report: Country Profiles." New York: UNDP. http://hdr.undp.org/en/countries.

UNICEF. 2008. "Malnutrition in the Sahel." www.unicef.org/wcaro/2819.html.

—— 2013. *Global SAM Management Update: Summary of Findings.* Nutrition Section, Program Division. New York: UNICEF.

—— 2014. "Sahel SAM Admissions Trends 2010–2013." Groupe Régional Sécurité Alimentaire et Nutrition. https://wca.humanitarianresponse.info/fr/system/files/documents/files/FSNWG%2030JAN2014_NUTRITION_UNICEF.pdf.

Wilding, J., Swift, J. and Hartung, H. 2009. "Mid Term Evaluation of DG ECHO's Regional Drought Decision in the Greater Horn of Africa." AGEG Consultants eG.

WHO. 2014. "Global and Regional Trends by UN Regions, 1990–2025 – Stunting: 1990–2025." http://apps.who.int/gho/data/view.main.NUTUNSTUNTINGv?lang=en.

Part II

Building awareness for disaster risk reduction

4 Effective planning for disaster risk reduction

Yusuke Amano and Taichi Minamitani

Introduction

Building more resilient societies has become a common goal around the world, as described in the subtitle of the Hyogo Framework for Action 2005–2015 report (World Conference on Disaster Reduction 2005), "Building the Resilience of Nations and Communities to Disasters." In many countries, significant progress has been observed in efforts towards disaster risk reduction (DRR). Such accomplishments include legislation on disaster risk management, the establishment of disaster management agencies at the national and local level, and the creation of national platforms to enhance multi-sector and multi-stakeholder coordination.

On the other hand, many disaster-prone countries are still affected by recurrent hazards, especially in areas where floods and cyclones/hurricanes/typhoons hit almost every year. Examination of such cases tells us that efforts are by and large directed towards response and relief activities, while little has been done in promoting preventive measures. This implies that many communities and nations have not reached the required level of resilience with which they "resist, absorb and accommodate the effects of a hazard" in an efficient manner (United Nations secretariat of the ISDR 2009).

The delay in the progress of investment in DRR seems to come from the invisibility of its effects. Without seeing clear linkages between DRR and development, consensus in society will not be reached on allowing an increase in investment for preventive measures. In this regard, governments should work to demonstrate the effects of DRR investment to promote the understanding of stakeholders. In addition, DRR measures should be properly planned at different levels so that they lead to effective implementation. In reality, however, even with the existence of well-organized plans, communities and nations are affected by disasters, sometimes more severely than anticipated. This is due to the gap between what was planned and what was implemented, resulting from the insufficient capacity of communities and nations to cope with disasters.

This chapter tries to explore the ways to implement investment in DRR, especially in terms of preventive measures. First, the chapter discusses the necessity of presenting the effects of DRR measures to promote the understanding of stakeholders on the need for investment. The economic benefits derived from

DRR investment will be amply demonstrated in chapter 5. This chapter focuses instead on other benefits, especially the physical effects of disaster prevention and mitigation measures. Second, the chapter moves on to the arguments related to the different types of planning for disaster risk reduction, because well-considered planning leads to better disaster management. The discussion tries to demonstrate the roles and functions of each type of planning. Finally, the chapter presents findings of the lessons learned from past disasters to ensure the more effective implementation of DRR measures. It reveals three capacity gaps that are frequently found between planning and implementation, and three principles to narrow these gaps.

Approaches to conveying the effects of preventive measures

It is generally difficult to recognize the effects of DRR before actual disasters happen. To enhance the understanding of stakeholders such as politicians and the general public, responsible agencies in the government should make every effort to convey the effects of investment in preventive measures. One such way is to demonstrate the economic benefits over costs, as will be introduced in chapter 5. Another approach is to explain the physical effects of counter-measures, by showing to what extent the impacts of hazards are supposed to be contained or absorbed, and how damage can consequently be reduced. It is also possible to explain to what extent the safety level can be raised by preventive measures.

The explanation is normally accomplished by using "with" and "without" comparisons of particular measures. For example, in the case of flood control, it may be said that a city or town that has undertaken preventive measures will be protected against stronger rainfall than "without" cases. It is also possible to demonstrate that inundated areas will be smaller than "without" cases against the same level of rainfall, or more specifically, which parts of the cities/towns will be free from inundation. In anti-earthquake measures, responsible agencies can show the effects of a building code and retrofitting by saying that buildings will be able to withstand earthquakes of stronger magnitude than "without" cases. Such efforts should take place in the planning stage of DRR projects to promote understanding and accelerate appropriate decisions for investment. In addition, if actual disasters happen, it is useful to analyze the real effects of the counter-measures and make the results public. The real cases may be used to evaluate the effectiveness of the measures and, if proven effective, to disseminate the method to other parts of the country.

There are already several cases in which such efforts have been made. For example, the Government of Japan constructed an outer-ring underground discharge channel in suburban Tokyo, to protect metropolitan areas from flooding. The channel is composed of a 6.3km-long tunnel and a water tank with a capacity of 670,000m^3. The effect of the project is that by diverting the water underground, the water level of the existing river channel can be reduced. Although some flooding is unavoidable following heavy rainfall, inundated areas are estimated to be smaller than without the project. More specifically, two cases of rainfall in 2000 (without the project) and 2006 (with the project) were compared. In the former case, under the heavy rainfall of 160mm, 137ha were inundated, affecting 248 households. On the other hand, in the latter case 33ha were inundated and 88 households were affected under even heavier rainfall of 172mm (MLIT n.d.).

In addition, scientific research is helpful in providing backup data for policy formulation and implementation. For example, there are cases where a building code is in place but is not being implemented effectively. Many reasons may be behind this gap, including overly ambitious goals but weak government capacity to enforce the code. In addition, lack of understanding on the necessity of observing the code may delay implementation. As the building code is applied not only to public institutions but also to private houses and buildings, the speed of retrofitting and new construction relies to a large extent on the actions of individuals and the private sector. Extra efforts by governments are necessary to promote understanding on the effectiveness of the code.

In order to disseminate better methods of constructing earthquake-resistant houses, the Ministry of Public Works in Indonesia issued guidelines on building safer houses. The guidelines, entitled "Pocket Book: Basic Requirements for a Safer House," were created in 2009 after Indonesia experienced a series of severe earthquakes. Japan International Cooperation Agency (JICA) supported the efforts through a technical cooperation project on "Building Administration and Enforcement Capacity Development for Seismic Resilience," commencing in 2007. The guidelines provide information on the selection of construction materials, the dimensions of each part, and ways of connecting parts with joints as well as construction methods. Packaged in a pocket-sized booklet, with many drawings and simple instructions, the guidelines are intended to be user-friendly and easily understood by the general public (JICA 2009).

There may be many other tools to demonstrate the effectiveness of DRR measures, depending on the range of hazard-specific and country-specific contexts. In an age of information and communications technology, such information can easily be presented and provided through websites or other tools. These efforts can also help governments to fulfill their need for accountability to society.

Planning DRR measures: five different aspects

1 Comprehensive disaster management plan

In many countries, disaster risk reduction and management plans at national and local levels have being formulated with the support of donors and international organizations. Many plans still focus on emergency response measures and pre-disaster preparations towards such responses; further steps are necessary to accelerate actions towards risk reduction measures. Even so, the virtue of these plans is that they can help to consolidate efforts and promote multi-sectoral and multi-stakeholder DRR. In fact well-coordinated planning is the key to making investments in DRR effective.

One of the most important functions of such comprehensive plans is to identify the responsibilities of each organization and agency. Dedicated agencies for DRR have been established in many countries mainly to coordinate actions of different government bodies, public corporations, NGOs and the private sector. On the other hand, most sectoral DRR measures should be taken by line ministries and other organizations specialized in that specific sector. Under such circumstances, designating clear roles and responsibilities for each organization is essential so that DRR may be situated as one of the core functions, not as an additional and unnecessary task of the specified organizations. Moreover, such plans enable the coordinating bodies to collect information and understand the progress of measures taken by each organization.

Defining roles and responsibilities is also useful in preparing for emergency situations. In large-scale disasters, emergency situations occur in many places and require different actions by different organizations to cope with each situation. In such cases, it is unrealistic to expect that the chief officer in the government will be able to grasp every detail of a situation and issue instructions. Therefore organizations working at the scenes of operations should respond proactively, based on pre-planned actions and roles and responsibilities. Otherwise, the situation will become worse before actions can be taken. Comprehensive plans can serve to avoid such cases as well.

With regard to the relationship among different levels of government, there are variations of systems depending on the situations of countries. In some countries, including Japan, local government is designated with the primary task of taking initiatives for DRR, while some other countries' central government has stronger responsibilities than local government. For example, the Government of Turkey formulated the National Earthquake Strategy and Action Plan (NESAP) (2012–2023) (AFAD 2012). The strategy was prepared to clarify the responsibilities of organizations for different countermeasures. In this case, greater responsibilities are designated to the central government for emergency response and disaster reduction than to local government.

As indicated in Table 4.1, there are different aspects of DRR activities that require attention at different levels of government. By taking into consideration such differences, each country will need to determine how to share responsibilities among these different levels.

2 Multi-sectoral DRR planning

The international community has been discussing how to mainstream DRR and build more resilient societies. To achieve this goal, while dedicated agencies for DRR should make efforts to secure finance and implement DRR measures, this in itself will not be sufficient. In fact, most of the measures necessary for creating a resilient society are related to a responsibility that all ministries and organizations should be pursuing as part of their regular programs. For example, building schools and hospitals is the responsibility of the education- and health-related ministries and agencies. The goals of making schools and hospitals safer against

Table 4.1 General considerations in defining roles and responsibilities at different levels of government

Responsiveness to needs	– DRR activities should respond to the specific needs of locality. – There are cases where cross-regional DRR measures, for example, river basin management, are required. – Multidisciplinary approaches are sometimes needed.
Availability of resources	– Investment in DRR often requires mobilization of large-scale financial resources outside the regular budget. – Nationwide technical standards and guidelines make it easier for local government to plan and implement DRR measures.
Accumulation of knowledge and lessons learned	– Region-specific knowledge and lessons learned should be accumulated to improve future DRR activities in the region. – Nationwide knowledge and lessons learned contribute to raising the general level of DRR activities.

Source: Authors.

hazards should also be placed within the responsibilities of the same ministries and agencies.

In this regard, defining the roles and responsibilities of all related organizations is an important but not sufficient factor. To achieve the goal of integrating DRR into all sectors, each sector should be given incentives to do so. First of all, it is necessary to promote the understanding of related sectors on the effectiveness of DRR investment, especially in preventive measures. If such measures are incorporated into all projects from the planning stage, there is a greater possibility that such a project will continue to function in disaster events. Second, finance should be provided in response to such proactive planning. In doing so, dedicated agencies for DRR may be able to play a coordinating role.

3 Defining target levels of protection with proactive measures

In planning disaster countermeasures, it is essential to define the target level of protection with specific measures. In other words, this means delineating to what extent the cities or regions should be protected from the hazards that the measures are addressing. It is true that there are no perfect measures to prevent all disasters from occurring, and it is often the case that finance is limited. Nevertheless, or perhaps because of this, defining the level of protection by risk reduction measures is important for effective planning.

The level of investment may be different from place to place. For example, in urban areas where population and capital assets are concentrated, costly countermeasures may be justified. This is because urban areas have greater assets in economic terms and they often face higher disaster risks compared to rural areas. In areas where flooding occurs frequently, it can be difficult to sustain economic growth as assets may be damaged by inundation. In such cases, it is rational to decide to protect the areas at least from high-frequency (but not necessarily mega-size) floods.

Defining the target level of protection is also important in justifying DRR investment. Cost–benefit analysis of investments may be made to confirm that the appropriate target protection levels are set. The effects of countermeasures are normally explained against defined levels of protections. In fact, defining target levels of protection implies defining levels of acceptable risk. In this regard it is desirable that countries, communities and populations make decisions based on the information of disaster-related risks they are facing and to what extent they are ready to step forward to reduce the risks. This would necessarily include a discussion on priorities of investment. For example, some countries may decide to protect essential public facilities and infrastructure as a first step.

However, there is no straightforward formula to define the target level of protection and priorities of investment applicable to all places in the world. A specific level will be defined, taking into consideration the following four aspects: (1) impacts of human losses and economic assets as a result of disaster events; (2) historical records of disasters and their scales, especially the largest scale disaster in the history of the region; (3) achievable amounts of investment and its effects; and (4) public opinion and the leadership of policymakers. In any case, it is essential that countries and communities make their own decisions through serious considerations and discussions.

Box 4.1 Brief case study of the Sanriku region

Evolution of risk reduction measures in conjunction with economic and techno-logical development.

Sanriku region, the old name of eastern Japan, is a disaster-prone area that has experienced tsunamis several times in modern history. One such case was the Meiji–Sanriku Tsunami that hit the region in 1896. At that point in time, public funds were barely available because there were no legal bases for rehabilitation and/or mitigation works. This recovery period was characterized by disaster reduction efforts implemented by individual citizens. Structural measures were implemented from the funds of powerful local figures (Cabinet Office 2010a).

The region was again hit by a tsunami (named the Showa–Sanriku Tsunami) in 1933. Based on the experiences of the Great Kanto Earthquake in 1923, recon-struction and rehabilitation work was carried out on the initiative of the central and local governments. However, spending a huge amount of money on building large-scale structures was hardly possible as Japan's economy was still underdevel-oped, even though such measures were effective as a means of coping with large-scale disaster events. This period gave rise to the idea of a combination of structural measures and non-structural measures.

The tsunami caused by the Chile Earthquake in 1960 reached as far as Sanriku region and caused severe damage. Computation technology, simulation skills and civil engineering technology were at the time becoming more advanced. Also around this time, Japan's economy had entered a period of rapid growth. Since this period, the policy has been to give priority to the construction of structural measures such as water gates and sea-walls (Cabinet Office 2010b). It has been proven that a series of coastal dykes, constructed during this period, worked effectively to prevent the effects of several small- and medium-scale tsunamis – up until the Great East Japan Earthquake in 2011.

4 Planning the best mix of structural and non-structural measures

In reducing disaster risks, both structural and non-structural measures should be taken into consideration because they have different functions and complement each other. While non-structural measures such as early warnings can play a key role in saving lives against predictable hazards, structural measures are indispensable in protecting areas where population and assets are concentrated.

Structural measures are also essential in saving human lives from unpredictable hazards – for example, hazards such as earthquakes and flash floods. Once buildings collapse, people may not have sufficient time to evacuate, even though they may have knowledge of disaster risks through education and training. It is often unrealistic to relocate all valuable assets to safer places due to limited land space. On the other hand, it may sometimes happen that the force of hazards exceeds the designed strength of structural measures. In such cases, the structures do not function as planned or even collapse, causing secondary damage. In this sense it is crucial to understand the performance range of structural measures.

Therefore, in planning structural measures such as bridges and buildings, the concept of design load is normally taken into account. Design load implies estimated levels of load that structural measures should withstand against certain magnitudes of hazards. As shown in Figure 4.1, if actual loads in disaster events are equal to or smaller than its design load, the structure can maintain its function. On the other hand, if hazards exceed the designed levels, the structure will not fully function and may collapse, perhaps even causing secondary damage. It is thus strongly recommended that structural measures be designed in ways that they will not be completely destroyed by extreme disasters and maintain at least partial function.

Again, there is no single method to determine a design load that will be applicable in all cases. Factors such as the anticipated damage from disasters, frequency and scale of hazards, available financial resources and public opinion all determine the level of the design load. Moreover, there are no structural measures that can withstand disasters of any scale. Even with the existence of structural measures, non-structural measures should be in place to prepare for cases where the forces of hazards are larger than the design load of structural measures. It is also important to note that the population should be properly informed about the limitations of structural measures. There have been some cases where evacuation behavior was delayed because people overestimated the capacity of structural

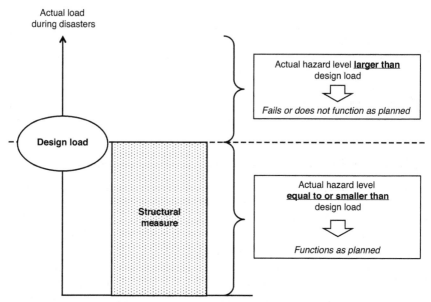

Figure 4.1 Diagram showing performance range of structural measures
Source: Authors.

measures to function. Since it is impossible to make a precise prediction of the time and scale of hazards, structural measures and non-structural measures need to be installed in a well-balanced manner and managed properly.

5 A medium- and long-term perspective for integrating DRR into land use plans and urban development plans

Different DRR measures require different levels of investment in different time frames. There are aspects that can be achieved at a relatively low cost and within a short period of time. These cases include retrofitting existing buildings and strengthening existing infrastructure. On the other hand, it is ideal that land use and regional plans are also developed to make the physical base of society stronger, by incorporating DRR measures. To realize such plans, a longer time frame is required – in some cases, 30 to 50 years.

A number of developing countries are now experiencing rapid urbanization, together with economic growth and increasing population. In such phases, urbanization tends to progress in areas where land acquisition is relatively easy, in order to respond to rapidly growing demands. As a result, cities and towns are developed without due consideration for disaster risks, creating new vulnerabilities. Japan experienced rapid urbanization during the 1960s and 1970s, and even now vulnerable parts remain in big cities such as Tokyo and Osaka. Such trends may be found in South-East Asia, Latin America and the Middle East. To cope with these issues, ensuring that the building code is enforced is one important solution. However, if buildings are constructed in ways that observe the building code but do not consider the proper use of land, the vulnerability of the city will increase further. To avoid such consequences, DRR measures should be incorporated into the framework of land use and regional development plans. Building resilient cities and towns requires enormous amounts of time and money. Continuous efforts are necessary to pursue this goal over the medium- to long-term perspective. In doing so, reaching a consensus among different sectors is essential but difficult. As a means of addressing this issue, it is useful to establish a method of planning to integrate DRR into regional development.

The Chubu Regional Development Bureau, a regional bureau of the Ministry of Land, Infrastructure, Transportation and Tourism (MLIT) of Japan, released "Guidelines on Developing Cities/Towns that Are Resilient to Earthquakes and Tsunamis" in 2014. The region is considered to be exposed to one of the greatest disaster risks in Japan, as a mega-earthquake (the Nankai Trough Earthquake) is anticipated to occur sometime in the future. To create a society that is resilient against earthquakes and tsunamis, the guidelines propose a set of planning methodologies. As shown in Figure 4.2, the final output is a grand design that gives an overall picture and provides direction for the future of the city. The guidelines underscore the importance of a partnership between local governments and various stakeholders, including the central government, local citizens, the private

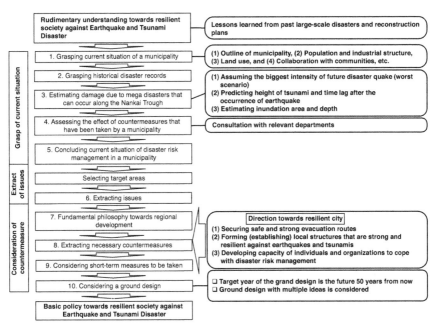

Figure 4.2 Flowchart to build consensus for deciding regional ground design among sectors

Source: The Chubu Regional Development Bureau, Ministry of Land, Infrastructure, Transport and Tourism of Japan; translated by the authors.

sector and NPOs. While short-term countermeasures are listed for immediate action, the grand design looks ahead at the next 50 years. The land use plan, reflecting the concept of a "city in which we want to live," is expected to be realized during this 50-year period (Chubu Regional Development Bureau 2014).

Three principles to implement more effective DRR

The efforts for DRR have no end. As mentioned in the previous section, there were some cases in which, even with the existence of countermeasures, risks were not prevented or mitigated. Following the Great East Japan Earthquake, JICA organized a task force to collect information and lessons learned from various experiences related to DRR measures. Through the study (JICA 2012a, 2012b), gaps were identified between plans and actual execution.

Three gaps in capacity for coping with disaster risks

Planning for a set of countermeasures – both structural and non-structural – should be carried out, taking into account the anticipated magnitude of hazards and projected damage. The assumptions behind the plan need to be as accurate as possible to increase the suitability of the planning. The reality tells us, however, that while planning is necessary, it is insufficient alone in reducing risks in actual situations. It should be noted that in real disaster events, including the Great East Japan Earthquake, even with the existence of well-thought-out plans, there will always be cases in which disasters will cause serious damage. Based on this observation, it is assumed that these events are caused by gaps between the planned and actual levels of disaster risk reduction. The three major gaps are as follows (Minamitani *et al.* 2011; JICA 2012a).

Gap 1

This gap is created when prepared plans are not put into action. Protection of the population and economic assets is achieved at a maximum level when all planned countermeasures are implemented. For example, measures against tsunami risks are designed on the assumption that water gates are properly operating and that the evacuation is carried out quickly enough, in addition to the construction of coastal dykes. In reality, however, some aspects of countermeasures do not work as planned (for example, warnings may not be received by the population due to a power shut-down). This gap, therefore, occurs when the actual capacity of disaster risk reduction is smaller than the planned level of capacity.

Gap 2

This gap emerges when the actual magnitude of hazards exceeds the planned level. For example, a hazard map is an excellent tool to raise awareness of the population concerning the disaster risks they are facing. However, as a map is created based on certain assumptions, there will always be the possibility that the area is hit by hazards exceeding the anticipated level. Another example is a town where a 10m-high coastal dyke was destroyed by tsunamis triggered by the Great East Japan Earthquake. People living in the area failed to evacuate in a timely manner, as they had so much confidence in the dyke that had previously protected the area against tsunamis equal to or below the anticipated levels. This gap may be classified as a case where the planned level of capacity in disaster risk reduction is smaller than the required level or capacity to cope with the actual hazards.

Gap 3

This gap arises with changes over time. The initial plan is developed based on the assumption of an anticipated hazard level and the economic and social conditions of the country/region at a certain point of time. The anticipated level of hazards would change along with the changes in natural conditions, including climate change, as well as advancements in scientific research. In addition, economic and social conditions also change in line with urbanization and demographic changes. There are also factors such as deterioration of countermeasures due to poor maintenance and failure to pass down memories and experiences to new generations. This gap is a case where the planned capacity in disaster risk reduction is smaller than the required level of capacity to cope with new risks emerging from continually changing factors.

Three principles to narrow the capacity gaps

To narrow the above-mentioned gaps, capacity development needs to be pursued in accordance with the three principles described below:

Principle 1: Raising risk literacy

This principle means that all stakeholders in society understand all possible disaster risks. This is necessary for the purpose of filling the gaps between the actual level of capacity in disaster risk reduction and the planned level of capacity. This principle will be pursued mainly by strengthening the implementation capacity of non-structural measures. Such measures include evacuation drills, disaster education and awareness-building programs. It is particularly important that the population understands the uncertain nature of disasters in terms of frequency and magnitude, and retains a certain level of alertness even after all planned countermeasures have been completed.

Principle 2: Securing redundancy

This principle is related to multi-layered and multi-sector countermeasures, to increase the level of protection. This principle contributes to a narrowing gap between the actual level of hazards and the anticipated level of hazards used in planning. For example, telecommunications infrastructure is critical in information management during an emergency. To provide appropriate medical services, such fundamental infrastructure as electricity, the water supply and sanitation is indispensable. To ensure essential infrastructure and utilities, backup facilities should be planned and installed to secure their primary functions. Another example is the road network, which should be designed in ways that will ensure evacuation, emergency operations and quick recovery of the supply chain.

Principle 3: Promoting "Kaizen"

This principle indicates the encouragement of continuous improvement in disaster reduction activities to narrow the gaps arising from changes over time. Countermeasures need to be reviewed and updated to cope with changes in natural as well as economic and social conditions. "Kaizen" is a Japanese term invented by the manufacturing sector to improve efficiency and enhance safety through day-to-day operations. This concept should also be applied to disaster risk management.

The relations between the three gaps and the three principles are shown in Figure 4.3.

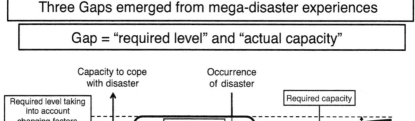

Figure 4.3 Diagram showing relations between gaps and principles towards better risk management

Source: JICA Task force.

Cases to which the three principles have been applied

There are cases where the three principles have already been applied to the design and implementation of technical cooperation projects supported by JICA. In the project planning stage, JICA is trying to convince partner countries to conduct so-called "disaster impact assessments" (DIA) to clarify the effects of the project on disaster risk management and include activities that lead to positive benefits.

One case was a school-based disaster education project in Turkey, as shown in Table 4.2. In 2010, JICA started a three-year technical cooperation project with the Ministry of National Education. In this project, the ultimate goal was to establish an official curriculum for disaster education and develop materials for teacher training. In the end, the concept of "making Turkey resilient," which was actually beyond the original scope of the project, was eventually shared with the Turkish government (JICA 2012d).

In many cases, projects tend to target short-term objectives and activities. By considering the steps to increase resilience in society, projects may take a longer term perspective with a wider scope of objectives.

Table 4.2 Three principles pursued in the project

Principle 1 Enhancing risk literacy	One-way and one-shot disaster education programs cannot enable students and teachers to increase their capacity sufficiently. This project tried to provide information so that teachers can include disaster education in several subjects and at all grades.
Principle 2 Securing redundancy	Disaster education alone cannot secure the lives of students and teachers in schools. Apart from knowledge acquisition through education, it is necessary to consider the schools' facilities. This project suggested preparing a disaster management plan at each school. Guidelines to formulate the plan were prepared. The guidelines instruct the principals of the schools to pay attention to the retrofitting of school facilities and the securing of furniture. The National Earthquake Strategy and Action Plan, formulated by the Turkish government, specifies that the Ministry of National Education shall take responsibility for such structural issues. In addition, the building code for schools has also become stricter than for other types of buildings. In the future, the progress of retrofitting work is to be monitored.
Principle 3 Promoting *Kaizen*	This project considers the establishment of a Disaster Education Advisory Group in the Ministry for the purpose of accumulating knowledge and lessons on (1) the methodology for training implementation, and (2) the contents of the handbook and materials. Although Turkey had experience in disaster education before this project, it was unable to create a sustainable implementation mechanism from the viewpoint of the administration.

Source: Mid-Term Review Report for School-Based Disaster Education Project, JICA (2012c); partially revised by the authors.

Conclusion

Disaster risks are intensifying in many countries as a result of many factors, including economic growth, urbanization and explosive population growth in certain countries. Increasing numbers of people are living on unsafe sites, such as coastal areas and flood plains. Lack of access to disaster risk information and discrimination for certain groups of population in society are also the causes of disasters. To cope with these trends and build a more resilient society, investment in DRR needs to be accelerated.

To promote investment in DRR measures, especially in preventive measures, the effects of investment should be clearly demonstrated. As discussed in this chapter, the physical effects of investment should be presented as one means to convince people regarding the necessity of investment. Normally, such presentations are made together with the economic effects of investment, such as reduced damage and assets preserved.

In many countries, dedicated agencies for DRR have already been established. The main function of such agencies is the coordination of different sectors and stakeholders, while the implementation of actual DRR measures falls under the responsibilities of relevant sectors. In this regard, national- and regional-level disaster management plans should clearly define the roles and responsibilities of different sectors. On the reverse side, sector development plans should incorporate DRR measures as part of their regular responsibilities.

In planning specific DRR measures, a target level of protection should be defined so that the scope of the investment required is made clear. Due attention should be paid to the role of structural measures, especially as a means of protecting economic assets. At the same time, non-structural measures need to be planned as complementary to structural measures. Over a longer time frame, it would be ideal to incorporate DRR considerations into land use and urban development plans. This is an important way of increasing the resilience of cities and towns.

In implementing planned measures, the capacity of the community and population does matter. In some cases, planned measures are not implemented. In other cases, the actual magnitude of the hazard exceeds the planned level, or the characteristics of the hazard change over time. To narrow the gaps between planning and implementation, capacity development is necessary to increase risk literacy and secure redundancy. The concept of *Kaizen* is effective to ensure a continuous and progressive approach.

There is no single formula to solve all of the issues discussed in this chapter. The level of investment depends on how serious disaster risks are experienced among stakeholders. Invisible factors such as leadership and public opinion may also affect decision-making. Against such factors, a practical approach that shows the effects of DRR investment and planning will help promote understanding and actions. This chapter is an attempt to present some of the aspects of practical approaches. To enhance the efforts of developing countries in formulating such plans for investment in DRR and to develop the capacity to implement them, there is ample room for the international community to support such efforts.

Recommendation

Pre-disaster investment in the reduction of risks should be recognized as a critical priority for sustainable development. To make such recognition common, continuous efforts have to be exerted to clearly show the powerful benefits of DRR. Therefore, a strategic and programmatic approach to DRR is crucial to ensure that *ex ante* investment is effective and beneficial with greater attention being paid to the planning stage in the project cycle of DRR.

Audiences of the recommendation: City governments, national governments, donors and international agencies.

References

AFAD. 2012. "National Earthquake Strategy and Action Plan." AFAD:Ankara. www.afad.gov.tr/UserFiles/File/udsep_1402013_kitap.pdf.

Cabinet Office of Japan. 2010a. "Saigai Kyoukunno Keishouni Kansuru Senmon Chyousa Houkoku Sho-Dai 4kai 1896nen Meiji-Sanriku Jishin Tsunami" [Reports of Expert Panel on Lessons Learned of Disasters – No. 4 1896 Meiji–Sanriku Earthquake and Tsunami]. Tokyo: Cabinet Office of Japan. www.bousai.go.jp/kyoiku/kyokun/kyoukun-nokeishou/pdf/kouhou028_18-19.pdf.

—— 2010b. "Saigai Kyoukunno Keishouni Kansuru Senmon Chyousa Houkoku Sho-Dai 30Kai 1960nen Chiri Tsunami" [Reports of Expert Panel on Lessons Learned of Disasters – No. 30 1960 Chile Tsunami]. Tokyo: Cabinet Office of Japan. www.bousai.go.jp/kyoiku/kyokun/kyoukunnokeishou/pdf/bs1009.pdf.

Centre for Research on the Epidemiology of Disasters (CRED). 2014. EM-DAT International Disaster Database. Result for Country Profile. www.emdat.be/result-country-profile.

Chubu Regional Development Bureau, Ministry of Land, Infrastructure, Transport and Tourism. 2014. "Jishin Tsunami Saigaini Tsuyoi Machidukuri gaidolain" [Guidelines on Developing Cities/Towns that Are Resilient to Earthquakes and Tsunamis]. Nagoya: MLIT. www.cbr.mlit.go.jp/kensei/machi_seibika/pdf/TunamiSaigai_guideline3.pdf.

Institute of Water Resources. 2009. "Flood Risk Management Approaches: As Being Practiced in Japan, Netherlands, United Kingdom and United States." IWR Report No. 20111-R-08. Virginia: IWR.

JICA. 2009. "Ministry of Public Works–JICA Developed Guidelines for Safer Housing." Jakarta: JICA. www.jica.go.jp/indonesia/english/office/topics/safe_house.html.

—— 2012a. "Projecto Kenkyuu Jishin Tsunamini taisuru koukateki aprochino kento Houkoku Sho" [Project Study on the Effective Countermeasures against Earthquake and Tsunami Disasters: Lesson Learned from the Disaster and Recovery]. Tokyo: JICA http://libopac.jica.go.jp/images/report/P1000010281.html.

—— 2012b. "Projecto Kenkyuu Bousai Shuryuukaa Houkoku Sho" [Project Study on Mainstreaming Disaster Reduction]. Tokyo: JICA. http://libopac.jica.go.jp/images/report/P1000013629.html.

—— 2012c. "Preparatory Survey Report on the Flood Prevention Project of East Side of the Pasak River in Ayutthaya in the Kingdom of Thailand." Tokyo: JICA. http://libopac.jica.go.jp/images/report/P1000011464.html.

—— 2012d. "Bosai Kyoiku Purojekuto Chuukan Houkoku Sho" [Mid-Term Review Report for School-Based Disaster Education Project]. Tokyo: JICA. http://libopac.jica.go.jp/images/report/P1000010171.html.

Minamitani, Taichi, Amano, Yusuke, Nagatomo, Noriaki and Nakasone, Shiro. 2011. "Kokusai Kyoryokuwo Tsujita Saigaini Tsuyoi Syakaizukurinimuketeno Senryakuno Kento" [Strategic Study on the Formation of a Society Invulnerable to Disaster through International Cooperation]. Paper presented at the Twenty-Second Japan Society for International Development's Annual Meeting: Nagoya. Ministry of Land, Infrastructure, Transport and Tourism. "Shutoken Gaikaku Hosuiro" [The Metropolitan Area Outer Underground Discharge Channel]. Tokyo: MLIT. www.ktr.mlit.go.jp/edogawa/gaikaku/intro/04kouka/index.html.

Ministry of Land, Infrastructure, Transport and Tourism. n.d. "Shutoken Gaikaku Hosuiro" [The Metropolitan Area Outer Underground Discharge Channel]. Tokyo: MLIT. www.ktr.mlit.go.jp/edogawa/gaikaku/intro/04kouka/index.html.

Ministry of Public Works. 2009. "Buku Saku: Persy Aratan Pokok Rumah Yang Lebih Aman" [Basic Requirements for a Safer House]. Jakarta: Ministry of Public Works. www.jica.go.jp/indonesia/english/office/topics/pdf/buku_saku_0.pdf.

Port and Airport Research Institute. Verification of Damage of the Break Water. www.pari.go.jp/info/tohoku-eq/20110401.html.

United Nations secretariat of the International Strategy for Disaster Reduction (ISDR) 2009. "UNISDR Terminology on Disaster Risk Reduction." Geneva: United Nations. www.unisdr.org/files/7817_UNISDRTerminologyEnglish.pdf.

World Conference on Disaster Reduction. 2005. "Hyogo Framework for Action 2005–2015: Building the Resilience of Nations and Communities to Disasters." www.unisdr.org/2005/wcdr/intergover/official-doc/L-docs/Hyogo-framework-for-action-english.pdf.

5 Economic analysis of investment in DRR measures

Noriaki Nagatomo, Eiji Otsuki and Junichi Hirano

Introduction

Does proactive investment in disaster risk reduction (DRR) measures pay? A number of arguments have already been made that provide a positive answer to this question. One of the early discussions on this subject, a report entitled *Prevention Better Than Cure*, was published by the Swedish Red Cross in 1984 and presented to the world the idea of how effective preventive investments could be. Throughout the International Decade for Natural Disaster Reduction in the 1990s and the International Strategy for Disaster Reduction commencing in 2000, continuous efforts were made to raise awareness among the international community on the need for investment in disaster risk reduction. Such efforts may be seen in a number of other documents. For example, the "Global Assessment Report (GAR) 2009" called for preventive investment by asserting the need to "Invest Today for a Safer Tomorrow" (United Nations secretariat of the ISDR 2009). The report *Natural Hazards, UnNatural Disasters: The Economics of Effective Prevention* (World Bank and United Nations 2010) was another attempt to convince finance ministers and citizens of disaster-prone countries to take steps towards preventive measures.

In reality, however, the volume of investment in DRR is still limited, especially in preventive measures. The national progress reports on the implementation of the Hyogo Framework for Action 2005–2015 (World Conference on Disaster Reduction 2005) of many countries in the periods 2009 to 2011 and 2011 to 2013 also tell us that spending on DRR measures has occurred mostly in the areas of response and rehabilitation, while little has been spent on preventive activities. It is assumed that slow progress in DRR investment stems from the fact that DRR tends to be a secondary priority, as countries are facing more urgent needs for economic and social development. This is also related to the fact that the effects of DRR investment are not always visible unless real disasters occur.

This chapter tries to look into approaches to demonstrate the effectiveness of such investment in monetary terms. The first section mainly discusses ways of demonstrating the economic benefits of investment in preventive measures. In fact, benefits are expressed in the form of damage, which can be avoided by increased investment. In this section, three aspects of damage are described.

The second section focuses on the methods of demonstrating the viability of investment in DRR measures. Three cases are presented here as examples of a cost–benefit analysis. The cases cover different countries and hazards, and attempt to demonstrate ways of justifying DRR investment by comparing costs and benefits. The third section introduces a new approach to demonstrating the effects of disasters on the macro-economy. A model showing how "disaster risk reduction investment accounts for development (DR^{2}AD)" is presented. The model is actually still in the process of development by the Japan International Cooperation Agency (JICA) in the hope that it will eventually become one of the tools used to provide proof that "preventive investment pays."

The ways to show the economic benefits of preventive investment

In promoting public investments, governments need to present the effects of investments to secure finance as well as public support. This section first analyzes the different perceptions of people towards general public investment and DRR investment. It then discusses the definition of the benefits of preventive investment, followed by the presentation of an actual case where benefits are identified against a specific type of hazard.

The specific nature of DRR investment compared with general investment

There are a number of reasons for the low level of investment in preventive measures but at least four elements are the key to promoting investment. These are: (1) consensus of people and society: (2) political will; (3) finance; and (4) technology and know-how (see Figure 5.1).

Among these factors, the consensus of people and society is often the most critical factor. In democratic countries, governments cannot increase public

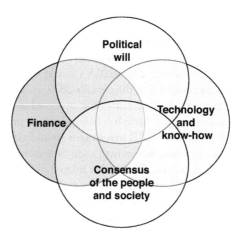

Figure 5.1 Four elements for promoting DRR investment
Source: Authors.

investment without the support and understanding of the people, because they are taxpayers and voters. In fact, investment in disaster risk reduction is different from other investments such as roads, bridges, education and health. While the effects of development-oriented investments are generally easy to understand, it is often difficult for people to grasp the need for DRR investment unless actual disasters occur. To measure the effects of DRR investment in terms of market value is also not an easy task. Therefore it is essential to promote the understanding of people on the effects of DRR investments, particularly in preventive measures, by demonstrating their benefits to people and society.

Benefits of preventive investment as reverse aspect of damage

Decisions concerning investments are made when clear benefits may be expected. This principle is applicable to DRR investment as well, but the question remains as to what constitutes benefits. In the investments that are made for economic and social progress, the benefits are measured by such aspects as the increases in road capacity, better access to schools, or time saved in collecting water. On the other hand, DRR investments are made to reduce the negative impacts of disasters and sustain economic and social functions as much as possible in disaster events.

In other words, the benefit of DRR investments is defined as the amount of damages that can be avoided by investing in DRR measures. Therefore it becomes necessary to understand the components of the damage. In its 2003 handbook, the Economic Commission for Latin America and the Caribbean (ECLAC) of the United Nations classified damage from natural disasters as "direct damages," "indirect losses" and "macroeconomic effects" (ECLAC and the World Bank 2003, 9). According to this classification, direct damage is the effect on fixed assets including real estate and stocks.

> The main items include the total or partial destruction of physical infrastructure, buildings, installations, machinery, equipment, means of transportation and storage, furniture, damages [sic] to farmlands, irrigation works, reservoirs and the like. In the case of agriculture, the destruction of crops ready for harvest must also be valued and included as direct damage.
> (ECLAC and the World Bank 2003, 11)

This category shows the damage that occurs at the onset of disasters.

The figures showing economic losses in a damage assessment of a disaster normally indicate this direct damage. For example, the Government of Japan released the total costs of damage resulting from the Great East Japan Earthquake three months after the disaster, stating that it was approximately 16.9 trillion Japanese yen (Cabinet Office, Government of Japan 2011). In fact, it is difficult to provide an accurate valuation and in many cases only estimated figures are available.

Indirect losses refer to the impacts of direct damage upon production capacity and social and economic infrastructure. Indirect losses also include increased costs or expenditure on basic services and utilities, as well as decreased or lost income due to the unavailability of such services and utilities. For example, losses in production due to damage to factories and lack of availability of raw materials are examples of indirect losses. Losses of future harvests due to flooding or prolonged droughts, and higher transportation costs incurred by the need to use alternative routes should also be considered when accounting for indirect losses (ECLAC and the World Bank 2003).

According to one report, the number of bankruptcy cases caused by the Great East Japan Earthquake had reached 1,485 firms in February 2014, 3 years after the disaster. The total financial losses of the bankruptcy cases are 1.243 trillion Japanese yen (approximately equal to US$12 billion at the June 2014 exchange rate). Around 21,000 people lost their jobs as a result. What should be noted is that the number of bankruptcy cases was larger outside the areas directly affected by the disaster, with Metropolitan Tokyo at the top (Teikoku Databank 2014). This case tells us that indirect losses are found not only in the areas physically affected by disasters but also in areas that were not damaged by the disaster itself.

Macro-economic effects are the impacts of disasters upon the major macro-economic indicators of the affected country. The most important macro-economic effects of a disaster are those that affect gross domestic product, growth in sectors (primary, secondary and tertiary industries), current account balance, indebtedness, foreign currency reserves, fiscal position and gross investment. Actual gross domestic product decreases as the outputs of affected sectors decline, but it can be increased through the reconstruction process. At the same time, inflation may be induced by shortages of materials arising from the huge demands for reconstruction and related speculation (ECLAC and the World Bank 2013).

In addition to the forms of damage listed above, damage to the population should not be ignored. This kind of damage is often classified as "intangible losses." Among these, direct damage, of course, refers to the loss of human lives and injuries that may be evaluated in monetary terms. However, disasters also cause indirect effects on populations, which are, in many cases, difficult to identify and quantify. These effects include loss of income due to the disruption of production activities and damage such as distress, suffering and other psychological impacts, as well as many other factors that have effects on well-being and the quality of life. Environmental and cultural losses should also be classified as intangible losses (Dassanayake et al. 2012). Figure 5.2 shows the conceptual relationship between damage and losses from disasters.

Actual case: Benefits of flood control measures

In order to accelerate investment in DRR measures, especially in preventive measures, showing the benefits of investment is the first step in deepening the understanding of the stakeholders. Table 5.1 is an example developed by the Ministry of Land, Infrastructure and Transport (MLIT 2005, 41) of Japan to demonstrate the benefits of flood control measures. In the table, the expected effects of floods are listed both as direct damage and indirect losses, to imply what

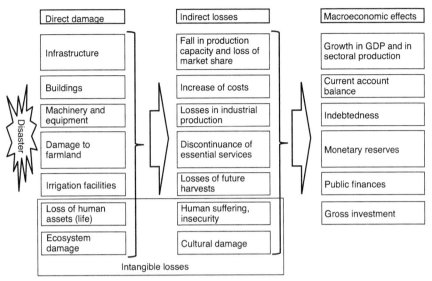

Figure 5.2 Losses and damage of disasters

Source: Authors.

Table 5.1 Major benefits: reductions in damage following a flood control project

Classification					Description of effect (damage)
Benefits of preventing damage	Direct damage	Effects of preventing asset from damage	General asset damage	Housing	Damage to buildings including housing by inundation
				Household articles	Damage to furniture or automobiles due to inundation, excluding fine art and precious metals
				Depreciable assets of private firms	Inundation damage to depreciable assets among a company's fixed assets excluding land and buildings
				Goods in stock of private businesses	Inundation damage to company inventory
				Depreciable assets of farmers/ fishermen	Inundation damage to depreciable assets among fixed assets of farmers/fishermen excluding land and buildings
				Goods in stock of farmers/ fishermen	Inundation damage to farmers'/fishermen's inventory assets
			Damage to farm products		Damage to farm products due to inundation
			Damage to infrastructure		Inundation damage to infrastructure, public facilities, farm facilities, utility facilities, farmland (e.g. roads, bridges, sewers, city facilities, electricity, gas, water, railroads, telecommunications, farmland, farm facilities, etc.)

Classification				Description of effect (damage)
			Effects of saving lives	Death or injury
Indirect Loss	Effects of preventing operation from damage	Damage from business interruption	Household budget	Damage that disturbs household work and leisure activities of families exposed to inundation
			Firms	Discontinuity of production at companies exposed to inundation (reduction of turnover)
			Public and utility service	Discontinuity of public and utility services
	Effects of avoiding post-event damage	Emergency costs	Household budget	Extra expenditure for cleaning houses after inundation or purchase of items such as drinking water
			Businesses	Damage is same as household budget
			National and local authorities	Damage is same as household budget
				Emergency financing with lower interest and sympathy money to victims
		Damage due to interruption of transport	Road, railway, airport, harbor, etc.	Damage spread to peripheral areas by disconnection of road or rail transport
		Damage by disconnection of utilities	Electricity, water, gas, communication, etc.	Damage spread to peripheral areas by disconnection of supplies of electricity, gas, water, etc.
		Effects on interruption of business		Decrease of production by disconnection of supply chain (insufficient intermediate products and raw materials)
				Influence on citizens by interruption of public/utility services such as medical care
	Effects of avoiding mental shocks	Followed from asset damage		Mental shock due to asset damage
		Followed from business interruption		Mental shock due to operational damage
		Followed from injury/death		Mental shock due to injury/death
		Followed from post-flood damage		Mental shock due to removal of debris
		Followed from spreading damage		Mental shock due to spreading damage
	Risk premium			Insecurity about suffering from future disaster
Upgrading benefit				Increased land prices by improvement of safety

Source: Unofficial translation by authors based on "Flood Control Economic Survey Manual (draft)" (Ministry of Land, Infrastructure, Transport and Tourism (MLIT) of Japan 2005).

will be lost without pre-disaster investment (damage) or what will be saved as a result of investment (benefits).

Costs and benefits of DRR investment

Comparing the benefits and costs of investment is a frequently used tool for evaluating the feasibility of a project. DRR investments, too, can be justified when benefits are larger than the costs. Attempts should be made to explain the rationale of preventive investment by demonstrating its benefits over costs. In this section, three cases are introduced as part of such attempts. The first two cases are related to measures dedicated to disaster risk reduction, through additional investment and new construction. The third case is multi-purpose investment in which costs for DRR are mixed with other costs. For the third case, a hypothetical analysis has been made by attempting to extract costs for DRR measures.

Case 1: Comparison of cost-reduction effects in different scenarios

Tehran City, the capital of the Islamic Republic of Iran, is located in an active seismic zone and is hit by major earthquakes every 150 years on average. To reduce damage to the residents and buildings of the city, JICA assisted the Government of Iran in developing seismic micro-zoning maps and a master plan for seismic disaster prevention and management (JICA and Tehran Disaster Mitigation and Management Center 2000, 2004).

Three active faults were confirmed near the city and identified as potential causes of hazards. Against the projected magnitude of an earthquake, three scenarios were developed to compare the impacts of the earthquake with and without investment in preventive measures. As shown in Table 5.2, disaster-related costs are divided into two categories based on whether the costs are incurred before or after the earthquake. Pre-disaster costs are related to retrofitting the buildings, while post-disaster costs include emergency response, reconstructing buildings, and the rehabilitation and reconstruction of the city. Damage to the population and buildings may also be compared using three scenarios.

The results show clear differences in the costs as well as damage. If there is no investment in retrofitting, it is estimated that nearly 400,000 people will die and 500,000 buildings will be damaged. The total cost of post-disaster expenditure will reach US$220 billion. To reduce the damage for each category (people and buildings) by 30 percent, US$14.5 billion needs to be spent on retrofitting, but the total costs for retrofitting added to the post-disaster expenditures will result in a total that has been reduced to US$163.4 billion. Decreasing damage by 90 percent requires retrofitting costs equivalent to US$63 billion, a figure more than four times that of the previous cost level. On the other hand, total post-earthquake costs will be reduced to US$86.4 billion. This implies that an additional investment of US$63 billion will reduce the damage by 90 percent and also total costs for pre- and post-disaster expenditures by US$134 billion (see Table 5.2).

Table 5.2 Comparison of cost and damage with/without countermeasures

		Case 1 (Do nothing)	Case 2 (30% decrease of damage)	Case 3 (90% decrease of damage)
Damages	Building damage	483,000	330,792	51,058
	Human casualties	383,000	265,572	57,071
	Displaced population	3,126,000	2,167,563	465,809
	Debris (1,000 tons)	124,000	85,981	18,477
Cost (billion US$)	Building damage	22.6	15.9	3.5
	Emergency response	2.9	2.1	0.4
	Rehabilitation and reconstruction	195.3	130.9	19.5
	Building strengthening	-	14.5	63.0
	Total	220.8	163.4	86.4
Remarks		The damage of earthquake is derived from estimation results of 6.7MW.	This alternative is target reduction level within the period of master plan.	In this case, the damage level can be handled in emergency response.

Notes

1. In case 1 earthquake damage is derived from "The Study on Seismic Microzoning of the Greater Tehran Area in the Islamic Republic of Iran, November 2000."
2. Building damage cost is calculated based on the replacement costs of the building.
3. Building strengthening cost is calculated by the building analysis results, using seismic index of structure value to determine reconstruction and retrofitting.
   The unit cost of strengthening building is determined based on the actual conditions and applied to the number of the objective buildings.
4. Emergency response cost is calculated at US$57 per victim per month and will continue for six months.

Source: Comprehensive Master Plan Study on Urban Seismic Disaster Prevention and Management for the Greater Tehran Area in the Islamic Republic of Iran: The Main Final Report. GE-JR-04-039. Tehran, Iran.

As shown in Figure 5.3, in the case of Tehran, retrofitting buildings is a highly effective way of reducing direct damage and eventually indirect losses. Although the comparison was made based on a rough estimation of costs and damage, it can serve in providing a general perspective of the effects of preventive investment.

Case 2: Benefit-to-cost analysis of a DRR project

Benefit-to-cost analysis is another approach for evaluating the effectiveness of a project. The analysis gives an idea of whether an intended project is viable and helps decision-making regarding investment. In the Abukuma River basin of Japan, the

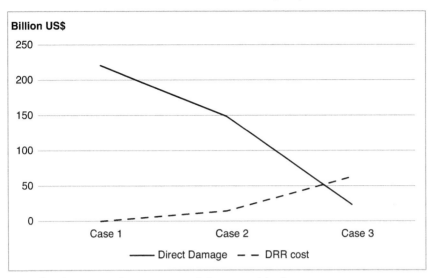

Figure 5.3 Comparison between cost and damage with/without countermeasures
Source: Authors (based on the Master Plan Study of JICA).

water level of the river bed downstream was rising due to the build-up of sediment being washed down from upstream. Consequently, the risk of floods and debris avalanches was becoming a serious threat, especially for urban areas. Against this background, the Government of Japan planned the Abukuma River System Sabo[1] Project (MLIT 2011). In planning the project, direct damage as well as indirect losses were taken into account. Direct damage is supposed to include private property (houses, household articles, assets and stocks of businesses and farmers/fishermen), farm products, public infrastructure and deaths or injuries to the population. Indirect losses would include interruptions to business and costs for response and rehabilitation measures (such as house cleaning and the purchase of new items).

The magnitude of the predicted damage would vary depending on several factors such as the breaking point of the bank, the range of flooded areas and the nature of affected assets. Figure 5.4 shows an image of flooding in which the bank is destroyed at point "P." Three cases of inundated areas are projected based on a probability of flood scale. The "A" is the inundated area in the case of a 1/30 (once in 30 years probability) flood scale. The inundated area expands to "B" and "C," with 1/50 and 1/100 probabilities, respectively. Naturally, the larger the flood scale, the more serious the damage the areas will face. In this regard, it is important to understand risks as to where and how much damage will arise.

In Abukuma River basin, the design standard for flood control is set to address a scale of 1/150, and 1/100 for debris avalanche. Tables 5.3 and 5.4 show the estimated damage if there is no investment in preventive measures made against the above-mentioned disaster scales. In sum, the total damage is assumed to be 223,029 million Japanese yen (JPY), comprising JPY200,099 million from the flood and JPY22,930 million from the debris avalanche.

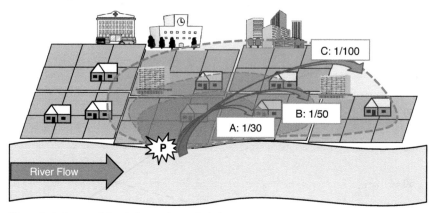

Figure 5.4 Range of flooded areas by probability
Source: Authors.

On the other hand, the total cost of damage decreases to an estimated JPY4,225 million per year after the completion of the project. The breakdown is shown in Tables 5.5 and 5.6. In addition, damage is expected to gradually decrease during the construction period, because even partial completion of the project will increase the level of protection.

Looking at the cost side, the costs for construction and maintenance should be taken into consideration. The main component of the project is to construct 56 sabo dams at a cost of JPY36,600 million (approximately US$366 million). The construction is expected to take 30 years and the life of the dams is expected to last 50 years after construction. Operational costs over 50 years are expected to be JPY3,390 million in total, making the entire cost of the project JPY39,990 (= 36,600 + 3,390) million.

In making a cost–benefit analysis, the concept of net present value (NPV) is used to evaluate the viability of the project. A discount rate[2] of 4 percent is used in Japan for public works.[3] Applying this rate, the NPV of the costs is estimated as JPY21,160 million, while that of the decreased damage, or benefits, is JPY58,324 million (see Table 5.7). This makes a benefit-to-cost ratio of 2.8. As the figure is larger than 1, the project is thought to be viable.

Case 3: Benefits and costs in multi-purpose facilities

As stipulated in the Hyogo Framework for Action, DRR measures need to be incorporated into the planning and implementation of other sectors. The notion of a "safe school" is a typical example of such needs. Against anticipated earthquakes, retrofitting school buildings will raise the safety level of the schools. This not only leads to the protection of children learning in the schools but may also protect the local population when the schools are used as shelters.

Multi-purpose cyclone shelters constructed in Bangladesh provide a good example of an actual case. The success story of Bangladesh in reducing deaths from

Table 5.3 Estimated maximum damage by flood without project: 1/150

	Direct Damage										Indirect Losses					
	General asset damage						Damage to farm products		Damage to infrastructure	Death or injury	Damage from business interruption	Emergency costs of households		Emergency costs of firms	Others	Total
	Housing	Household articles	Assets of private firms		Assets of farmers/ fishermen		Paddy rice	Others				Cleaning houses	Purchase of items			
			Depreciable assets	Goods in stock	Depreciable assets	Goods in stock										
	34,620	20,760	11,236	4,335	85	27	221	813	120,379	0	3,213	1,052	1,704	537	1,118	200,099

(Million Yen)

Source: Original document was prepared by Ministry of Land, Infrastructure, Transport and Tourism in Japanese (MLIT 2011). Unofficial translation by Author.

Table 5.4 Estimated maximum damages by debris avalanche without project: 1/100

Direct damage										Indirect losses					
General asset damage						Damage to farm products		Damage to infrastructure	Death or injury	Damage from business interruption	Emergency costs of households		Emergency costs of Firms	Others	Total
Housing	Household articles	Assets of private firms		Assets of farmers/fishermen		Paddy rice	Others				Cleaning houses	Purchase of items			
		Depreciable assets	Goods in stock	Depreciable assets	Goods in stock										
47	28	1,357	85	0	0	4	14	2,602	18,721	30	1	22	19	0	22,930

(Million Yen)

Source: Original document was prepared by Ministry of Land, Infrastructure, Transport and Tourism in Japanese (MLIT 2011). Unofficial translation by Author.

Table 5.5 Expected decrease of damage by flood

| Scale of probable flow | Probability of exceedance | Damage (Million Yen) | | | (d) Average damage by section | (e) Probability of section | (f) Yearly average of damage (d)*(e) | Cumulative yearly average of damage = expected decrease of damage in yearly average |
		(a) Without project	(b) With project	(c) Decrease cost(a)–(b)				
1/10	0.100	0	0	0	28,723	0.067	1,924	1,915
1/30	0.033	68,242	10,797	57,445	64,962	0.013	866	2,781
1/50	0.020	149,017	76,539	72,478	77,326	0.006	442	3,223
1/70	0.014	166,898	84,725	82,173	79,523	0.004	341	3,564
1/100	0.010	184,921	108,049	76,872	77,602	0.003	259	3,822
1/150	0.007	200,099	121,768	78,331				

Source: Original document was prepared by Ministry of Land, Infrastructure, Transport and Tourism in Japanese (MLIT 2011). Unofficial translation by Author.

Table 5.6 Expected decrease of damage due to debris avalanche

Scale of probable flow	Probability of exceedance	Damage (Million Yen)			(d) Average damage by section	(e) Probability of section	(f) Yearly average of damage (d)*(e)	Cumulative yearly average of damage = expected decrease of damage in yearly average
		(a) Without project	(b) With project	(c) Decrease cost(a)−(b)				
1/10	0.100	0	0	0				
1/20	0.050	2,964	862	2,102	1,051	0.050	53	53
1/100	0.010	22,930	7,525	15,405	8,754	0.040	350	403
	Total damage =	223,029						
					Total expected decrease of damage in yearly average =			4,225

Source: Original document was prepared by Ministry of Land, Infrastructure, Transport and Tourism in Japanese (MLIT 2011). Unofficial translation by Author.

Table 5.7 Cost–benefit analysis of Abukuma Sabo Project

(Million yen)

Term	Year	t	Discount rate 0.04	(a) Benefit		(b) Remaining value	(a)+(b)	Cost C						Cost–benefit ratio
								(c) Project cost		(d) Maintenance cost		(c)+(d)		(B/C)
				Benefit	NPV	NPV		cost	NPV	cost	NPV	Cost	NPV	
Construction Period	2012	1	0.962	74	71		71	1,043	1,003			1,043	1,003	
	2013	2	0.925	74	69		69	1,000	925			1,000	925	
	2014	3	0.889	160	142		142	1,002	891			1,002	891	
	2015	4	0.855	264	226		226	1,005	859			1,005	859	
	2037	26	0.361	3,558	1,283		1,283	1,261	455			1,261	455	
	2038	27	0.347	3,623	1,256		1,256	1,261	437			1,261	437	
	2039	28	0.333	3,767	1,256		1,256	1,261	421			1,261	421	
	2040	29	0.321	4,006	1,285		1,285	1,261	404			1,261	404	
	2041	30	0.308	4,225	1,303		1,303	1,261	389			1,261	389	
Evaluation Terms after Completion of the Project	2042	31	0.296	4,225	1,253		1,253			68	20	68	20	
	2043	32	0.285	4,225	1,204		1,204			68	19	68	19	
	2044	33	0.274	4,225	1,158		1,158			68	19	68	19	
	2045	34	0.264	4,225	1,115		1,115			68	18	68	18	
	2046	35	0.253	4,225	1,071		1,071			68	17	68	17	
	2088	77	0.049	4,225	206		206			68	3	68	3	
	2089	78	0.047	4,225	198		198			68	3	68	3	
	2090	79	0.045	4,225	191		191			68	3	68	3	
	2091	80	0.043	4,225	183	459	642			68	3	68	3	
Total				275,305	57,865		58,324	36,600	20,711	3,390	449	39,990	21,160	B/C = 2.8

B C

Source: Original document was prepared by Ministry of Land, Infrastructure, Transport and Tourism in Japanese (MLIT 2012). Tentatively translated and modified by Author.

cyclones is already well known throughout the world. This remarkable achievement is the result of joint efforts of the people and the Government of Bangladesh, supported by the international community. A set of measures were taken including the installation of meteorological radars and early warning systems, and the construction of shelters, as well as evacuation drills organized by the Red Crescent Society of Bangladesh, with the participation of community members.

Moreover, the Government of Japan has been supporting the efforts of Bangladesh in upgrading the education sector. To contribute to the concept of "Education for All" in Bangladesh, primary school buildings were constructed with Japan's grant assistance. The school buildings were designed using a piloti (or pillar) structure, in which the ground floor has only pillars without walls. The first floor is designed to be used as a school during normal weather, and as a shelter together with the roof-top to save lives from storm surges and floods once cyclones hit the region.

To see the effectiveness of this approach in relation to DRR, a hypothetical analysis is presented here. In analyzing costs and benefits, the costs for constructing multi-purpose school buildings should be compared with the costs for constructing single-purpose school buildings. According to the estimation used in the design of the project, the pillars of pilotis accounted for 12.5 percent and stairs for 4.5 percent of the total cost. Therefore, the cost was approximately 20 percent higher than a one-storey school if other conditions were the same: $1/(1 - (0.125 + 0.045)) = 1.20$.

The question is whether this 20 percent increase in cost is justifiable. The average cost of constructing a multi-purpose school building was JPY19 million. The average floor size of one school without the pilotis and stairs is 618.86 m². This space is supposed to be used for education as well as evacuation purposes. The hypothetical cost of this space is JPY15.77 million (17 percent less than the construction cost of a multi-purpose building), or JPY25,482 per 1 m². The actual construction cost for a multi-purpose building divided by the same floor size of 618.86 m² is JPY30,702 per 1m². The difference is JPY 5,220 or US$52 per 1 m².

The 20 percent of the initial cost seems to be rather costly, if a multi-purpose cyclone shelter is used only for evacuations a few times a year. According to the design, four or five persons can be accommodated in 1 m² for several hours in case of evacuation. This means that to save the life of one person, an additional cost of US$13–15 is necessary. Considering the fact that the building is used as a primary school in normal times and is used to save lives of children and adults in case of cyclones, this additional cost may be justifiable. Although this is a hypothetical estimation, this case should be counted as an economically viable project. However, to make this kind of analysis widely acceptable, methodological improvements will be necessary.

A model to show the effects of DRR investment on the macro-economy

This section introduces a model named "Disaster Risk Reduction Investment Accounts for Development" (DR²AD). The model is being developed by JICA with the aim of demonstrating that proactive DRR investment pays. By focusing on the impacts of disasters upon aggregate economic growth of a country, the model is intended to prove that investment in DRR promotes sustainable development. The first version of the model was presented at the fourth session of the Global Platform for Disaster Risk Reduction (GPDRR) in Geneva in May 2013, and an abstract was included in the Global Assessment Report of 2013 (United Nations secretariat of the ISDR 2013).

The model is still in the process of elaboration and the version introduced in this section is 1.4. Although the model needs further verification, the basic concept and structure are unlikely to change. In this section, an outline of the model are presented, using a case study from Pakistan.

Background

As discussed in the first section of this chapter, the macro-economic situations of a country are also affected by disasters. For example, in the case of the massive floods in Pakistan in 2010, the overall economic losses and damage were estimated at Rs.855 billion, which was equivalent to 5.8 percent of the 2009/2010 GDP of the country (WB and ADB 2010). As for the floods in Thailand in 2011, the damage was at least 185 billion baht according to the latest estimation by the Federation of Thai Industry. This economic loss was projected to result in a decrease of between 0.6 and 0.9 percent in the annual economic growth of Thailand (Yuvejwattana and Suwannakij 2011). These figures would be much higher if calculated as a percentage of the economy in the regions and the river basins directly affected by the disasters. Disasters significantly affect the economic growth of a country, particularly when the size of the economy is small, and tend to have greater impacts on local economies even when national economies are only slightly affected.

To demonstrate the impacts of these disasters upon economic growth in a convincing manner, the DR^{2}AD model was conceptualized. The DR^{2}AD model is expected to help governments in developing policies for disaster risk reduction through its functional ability to simulate the impacts of disasters upon economic growth. Simulations can be made to assess the degree of negative effects of disasters on GDP, as well as how the effects will change depending on the level of the disasters. More concretely, damage from a series of disasters over the middle- to long-term period may be quantified as losses to GDP. The effects of DRR investment may then be shown in specific numerical values on the assumption that the economic losses have been saved by the investment. Through the promotion of well-reasoned and evidence-based investment amounts, DRR policies are much more likely to be accepted following the emergence of a stronger consensus between stakeholders.

Objective and features of DR^{2}AD model

The DR^{2}AD model is being developed to achieve the following objectives:

1   to show the relationship between proactive investment in DRR and macro-economic situations of a country, by simulating the impacts of

long-term disaster risks and trends in economic growth, "with or without DRR investment";

2   to demonstrate that DRR investment pays and makes an effective contribution towards the sustainable development of the country;

3   to promote decisions towards investment in DRR, especially in developing countries.

DR²AD is a dynamic model that shows the increase in disposable income and changes in household expenditures realized as a result of improved levels of safety. As shown in Figure 5.5, the basis of the DR²AD model is the assumption that economic growth will be disrupted when a country is hit by disasters and a certain period of time is necessary before the economy gets back on track. The two different patterns of growth show different degrees of direct damage in the cases with and without proactive DRR investment. With DRR investment, especially in preventive measures, direct damage as well as indirect losses caused by delays in recovery can also be smaller, and the economy can return to growth trends more rapidly. On the other hand, if no investment is made in DRR measures, the damage may be larger and the fruits of economic growth lost every time a disaster occurs, resulting in zero or very low overall growth.

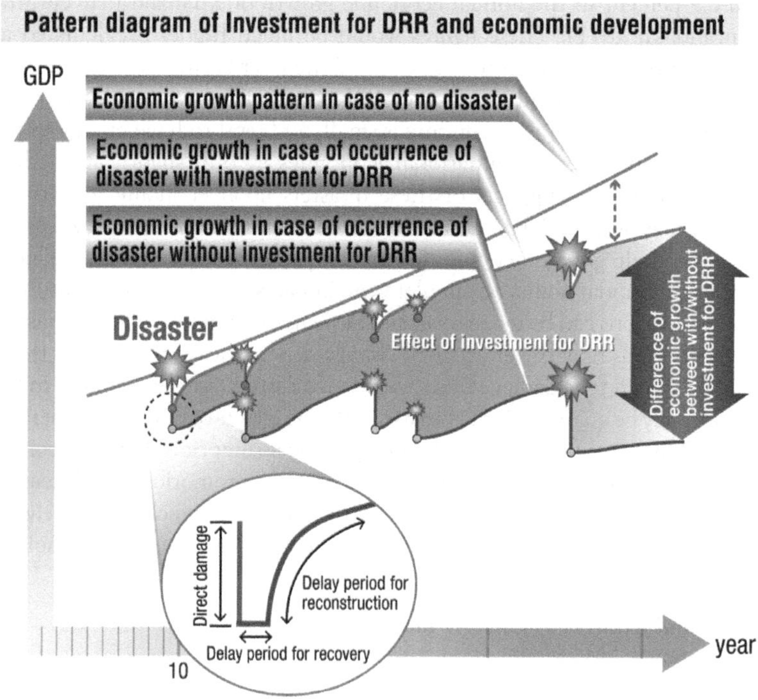

Figure 5.5 Effects of investment in DRR
Source: JICA.

Characteristics of the DR²AD model

The DR²AD model has been developed based on a dynamic stochastic general equilibrium model with the following characteristics.

Accounting for disaster damage

Generally speaking, reliable data on the scale and frequency of disasters are lacking or limited in developing countries, whereas disaster damage statistical data tend to be stored. Therefore, for the ease of applying the model to developing countries, the existing databases of the United Nations secretariat of the ISDR and EM-DAT (CRED) on the number of deaths and economic losses from disasters may be used to provide the primary data on direct disaster losses. By setting several disaster levels and attrition rates for each disaster level, the model may be used for the advanced simulation of damage with high-frequency and small-scale disasters as well as low-frequency and large-scale disasters. Moreover, in addition to the statistical data, tools such as DesInventar, hosted by the United Nations secretariat of the ISDR and flood simulation data based on precipitation, may be used as well. In this manner, the effects of climate change in future scenarios may also be assessed by using the precipitation data, based on climate change predictions.

Focusing on householder behaviors

In calculating GDP, a structure focusing upon household expenditures may be adopted, based on the following three assumptions:

1   Households decide the proportion of consumption, human capital investment and savings, with full understanding of future disaster risks. This implies that households know the optimal proportion of investment, by assuming a scale of frequencies of future disasters within the set period.
2   Full employment and complete mobilization of capital are achieved by firms.
3   Goods and factors of production will be fully consumed every year.

Investment for DRR

The DR²AD model can simulate the effects of DRR countermeasures upon economic growth by assuming that such investments will reduce losses and damage from disasters. For example, early warning systems can reduce the number of deaths but do not have significant effects on reducing economic losses. On the other hand, investment in DRR infrastructure such as river levees and aseismic retrofitting may have greater effects in terms of reducing both human damage and economic losses. Hence, by evaluating effects of DRR countermeasures that correspond to the specific nature of different disasters, government interventions and understanding of the people on DRR investment are expected to be promoted, leading to decreases in losses and damage from disasters.

Impacts upon the economy

In the DR^{2}AD model, GDP is an economic indicator used to evaluate the effects of various types and scales of disasters and DRR investment.

The DR^{2}AD model, including the components mentioned above, is a more simplified structure than popular macro-economic models (Figure 5.6). In the DR^{2}AD model, it is assumed that households and firms are the main actors in the economy, without considering government, intermediate goods markets or external trade (Figure 5.7). In "year t," when a certain magnitude of disaster occurs without DRR investment, the amounts of some items, such as capital and land in the market for the factors of production as well as chattels and the human capital of households, will decrease as a result of disaster damage, and hence there will be a resulting drop in GDP (Figure 5.8). On the other hand, in the case of a "with DRR investment" situation, the above-mentioned items are protected by countermeasures, with less damage from disasters. As a result, the decrease in GDP will also be smaller (Figure 5.9). Differences in the decrease in GDP between the cases of with and without disaster countermeasures show the quantitative effects of DRR investment.

Case study

JICA conducted a DR^{2}AD model (ver. 1.4) simulation case study using a dataset from Pakistan. The reasons for the decision to work with the Pakistan dataset were as follows:

- Pakistan is vulnerable to natural disasters such as earthquakes and floods.
- Statistical data, including disaggregated income class data, are available.
- The United Nations secretariat of the ISDR has presented Pakistan's baseline scenario, which assumes an economic growth path in the absence of disasters.

In this simulation, the disaster occurrence pattern over 20 years is assumed by using actual damage data over 6 years (from 2004 to 2010) and 14 years of simulated data (from flood analysis) (Figure 5.10). In the results of the DR^{2}AD model simulation, the difference between GDP growth occurring with or without DRR investment may be observed clearly. In cases where disaster damage has decreased by 20 percent as the result of DRR investment, GDP growth value is 10 to 20 percent larger than the value in the case without DRR investment. In the case of a reduction in damage by 50 percent, the difference is 40 to 50 percent (Figures 5.11 and 5.12).

Future challenges

The following challenges may be expected when using the DR^{2}AD model (ver. 1.4) as a widely used simulation model in developing countries.

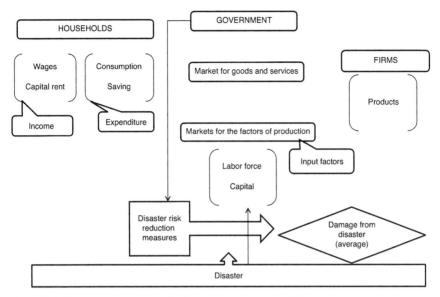

Figure 5.6 Basic structure of standard macro-economic model

Source: Developed by the authors.

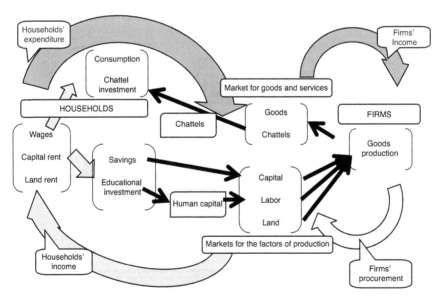

Figure 5.7 Structure of DR²AD model (1) Model focusing on household behavior (without disaster)

Source: Developed by the authors.

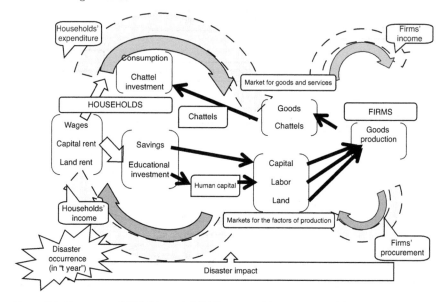

Figure 5.8 Structure of DR²AD model (2) Damage of disaster in model
Source: Developed by the authors.

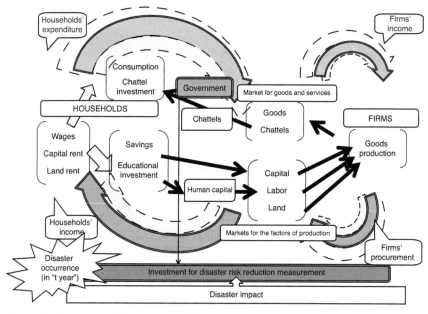

Figure 5.9 Structure of DR²AD model (3) Damage mitigation effect of DRR investment
Source: Developed by the authors.

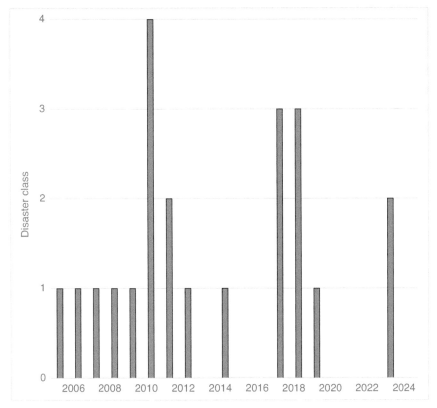

Figure 5.10 Assumption of disaster occurrence (based on a dataset from Pakistan)
Source: JICA.

1 Disaster damage data

With regard to the disaster damage data, simple damage function data in the model are used based on the information from DesInventar and EM-DAT. When performing sophisticated damage predictions in light of climate change, etc., it is necessary to set an appropriate damage function using geographical conditions and detailed damage data.

For example, flood damage was the only disaster considered in the case study of Pakistan. In order to more properly verify the effects of DRR, it will be necessary to analyze numerous types of disasters and treat them as independent events, as well as show disaster scales caused by multiple hazards. There is no doubt that data collection on related disasters is a new challenge that requires international and national efforts in the next decade.

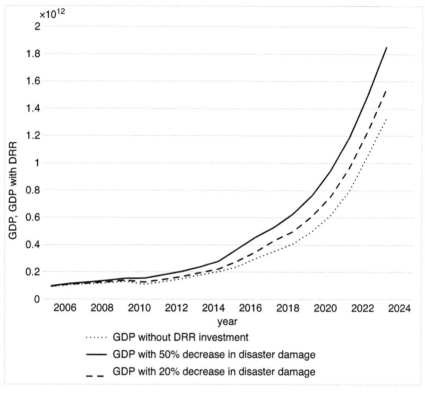

Figure 5.11 GDP growth with or without DRR (based on a dataset from Pakistan)
Source: JICA.

2 Guidance for more effective combinations of DRR policies

It is possible to identify an effective countermeasure menu and measures based on characteristics of the country to be analyzed. For example, the scale of financial damage and human suffering will be defined on the assumption that there is no damage either to capital stocks or residents by the projected disaster events if the structural measures are properly implemented against the projected magnitudes of hazards. On the other hand, the scale of human suffering is defined on the assumption that adequate actions for evacuation are taken by residents and human lives are saved in disaster events. The actions depend on non-structural measures and the degree of familiarity (or permeation) of such measures to the population. But since the reduction of financial damage requires more than the use of non-structural measures alone, the scale of financial damage is assumed to be the same as in the case of no investment in DRR measures.

By compiling data on countermeasures that are proven to be effective, it is expected that an optimum investment for DRR will be selected by reflecting on

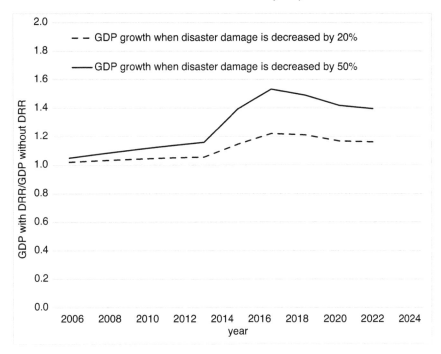

Figure 5.12 Effects of DRR investment on GDP (based on a dataset from Pakistan)
Source: JICA.
Note: GDP without DRR investment = 1.0

the effects of structural/non-structural measures. In this sense, it is important to develop a database on various countermeasures and their effects.

3 Estimation of costs for DRR investment

The DR²AD model can demonstrate the benefits of DRR investment to GDP growth in a quantitative manner. Currently it is calculated as "saved damage" from disasters due to the limitations of the data. However, to make in-depth judgments on the necessity of DRR investment, actual costs for DRR counter-measures should be made available. Unfortunately, in developing countries, the datasets necessary for estimating such costs are often inadequate. It is desirable that databases of costs are developed based on current investment levels and target areas for DRR, using advanced examples from Japan and other countries where such basic datasets are commonly used.

Conclusion

Once disasters occur, they disrupt the social and economic functions of a soci-ety and hamper sustainable development. While this fact is widely known, investment in DRR is seldom promoted because its effects are not visible unless real disasters happen. Therefore investment in DRR tends to be neglected in the face of competing needs in production sectors.

One of the most convincing ways to reverse this tendency is to explain that the effects of DRR investment should actually be counted in terms of its benefits to society and that these benefits are related to social and economic development. Expressing the benefits of DRR investment in monetary terms is one of the ways to demonstrate the effects of investment. Cost–benefit analysis is an approach to evaluate the viability of an investment project. This tool may be used to back up decisions for DRR investment in a specific project or in sector-wide programs. As investment is not the sole responsibility of the government but is also made by individuals and the private sector, demonstrating the effects is particularly important in promoting a general understanding of the need for proactive investment.

However, it should be noted that limitations exist in determining benefits and costs with precision, as figures are normally calculated based on certain assumptions. Moreover, there is always a risk of omitting some factors. If DRR measures are integrated into sectoral works or multi-purpose projects, separating benefits and costs from overall projects becomes more difficult. Even so, cost–benefit analyses can promote an understanding of DRR measures, compared with a situation in which no evidence is available for policy formulation or decision making.

The purpose of the DR^{2}AD model presented in this chapter is to demonstrate the effects of DRR investment in a macro-economic perspective. This model has been developed with the intention of inviting discussion with the international community so that it can be further developed into a more widely acceptable model. The goal of the model is to promote global understanding that proactive DRR is an indispensable factor in achieving economic growth. This concept is closely linked with internationally agreed goals related to sustainable development (SDGs).

Approaches to evaluating the benefits of DRR investment are still in progress both at the project and the macro-economic level. Some of the cases presented here may be case-specific. To establish internationally agreed-upon analytical methods, more active discussion among the international community will be necessary.

Recommendation

Damage from disasters, both direct and indirect, affects populations and communities, and hinders economic growth and sustainable development. The economic benefits of DRR, expressed in the form of decreased damage, can support governments, strengthen societies and promote stakeholders' understanding of the effectiveness of DRR investment. The international community should join forces in developing datasets, tools and models to clarify relations between economies and disasters to encourage increased investment in DRR.

Audiences of the recommendation: National governments, donors, international agencies and the United Nations secretariat of the ISDR.

Notes

1 "Sabo" refers to preventive measures to protect lives and assets from sediment-related disasters such as landslides, debris flows, slope failures and avalanches that may be caused by torrential rainfall, volcanic eruptions, snowmelt, earthquakes, etc.
2 Discount rate is used to calculate the present value of future cash flow.
3 It should be noted that different countries use different discount rates. For example, in the case of the UK, the rate is 3.5 percent (Mackie and Worsley 2013).

References

Cabinet Office, Government of Japan. 2008. Bousai Hakusho (Heisei 20 nendo-ban) [White Paper on Disaster Management, 2008 edition]. www.bousai.go.jp/kaigirep/hakusho/h20/index.htm.

—— 2011. Higashi Nihon Daishinsaini Okeru Higaigakuno Suikeini Tsuite [Estimated Costs of Damage Resulting from the Great East Japan Earthquake], June 2011. www.bousai.go.jp/2011daishinsai/pdf/110624-1kisya.pdf.

Dassanayake, Dilani Rasanjalee, Burzel, Andreas and Oumeraci, Hocine. 2012. "Coastal Flood Risk: The Importance of Intangible Losses and their Integration." *Coastal Engineering Proceedings* 1(33), Management.80.

ECLAC and the World Bank. 2003. *Handbook for Estimating the Socio-economic and Environmental Effects of Disasters*. LC/MEX/G.5. Mexico City: United Nations Economic Commission for Latin America and the Caribbean (ECLAC) and the International Bank for Reconstruction and Development (World Bank).

Hagman, Gunnar and Beer, Henrik. 1984. *Prevention Better than Cure: Report on Human and Environmental Disasters in the Third World*. Stockholm: Swedish Red Cross.

HM Treasury. 2014. *The Green Book: Appraisal and Evaluation in Central Government*. London: TSO. www.gov.uk/government/uploads/system/uploads/attachment_data/file/220541/green_book_complete.pdf.

—— 2011. *Revealing Risk, Redefining Development*. Global Assessment Report on Disaster Risk Reduction. Geneva: United Nations.

—— 2013. *From Shared Risk to Shared Value. The Business Case for Disaster Risk Reduction*. Global Assessment Report on Disaster Risk Reduction. Geneva: United Nations.

JICA and Tehran Disaster Mitigation and Management Center. 2000. "The Study on Seismic Microzoning of the Greater Tehran Area in the Islamic Republic of Iran: Final Report Executive Summary." SSF-JR-00-186.

—— 2004. *Comprehensive Master Plan Study on Urban Seismic Disaster Prevention and Management for the Greater Tehran Area in the Islamic Republic of Iran: The Main Final Report*. GE-JR-04-039. Tehran, Iran.

Mackie, Peter and Worsley, Tom. 2013. *International Comparisons of Transport Appraisal Practice: Overview Report*. Institute for Transport Studies, University of Leeds.

MLIT. 2005. *Chisui Keizai Chousa Manuaru* [Flood Control Economic Survey Manual]. Draft Version. Tokyo: Ministry of Land, Infrastructure, Transport and Tourism. https://www.mlit.go.jp/river/basic_info/seisaku_hyouka/gaiyou/hyouka/h1704/chisui.pdf.

Teikoku Databank. 2014. "Tokubetsu Kikaku: Higashinihon Daishinsai Kanren Tosan (Hassei kara 3nen) no Uchiwaketo Kongono Mitoshi" [Breakdown and Prospects of Bankruptcy Cases Related to the Great East Japan Earthquake (3 years after the onset)], March. www.tdb.co.jp/report/watching/press/pdf/p140301.pdf.

Tohoku Regional Development Bureau, Ministry of Land, Infrastructure, Transport and Tourism. 2012. "Heisei 23 Nendo Jigyou Hyouka Kanshi Iinkai (Dai 6 Kai Shiryou) Shiryou 1-1 – Kasen Kankei Jigyou Abukuma Gawa Suikei Chokkatsu Sabou Jigyou Setsumei Shiryou" [Abukuma River System Sabo Project – Document Submitted for the 6th Monitoring and Evaluation Committee of the Fiscal Year 2011]. Sendai: MLIT. www.thr.mlit.go.jp/bumon/b00097/k00360/h13jhyouka/2306hpsiryou/siryou230601. pdf.

United Nations secretariat of the International Strategy for Disaster Reduction (ISDR). 2009. *Risk and Poverty in a Changing Climate: Invest Today for a Safer Tomorrow. Global Assessment Report on Disaster Risk Reduction.* Geneva: United Nations.

World Bank and United Nations. 2010. *Natural Hazards, UnNatural Disasters: The Economics of Effective Prevention.* Washington, DC: World Bank.

World Conference on Disaster Reduction. 2005. "Hyogo Framework for Action 2005–2015: Building the Resilience of Nations and Communities to Disasters." www.unisdr. org/2005/wcdr/intergover/official-doc/L-docs/Hyogo-framework-for-action-english.pdf.

Yuvejwattana, Suttinee and Suwannakij, Supunnabul. 2011. "Thai Flooding Threatens Bangkok, May Cut Deeper into Growth". New York: Bloomberg Business Week.

6 Institutionalizing and sharing the culture of prevention

The Japanese experience

Satoru Nishikawa and Yukinari Hosokawa

Introduction

Through her long history of confronting natural disasters, Japan has chronicled the experiences of disasters, devised measures to reduce disasters, and nurtured a culture of prevention. In the past 70 years, Japan has experienced three epoch-making disasters. Each of them imparted valuable lessons. The first was a typhoon, the second an urban earthquake, and the third a gigantic tsunami generated by a tectonic earthquake. After each event, a thorough investigation of the causes of the catastrophic damage was conducted and recorded, and countermeasures, including augmented organizational arrangements, were developed. Lessons were learned not only from these gigantic disasters but every disaster, regardless of size, provided lessons on how to cultivate societal preparedness against disasters. The process of implementing these learnings has evolved into constant "Kaizen" (improvement), perpetual enlargement of participation and the unremitting expansion of the scope of disaster reduction activities. These experiences have been shared with the international community under the auspices of the United Nations through the International Decade for Natural Disaster Reduction (IDNDR) and the International Strategy for Disaster Reduction (ISDR) activities. The culture of prevention has been shared with a number of countries and has contributed to disaster reduction activities in these countries.

This chapter describes the Japanese history of facing and learning the lessons from various disasters, and how countermeasures came to be institutionalized in modern Japan and further shared with the international community.

A culture of prevention fostered through bitter experiences of disasters in Japan

History of confronting disasters in pre-modern Japan

Since the Japanese Archipelago is located on the Pacific Ring of Fire and along the north-west Pacific 'typhoon alley', Japan has been repeatedly menaced by typhoons, floods, landslides, heavy snow, earthquakes, tsunamis and volcanic eruptions. Japan's surface area takes up just 0.25 percent of the world; however,

Japan has a disproportionate share of tectonic incidents, with 20.5 percent of all earthquakes stronger than M6 in the first decade of the twenty-first century and 7.0 percent of active volcanoes on Earth. As a result of these harsh conditions, the Japanese people have monitored and recorded disasters, accumulated knowledge and developed technologies to cope with disasters, thereby nurturing a culture of prevention.

The Nihon-Shoki, one of the oldest official history books, dates back to the eighth century, and contains details of a number of earthquakes and tsunamis. The reports include the Yamato-Kochi Earthquake in AD August 416 and the Hakuho-Nankai Great Earthquake in AD November 684. This latter disaster was followed by a subsequent great tsunami and land subsidence. In the succeeding official history book, edited by Nihon-Sandai-Jitsuroku in the ninth century, it is reported that in July 869AD,

> a great earthquake hit the Mutsu-no-Kuni [the old name for Tohoku], people toppled over and were unable to stand up, and houses collapsed, crushing the people inside to death. Others became trapped in earth cracks, while warehouses, gates, derricks and walls of fortresses were destroyed here and there. Seawater surged into the castle of Taganoki and 1,000 people there drowned to death.

(Sangawa 2011, 49)

The gigantic earthquake and tsunami, known as the Jogan Earthquake, shows a number of similarities to the 2011 Great East Japan Earthquake and Tsunami.

In the history of Japan, there have been many renowned historical figures that have contributed to disaster reduction. In the sixth to tenth centuries, Buddhism was brought to Japan from China through the Korean peninsula. Japanese priests were sent to China to acquire the Buddhist scriptures. They not only studied Buddhism but also acquired medical and civil engineering knowledge. Some of these priests strongly believed that the goal of alleviating the sufferings of fellow people was an important task for religious leaders. Since the peasants at that time constantly suffered from droughts and floods, some priests undertook the mission of applying their civil engineering knowledge to disaster reduction.

In the seventh to eighth centuries, the high Buddhist priest Gyoki, on his pilgrimage as a missionary, put in place civil engineering works for river control. In 731, Gyoki and his followers constructed Koya-ike (Koya-pond), a multi-purpose dam reservoir for flood control and irrigation in the present Hyogo prefecture (Kako and Ogata 1997a). This Koya-ike is still used as a reservoir to provide tap water, and is surrounded by a city park where the citizens can enjoy the scenery. Similarly, in 821, the high Buddhist priest Kukai (Kobo Daishi) reconstructed the Mannou-ike (Mannou-pond) dam reservoir by applying the latest civil engineering technology. The completed dam is still compatible with modern dams and has ensured the livelihood of farmers suffering from water shortages and flooding. Mannou-ike is presently used as an irrigation reservoir for 32km^2 of rice paddies.

The famous sixteenth-century warlord Takeda Shingen, whose main territories were located in the Kofu basin, an area frequently menaced by violent flooding, developed a new water control levee. The structure is known as *Shingen tsutsumi* (grouped echelon embankments) and is applied in modern Japanese river works. He was also responsible for the invention of a water control structure called the sacred cow (lumber made into a triangular pyramid to be placed in river beds at risk of torrents to streamline and ease the flow). With these constructions, he was able to stabilize the livelihood of his farmers and gain support and power (Kako and Ogata 1997b). All of the above people contributed to the welfare and livelihood of commoners through the development and application of disaster reduction technologies and are regarded as great figures in Japanese history.

The Horyuji Temple pagoda, built in the seventh century, is the oldest wooden "high-rise" building in Japan. The 32-meter high, five-layered pagoda is a unique structure consisting of a combination of semi-flexible timberwork joints and a central wooden pillar that disperses and absorbs earthquake shocks. This wooden structure has withstood numerous earthquakes over the centuries. Modern Japanese structural engineers have carefully studied its strengths, and in 2002 they emulated these seismic-structural features in the design of a 179-meter-high office building in Tokyo (Mitsubishi Jisho Sekkei Inc. 2003). In these ways, the Shingen tsutsumi (embankment) and Horyuji Temple pagoda represent the inheritance of disaster mitigation technologies over the centuries in Japan.

The culture of prevention fostered

Through these experiences, the Japanese people have fostered a culture of disaster prevention. Fear of disasters is reflected in the traditional listing of dreadful things for Japanese children, *"Jishin Kaminari Kaji Oyaji,"* which means "Earthquake, Thunder, Fire and Father (Storm)." The usual meaning of *Oyaji* in Japanese is "strict father." However, the term also stands for a "big storm." There are numerous local legends and proverbs expressing the necessity of being prepared for disasters. One example is the story of *"Inamura-no-hi,"* or "Fire on Rice Sheaves." The story is based around the immediate tsunami evacuation led by the Hiro village chief Hamaguchi Gihei immediately after the 1854 *Ansei-Nankai* Earthquake. Hamaguchi felt the tremors of a strong earthquake and when he looked down from a hilltop he noticed that the seawater was receding and remembered that this was the sign of an approaching tsunami. Since it was growing dark, Hamaguchi, having a quick wit, lit a fire on stacks of harvested rice sheaves on the high ground. His fellow villagers were surprised to see the fire and ran up the slopes to extinguish it. Hamaguchi ordered them to let the fire burn on so that their followers would continue to run up the slopes, thus enabling them to flee from the tsunami. When the villagers looked back, their houses facing the seashore were totally inundated. Seeing the devastation wrought by the tsunami, Hamaguchi took charge of the reconstruction of the village and provided funds for the construction of a tsunami embankment along the coastline, hiring the villagers who had lost their means of livelihood. This story was published in the national elementary school reading book from 1937 to 1947 and is widely known among the Japanese population. This tsunami embankment

Figure 6.1 Ukiyo-e print, "Shin-Yoshihara Oo-Namazu Yurahi"

Source: International Research Center for Japanese Studies/Earthquake Research Institute Library, The University of Tokyo.

protected Hiro village in 1946 when the *Showa-Nankai* Tsunami hit again (Japan Meteorological Agency n.d.).

Another tale is a proverb told by a famous physicist Torahiko Terada who investigated the 1923 Great Kanto Earthquake. "*Tensai ha wasuretakoro ni yattekuru,*" or "natural disasters will hit us when we have forgotten about them" he claimed, thereby alerting the population to the importance of disaster awareness. Every time a major disaster occurred, people would erect stone monuments and shrines to pass down the terrible experiences to their descendants. When Edo (the old name for Tokyo) was hit by the *Ansei-Edo* Earthquake in 1855, an ukiyo-e (a popular woodblock color print of the Edo era) drawing was published, showing the citizens of Edo trying to beat the legendary monster catfish which at that time was believed to have caused the earthquake (Figure 6.1). This drawing symbolizes the wishes of the Edo commoners to eliminate earthquakes. These form an important part of the Japanese culture and are still occasionally used in public awareness programs.

Institutionalization of disaster reduction efforts brought by the first epoch-making turning point: 1959

Modern Japan continued to suffer

Even in the modern age, disasters have continued to ravage Japan. In 1891, 7,273 people were killed by the M8 *Noubi* Earthquake; in 1896, 22,000 lost their lives in the *Meiji-Sanriku* Tsunami, and in 1923 Tokyo and its vicinity were devastated by the M7.9 Great Kanto Earthquake. This latter disaster resulted in the loss of 105,000 lives and 40 percent of the country's GDP. In 1933, 3,064 people were killed by the *Showa-Sanriku* Tsunami. In response to the devastating damage, the Japanese government not only provided relief and recovery to the affected areas but also tried to investigate the root causes of this damage through the interdisciplinary Association for Earthquake Disaster Prevention, established in 1892. The Association continued its activities until 2010 when its responsibilities were handed over to the Japan Association for Earthquake Engineering.

Multi-sectoral approach brought by the first epoch-making turning point: 1959

In the 1940s and 1950s Japan was repeatedly ravaged by typhoons and earthquakes. Almost every year, thousands of lives were lost. In response, the Japanese government put measures in place incrementally to cope with disasters. In 1959, when Japan was on a course towards a revival from the ashes of World War II, the Ise-wan Typhoon hit the country's third largest metropolitan area, Nagoya, killing 5,098 people. The heavy damage brought by the typhoon triggered an extensive debate within the Japanese government on how to cope with natural disasters. After 2 years of discussions, the Disaster Countermeasures Basic Act (Government of Japan 1961) was passed in 1961. This Act has three major characteristics:

1   The Central Disaster Management Council was established, chaired by the Prime Minister, with membership of all Ministers of the Government as well as heads of semi-public organizations, such as NHK Public Broadcasting, Bank of Japan, Japanese Red Cross and NTT Telecommunications Company, as well as academics. The Council was given the role of formulating the overall policy for disaster risk management and functioned as the national coordinating body for disaster management.
2   The roles and responsibilities of the national, prefecture and municipal governments, as well as community organizations and citizens with roles related to disaster reduction, were clearly defined. The three layers of government were obliged to prepare master plans for disaster reduction. Moreover, all the ministries and semi-public service providers, such as electricity, gas, railway, bus and forwarder companies, were obliged to prepare disaster management plans.
3   The Cabinet was tasked with submitting an annual official report to the National *Diet* regarding the status of disaster risk management and budgetary allocations for disaster reduction programs. The National *Diet*, both in the lower house and the upper house, formed a special committee for disaster management, and has continued to monitor governmental efforts towards disaster reduction.

This Basic Act proved to be quite effective in addressing not only the emergency response but also prevention/mitigation, preparedness and recovery/reconstruction – all the four phases of disaster reduction performed through a multi-sectoral approach. As a result of the comprehensiveness of the Act, even in years when no major disasters have occurred, disaster risk management was always tabled on the national political agenda, and thus disaster reduction has been mainstreamed into the national policy framework, thereby securing the financial basis for disaster reduction. In addition, in 1960, the Erosion and Flood Control Emergency Measures Act was passed to enhance preventive works; and, following this, in 1962, the Act Concerning Special Financial Aid to Deal with Disasters was passed to assist local governments with disaster recovery. From 1960 onwards, September 1, the date when Tokyo was devastated by the Great Kanto Earthquake (and also the day when typhoons most frequently make landfall in Japan), has been designated "Disaster Prevention Day." Hence, every year public awareness programs for disaster reduction are conducted on this day (Nishikawa 2007). As a result of these efforts, despite the fact that the number of typhoons reaching Japan has not changed on average over the past 70 years, the number of casualties caused by natural disasters has greatly decreased, as shown in the statistics of the White Paper on Disaster Management (Figure 6.2).

The International Decade for Natural Disaster Reduction (IDNDR) and the Japanese involvement

Proposal of IDNDR

In the late 1980s, a group of American and Japanese earthquake engineering scientists stated that there was already a wealth of scientific knowledge that could be applied to alleviate the suffering from natural disasters, and issued a call on the need for international action for disaster reduction. The Japanese government,

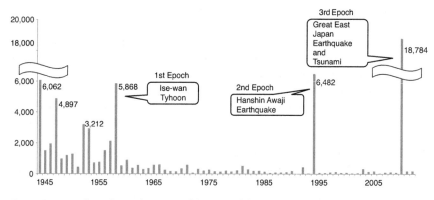

Figure 6.2 Number of casualties caused by natural disasters in Japan (1945–2013)

Source: Prepared by the authors on the basis of data from the Cabinet Office of the Government of Japan, "BOUSAI HAKUSHO" [White Paper on Disaster Management].

with its experience of substantially decreasing casualties from natural disasters, immediately recognized the significance of this idea and decided to strongly endorse it in the international community. Japan, together with Germany, Italy, the Group of 77 countries and others, submitted a draft resolution to the forty-second session of the United Nations General Assembly to take this issue to the wider international community. In December 1987, the United Nations General Assembly unanimously adopted the resolution A/RES/42/169, designating the 1990s as the International Decade for Natural Disaster Reduction (IDNDR). This resolution taken the 1990s was in a decade in which the international community, under the auspices of the United Nations, would pay special attention to fostering international cooperation in the field of natural disaster reduction. It also resolved that the main objectives of this decade were, through concerted international actions and especially in developing countries, to reduce the loss of life, property damage and social and economic disruption caused by natural disasters. The United Nations General Assembly adopted subsequent resolutions in 1988 (A/RES/43/202) and 1989 (A/RES/44/236) and the Decade was launched in January 1990 (Nishikawa 2010).

Tabling disaster reduction to the international political agenda and the call for multi-sectoral approaches

While there have been previous efforts by the scientific community to enhance international knowledge exchanges regarding disasters, the proclamation of the IDNDR by the UN General Assembly was epoch making, since it brought a natural disaster agenda to the attention of the international political forums. In A/RES/44/236, the UN recognized "the necessity for the international community to demonstrate the strong political determination required to mobilize and use existing scientific and technical knowledge to mitigate natural disasters, bearing in mind in particular the needs of developing countries" (United Nations General Assembly 1989). Furthermore, IDNDR brought the idea of the multi-sectoral approach to disaster reduction. Resolution A/RES/44/236 called on all governments:

1   To formulate national disaster mitigation programs, as well as economic, land use and insurance policies for disaster prevention, and, particularly in developing countries, to integrate them fully into their national development programs.
2   To participate during the decade in concerted international action for the reduction of natural disasters and, as appropriate, to establish national committees in cooperation with the relevant scientific and technological communities and other concerned sectors with a view to attaining the objective and goals of the decade.
3   To encourage local administrative bodies to take appropriate steps to mobilize the necessary support from the public and private sectors and to contribute to the achievement of the purposes of the decade.

4   To keep the Secretary-General informed of the plans of their countries and of assistance that can be provided so that the United Nations may become an international center for the exchange of information and the coordination of international efforts concerning activities in support of the objective and goals of the decade, thus enabling each state to benefit from the experience of other countries.

5   To take measures, as appropriate, to increase public awareness of damage-risk probabilities and of the significance of preparedness, prevention, relief and short-term recovery activities with respect to natural disasters and to enhance community preparedness through education, training and other means, taking into account the specific role of the news media.

6   To pay due attention to the impact of natural disasters upon health care, particularly to activities to reduce the vulnerability of hospitals and health centers, as well as the impact upon food storage facilities, human shelter and other social and economic infrastructures.

7   To improve the early international availability of appropriate emergency supplies through the storage or earmarking of such supplies in disaster-prone areas.

The Japanese government, with the advice of Japanese scientists, was very active in drafting these resolutions and was eager to reflect the Japanese experience in decreasing casualties from natural disasters through a multi-sectoral approach established by the Disaster Countermeasures Basic Act of 1961.

Sharing the Japanese experience for international cooperation

With the launch of the IDNDR in 1990, the Japanese government initiated various programs to promote the decade. Various JICA training courses and seminars were newly developed with the purpose of sharing the Japanese expertise on disaster reduction. One of the flagship JICA courses was the "Seminar on Disaster Management Administration," which introduced a wide spectrum of disaster reduction activities, starting from meteorological and geophysical observations to school disaster education programs, and covering the organizational arrangements following the 1961 Act to enable multi-sectoral coordination and cooperation for disaster reduction.

In addition, academia, the Japanese Red Cross Society and the private sector formulated the Japanese National Committee for IDNDR. The Japanese National Committee aimed to broaden international exchanges for disaster reduction and ran various programs. Among them is the unique "Multi-language Glossary on Natural Disasters," which covers specialized terminology on disasters in Chinese, English, French, Japanese, Korean and Spanish, for the sake of better communication among international experts (Toki 1993, 1996). From September 27 to October 3, 1990 the Japanese government and the Japanese National Committee, with the cooperation of the United Nations IDNDR Scientific and Technical Committee, organized the International Conference on IDNDR in

Yokohama and Kagoshima, with Japan to provide the momentum for the decade and to identify the challenges.

World Conference on Natural Disaster Reduction 1994 and the Yokohama Strategy and Plan of Action

The launch of IDNDR in 1990 was welcomed by various scientific societies around the world which were involved in disaster reduction activities. The Manjil-Rudbar Earthquake, which hit north-west Iran in June 1990, claimed more than 41,000 lives and reminded the international community of the importance of IDNDR. But in the international political forums, IDNDR was overshadowed by the Gulf Crisis, which began in August 1990. The mass of displaced people in the Middle East required a large amount of urgent assistance. Discussions within the international humanitarian community were dominated by the need to develop ways and means to cope with this crisis, meaning that IDNDR was not able to attract due attention. However, a cyclone in Bangladesh in 1991, the Mt Pinatubo eruption in the Philippines in 1991 and the Maharashtra Earthquake in India in 1993 provided continuous reminders to the international community of the necessity of promoting IDNDR.

The Japanese government felt the need to keep up the momentum of IDNDR. In December 1993, the forty-eighth session of the United Nations General Assembly adopted a resolution (A/RES/48/188) to convene the World Conference on Natural Disaster Reduction in 1994, hosted by the Government of Japan in Yokohama from May 23 to 27, 1994. The conference adopted the "Yokohama Strategy and Plan of Action for a Safer World: Guidelines for Natural Disaster Prevention, Preparedness and Mitigation." The Yokohama Strategy was the first internationally agreed document outlining a broad spectrum of actions necessary for natural disaster reduction at the local, national and international levels. The Yokohama Strategy called for the "development of a global culture of prevention as an essential component of an integrated approach to disaster reduction," reflecting the Japanese experience of fostering the culture of prevention (United Nations 1994).

The second epoch-making turning point for Japan: 1995

The Great Hansin-Awaji Earthquake hit Kobe in 1995

Early in the morning of January 17, 1995, a strong M7.3 earthquake hit the city of Kobe and its vicinity. The epicenter was shallow, approximately 12km in depth; the active fault ran directly beneath the center of Kobe. This is called the "Great Hanshin-Awaji Earthquake." The collapse of buildings and subsequent fires killed 5,521 people. The total number of casualties, including indirect deaths, totaled 6,437. This was the worst natural disaster for Japan since the 1959 Ise-wan Typhoon. The sixth floor of Kobe City Hall building collapsed, and cracks appeared in the Hyogo Prefectural Government Building. Local fire and police

stations were badly damaged; local city offices, which were designated as emergency command stations, were also damaged and lost electricity, thus paralyzing
the initial local government response command for a few hours. The passable
roads in Kobe quickly became jammed with cars, since initial traffic control was
not strictly enforced, thus delaying ambulances and fire engines.

The bottom-up damage reporting system had been developed in 1961, with
a reporting chain from municipal government to prefecture government and
then to national government. The three-layered response system, in which the
municipal government, then the prefecture, respond at the request of the mayor,
and the national government respond at the request of the governor, did not
function. This was because the initial responders themselves lost base and were
not able to grasp the damage in its entirety. Later in the morning, when daylight
came, the aerial footage from the NHK (the public broadcasting TV) helicopter
showed serious damage; however, the casualty reports from local government
to Tokyo counted a death toll of fewer than 100, which demonstrated the mal-
functions in the reporting system (Department of Humanitarian Affairs, United
Nations 1995).

Progress based on the lessons learned in Kobe, 1995

The 1995 earthquake was the first major natural disaster to hit the center of
a large modern metropolis of a developed country. As a result of the earthquake, the weaknesses in the 1961 system were exposed, and numerous lessons were learned. The Japanese government thoroughly reviewed the Disaster
Countermeasures Basic Act and made major revisions in 1995, focusing mainly
on the immediate response system. For example, if in case of a major disaster, the
Prime Minister sees that the damage is overwhelming the capacity of the local
government, he can immediately mobilize the Japan Self Defense Force without
a request from the governor. The Prime Minister was also given the power to
create an on-site emergency coordination headquarters and designate the head.
New decision-supporting systems, damage estimation systems, and emergency
communication systems using geographic information systems (GIS) and the
latest IT tools were developed. Whenever a strong earthquake was observed,
the damage estimation system would be automatically activated to determine the
scale of the human casualties and building damage to give guidance to the immediate response bodies. New research programs related to earthquake sciences
were launched along with nationwide research on active faults. Results of these
investigations were published as a map, indicating that all 47 prefectures of Japan
have active faults (The Headquarters for Earthquake Research Promotion 1997).
The publication urged all local governments to be aware of this fact and revise
their local disaster management plans accordingly. Institutional arrangements for
disaster management were also enhanced. A high-ranking position, the Deputy
Chief Cabinet Secretary for Crisis Management, was created. Subsequently, in
January 2001, on the occasion of national government reforms, a new position,
Minister of State for Disaster Management, was created in the Cabinet Office to

be in charge of inter-ministerial planning and coordination. The Minister's role is to act on behalf of the Prime Minister who is Chair of the Central Disaster Management Council. The Minister has the responsibility of advocating disaster reduction at the political level and will be the controller and coordinator of responses. This Minister's presence upgraded the status of disaster reduction policy at the national level.

New initiatives for public awareness launched

Prior to the 1995 earthquake, many Japanese believed that it would be the Tokai (the area between Tokyo and Nagoya) and the Tokyo metropolitan areas that would be hit by major earthquakes in the near future. The citizens of Kobe erroneously believed that they did not face the risk of earthquakes, simply because they had not experienced even small earthquakes within living memory. However, the lifetime of human beings is far shorter than the recurrence period of extreme natural events. Therefore it is absolutely necessary to pass down the lessons learned from disasters over the generations and also to share them across geographical boundaries.

The Disaster Reduction and Human Renovation Institution (DRI) was newly organized by the Hyogo Prefectural Government, with financial and technical support from the Cabinet Office. It was opened in April 2002, together with a museum facility in Kobe, with the goals of meeting future necessities, and in particular to hand down the experiences of the 1995 earthquake to younger generations and to ensure that the best use is made of the lessons learned in future disaster management initiatives. The DRI has committed itself to creating a disaster management culture, improving local capacities for disaster risk reduction, supporting the planning of disaster management policies and helping to realize a safe and secure community in which citizens work together for disaster risk reduction. The DRI also aims to play a pivotal role in developing and disseminating effective and overall countermeasures against disasters, serving as a center for research and study of disaster risk management (Disaster Reduction and Human Renovation Institution 2014). When a disaster occurs, the DRI's researchers are dispatched to the affected areas to support the local government and offer their disaster management methodology. The DRI museum contains exhibits showing the devastation that occurred as a result of the 1995 earthquake, the suffering of the people and the reconstruction process. Survivors of the 1995 earthquake are always available at the exhibition space as volunteers to explain their own personal experiences to visitors in their own words. The DRI has become one of the most popular site visits for junior high school excursions, thereby fulfilling its mandate of passing on knowledge of the disaster.

In May 2003, for the sake of extracting valuable lessons from historical disasters, the Central Disaster Management Council decided to commission the Special Committee on Inheritance of Lessons Learned from Disasters to thoroughly review historical disasters from interdisciplinary viewpoints. Academics from different science faculties were convened and mobilized for the acquisition of dispersed historical documents on selected individual disasters from the seventeenth to the twentienth centuries in Japan. The purpose of this exercise was to review the disasters from various perspectives to draw a complete picture of the damage and human responses to each disaster. By December 2010, a total of 24 disasters had been reviewed and reports on individual disasters, as well as analytical reports on lessons by type of disaster – hydro-meteorological events, volcanic eruptions, ocean-tectonic earthquakes and tsunamis, inland earthquakes and urban fires – were published. Moreover, educational materials for child and adult education were produced and posted on the Cabinet Office website to be freely used for various public awareness programs (Cabinet Office of Japan n.d.).

New public awareness initiatives applied in Turkey

These programs for nurturing a culture of prevention were emulated by countries who had suffered similar disasters. Turkey was hit by two strong earthquakes in 1999 with the loss of approximately 20,000 lives. Hyogo Prefecture, together with the Japanese government, immediately offered assistance, including provision of high-quality prefabricated temporary housing units to the affected areas. JICA technical assistance programs for earthquake disaster mitigation, such as training of trainers' programs for governors and mayors, and in-depth studies for earthquake mechanisms, were conducted. In their study tours to Kobe, Turkish experts were impressed by the DRI museum and its programs. The Turkish Disaster and Emergency Management Presidency (AFAD) decided to construct a public disaster education center, similar to DRI, in Bursa, an area in north-western Turkey. The Bursa Public Disaster Education Center opened in September 2013. DRI, through JICA's technical assistance scheme, provided advice and experts on how to operate the center and develop educational programs for student disaster awareness, as well as what would be required for the center to become the Turkish repository of materials on disasters.

The improved disaster management system tested in Japan

There were several major disasters following the earthquake in Kobe that provided an opportunity to test the improved disaster management system. A major volcano in Hokkaido, Mt Usu, erupted in 2000/2001. An on-site emergency coordination headquarters was put in place, and the scientific prediction of lava and ash flows and local evacuation plans were then meticulously prepared at the headquarters. A massive, orderly evacuation of residents was implemented successfully and no human casualties resulted. In May 2003 a strong M7.1 earthquake hit Miyagi in northern Japan, resulting in no casualties. Disaster information was immediately shared among local and national authorities. Miyagi was hit again by an M7.2 earthquake in August 2005, again with no casualties. A previous M7.4 earthquake in Miyagi, in 1978, killed 28 people. These three earthquakes in Miyagi demonstrated the progress in disaster risk management in Japan and also alerted people in Miyagi to be prepared for future strong earthquakes.

Earthquake disaster reduction strategy for Japan

The series of research programs for disaster reduction and the enhanced institutional arrangements following the 1995 earthquake prompted new findings and policies. Starting from 2003, the Central Disaster Management Council published a series of detailed damage estimates for probable major earthquakes – the predicted Tokai, Tonankai and Nankai, and Inland Tokyo earthquakes. All of these estimates indicated that the damage would be far more serious than the Kobe earthquake. Countermeasures to decrease the amount of damage were sought. Detailed investigation on the causes of deaths in the Kobe earthquake revealed that 80 percent of the deaths had been caused by the physical collapse of houses and falling furniture, and the majority of deaths had occurred within 15 minutes of the quake. This fact indicated that no matter how quickly the rescue teams were mobilized, it would have been difficult to save many lives. Houses built before the 1981 building code suffered heavy damage, whereas new houses suffered only minor damage. These facts led to the clear conclusion that in order to substantially decrease casualties, preventive measures are much more important than response. Old buildings need to be structurally checked and retrofitted as necessary. Based on these findings, the Central Disaster Management Council decided to implement Earthquake Disaster Reduction Strategies for Tokai, Tonankai and Nankai, and Inland Tokyo earthquakes. These strategies comprise a set of programs for action to effectively halve the estimated damage of major earthquakes within 10 years. For example, the Inland Tokyo Earthquake Strategy lists five main pre-disaster programs to halve the numbers of deaths and casualties:

1   seismic strengthening of housing and building stocks;
2   affixing of furniture;
3   redevelopment of old densely populated areas;
4   upgrade immediate fire-extinguishing capacity;
5   protect steep hills from slope failures.

These five ideas were accompanied by three main programs to halve economic damage:

1   mitigation measures to decrease reconstruction costs;
2   business continuity of enterprises;
3   early recovery measures for transportation facilities.

The UN World Conference on Disaster Reduction 2005 hosted in Japan and the Hyogo Framework for Action adopted

The launch of ISDR and the proposal of the World Conference on Disaster Reduction

In December 1999, the United Nations General Assembly adopted a resolution (A/RES/54/219) providing arrangements to create a successor to IDNDR in the United Nations system as the International Strategy for Disaster Reduction (ISDR). In July 2003, the Japanese government, wishing to share the terrible experiences learned as a result of the 1995 Great Hanshin-Awaji Earthquake, expressed its willingness to host another UN conference on disaster reduction. In December 2003, the fifty-eighth session of the United Nations General Assembly adopted a resolution (A/RES/58/214) to convene the World Conference on Disaster Reduction (WCDR) in 2005 at the senior-official level and hosted by the Government of Japan in Kobe, Hyogo.

How the Indian Ocean Tsunami 2004 impacted the World Conference on Disaster Reduction

On December 26, 2004, a gigantic earthquake occurred off the coast of Sumatra, Indonesia and generated the Indian Ocean Tsunami. The resulting tsunami not only directly hit Indonesia but also traveled across the Indian Ocean, reaching as far as Somalia. The tsunami claimed more than 230,000 lives, including European tourists who were staying in the seaside resorts in South-East Asia, making it the worst natural disaster since the start of the twenty-first century. The Japanese government immediately provided emergency humanitarian assistance to the affected countries and offered to fund a package of international programs under the auspices of the United Nations to strengthen the early warning capacities of Indian Ocean countries.

The UN World Conference on Disaster Reduction was held in Kobe from January 18 to 22, 2005, where delegates from 168 UN member states, including Ministers from European countries, unanimously adopted the Hyogo Framework for Action (HFA) 2005–2015. Japan has substantially contributed to the drafting of HFA, reflecting on the experiences throughout her history and the multi-sectoral and preventive approach for disaster reduction. Moreover, in a swift response to the Indian Ocean Tsunami, Japan discussed the issue with UNESCO and the United Nations secretariat of the ISDR, and organized a special session on the Indian Ocean Disaster in WCDR. As a result of this session, the "Common Statement of the Special Session on the Indian Ocean Disaster: Risk Reduction for a Safer Future" (World Conference on Disaster Reduction 2005) outlined an overall framework to address the tsunami disaster.

Implementing HFA in Japan, a nationwide movement for disaster risk reduction

In 2004, Japan was hit by a record-breaking number of ten typhoons. In October 2004, a strong earthquake hit Niigata in northern Japan. Thus, in Japan, the year 2004 was named the "Year of Disasters." The December 2004 Indian Ocean Tsunami reminded the nation of the threat of possible tsunamis that could occur as a result of the Tokai and Tonankai and Nankai earthquakes in Japan. The set of programs listed in the Earthquake Disaster Reduction Strategy require a full government commitment to halve the estimated damage within 10 years. In addition, certain programs require strong voluntary action from the private sector and the public at large. The Government of Japan decided to take this opportunity to reinforce disaster reduction activities for the implementation of HFA in Japan. In July 2005, the Central Disaster Management Council commissioned its subcommittee to launch the Nationwide Movement for Disaster Reduction.

In 2006, the government increased subsidies and tax incentives for the seismic retrofitting of houses. However, the house owners themselves must recognize the personal risk of being killed in their own houses and take the initiative themselves to invest in improving safety and apply for subsidies and tax exemptions. It is up to the resident to decide on ensuring that furniture is affixed to walls. Likewise, the CEO of an enterprise must recognize the significance of business continuity planning for the sake of the company. New disaster awareness activities involving various sectors and groups, chambers of commerce, parents and teachers associations, Red Cross chapters and local shop unions were proposed. Public awareness programs and educational materials were developed, and comic books by renowned artists were published. A movie based on a real story from the Kobe earthquake was produced and ranked third in December 2006 in national ticket sales. Figure 6.3 shows the winning entry of the national disaster awareness poster competition in 2005, symbolizing the necessity of disaster awareness. It illustrates the fact that people often tend to think that disasters are somebody else's tragedy to watch on the TV screen when such events may be right on their doorsteps.

The Central Disaster Management Council published the Business Continuity (BC) Guidelines (1st edition) in 2005, where the concept of Business Continuity Planning (BCP) is thoroughly defined and elements are described. Furthermore, the Council called on trade unions to adapt this guideline to the specific characteristics of each industry. The government, in association with the Development Bank of Japan, offered new special low interest loans to companies that fulfill the basic points of the BC Guidelines. In addition, with the endorsement of the Cabinet Office, the BCAO (Business Continuity Advancement Organization) was established in 2006 to widely disseminate BCP in Japan. Through these activities, the idea that "disaster reduction is everyone's business and should not be limited to emergency managers" has come to be accepted in Japan.

Promoting HFA and international cooperation for disaster reduction

On January 18, 2005, the first day of the WCDR, the Government of Japan published the policy paper "Initiatives for Disaster Reduction through ODA" (Official Development Assistance) (Government of Japan 2005) where it announced that Japan will support the self-help efforts of developing countries in the field of disaster reduction. Japan initiated numerous cooperation programs for disaster reduction based on this policy paper.

In February 2005 Japan, together with the United Nations secretariat of the ISDR, Intergovernmental Oceanic Commission (IOC) of UNESCO, International Tsunami Information Center (ITIC), World Meteorological Organization (WMO), Asian Disaster Reduction Center (ADRC) and the Pacific

いつまでも、他人事とは限らない、扉を開ければ、すぐ隣。

Figure 6.3 Disaster awareness poster by Nobutaka Uchida, 2005

Source: "Bousai Jouhou no Pe-ji" [Disaster Management Information Homepage], Cabinet Office, Government of Japan.

Tsunami Warning Center (PTWC) organized the "Mission on Policy Dialogue for High Level Administrative Policy Makers on Establishing a Tsunami Early Warning Mechanism in the Indian Ocean." In March 2005, JICA organized "the JICA Regional Seminar on Tsunami Early Warning Systems." The Cabinet

Office of Japan, with the cooperation of ADRC, developed education materials on tsunamis in the local languages of the affected countries based on the Japanese story of "*Inamura-no-hi*" or "Fire on Rice Sheaves," which were later widely used for public awareness programs in these countries. Prior to 2004, there were only a few organizations with experiences of tsunami disaster reduction programs in the world. ADRC had a successful experience of adapting the Japanese tsunami awareness program for Papua New Guinea in 1999 (Figure 6.4), and the same methodology was effectively converted for application in the Indian Ocean countries.

Bilateral technical assistance programs for the countries affected by the Indian Ocean Tsunami were initiated by JICA in 2006. JICA studies aimed at enhancing the institutional capacities for disaster reduction in Thailand and Sri Lanka, to name a few countries.

Comprehensive disaster reduction initiative with Indonesia

Furthermore, Japan has stepped up to launch a comprehensive package program to strengthen Indonesia's efforts to build a disaster-resilient nation. In June 2005, the President of Indonesia and the Prime Minister of Japan issued a "Joint Communique Regarding the Bilateral Cooperation for Mitigating Damage Caused

Figure 6.4 Tsunami awareness poster produced by ADRC for Papua New Guinea, 1999

Source: Department of Education, National Disaster Management Organization and Geology Department, University of PNG. Drawn by Michael John. Layout by the Religious Television Association. Printed by PNG Printing.

by Natural Disasters." Based on this communique, the Joint Committee of Japan and Indonesia on Disaster Reduction was established. The purpose of this Joint Committee was to reduce natural disasters in Indonesia while strengthening the cooperation between the two countries to develop a system to mitigate damage caused by natural disasters. In July 2006, the Minister of State in charge of disaster management of Japan and the Coordinating Minister for the People's Welfare of Indonesia adopted the report, "Building the Resilience of Indonesia and its Communities to Disasters for the Next Generation" as a guideline for future disaster reduction measures, which was then reported to the leaders of both countries. Based on this report, the governments of both countries worked together to promote disaster reduction in Indonesia, especially in the following four prioritized areas: establishing a disaster risk-management administrative structure, developing a tsunami early warning system, strengthening building standards for seismic safety, and enhancing countermeasures against floods and landslides.

Culture of prevention adopted by Central America

Like Japan, the Central American Isthmus region is located on the Pacific Ring of Fire and in the paths of numerous hurricanes every year. As a result, it has often been threatened by earthquakes, tsunamis, hurricanes, landslides and volcanic eruptions. Hurricane Mitch in 1998 devastated the northern part of Central America, including Honduras, Guatemala, El Salvador and Nicaragua, and claimed the lives of more than 11,000 people. In order to improve preparedness at national, municipal and community levels, JICA supported the "Project on Capacity Development for Disaster Risk Management in Central America" in six countries from 2007 to 2012. When this project started, the Central American countries and JICA agreed to nickname the project "BOSAI," which is the Japanese word for "disaster prevention." This clearly indicates that the culture of prevention fostered in Japan has been well accepted and adopted by Central American countries under their ownership. During the implementation of BOSAI, the counterparts in Central America added the slogan "aprendiendo a convivir con el riesgo" or "learning to live together with risks" to remind the people of the importance of the coexistence between human beings and nature. This saying is derived from the philosophy of dealing with disasters developed through the historic experiences of disasters in Japan. This increased sense of ownership by Central American counterparts led to the great success of this project.

Other Japanese nicknames were given to technical cooperation projects being implemented by JICA. The "Project for the Enhancement of Technology for the Construction of Earthquake-Resistant Popular Housing (from 2003 to 2008)" for the Republic of El Salvador was named "TAISHIN," or "resistance to earthquakes." Its subsequent project, "Enhancement of the Construction Technology and Dissemination System of the Earthquake-Resistant 'Vivienda Social' (from 2009 to 2012)" was nicknamed "TAISHIN II." Recently, another, the "Project for Capacity Development of the Department of Climate Change Adaptation and Strategic Risk Management for Strengthening of Public Infrastructure in El Salvador," was given the Japanese name "GENSAI," which stands for "disaster mitigation."

Previously, many in this region believed in ancient legends that earthquakes are God's punishment for the wicked actions of the people and did not pay attention to preventive efforts against natural disasters (Technical Cooperation Projects of Japan International Cooperation Agency (JICA) 2008). The sharing of such symbolic names across geographical regions demonstrates how disaster reduction can be commonly accepted as a suitable agenda to be pursued and that the idea of "fatalism about natural disasters is no longer justified" (UN General Assembly Resolution 1989 A/RES/44/236).

The third epoch-making turning point for Japan: 2011

The Great East Japan Earthquake and tsunami

On March 11, 2011, a gigantic earthquake measuring M9.0 was generated on the boundary of the Pacific and the continental plates, with its hypocenter approximately 130km off to the east of Tohoku Japan. This was the strongest earthquake observed in Japan's history and was the fourth strongest earthquake observed by modern science (i.e. the twentieth and twenty-first centuries). The consequent tsunami claimed approximately 18,500 lives, and brought massive destruction to the Pacific coastline of north-eastern Japan. The extreme strength and length of the tremor caused widespread damage to industries. The power of this earthquake was almost equivalent to the North Sumatran Earthquake, which generated the Indian Ocean Tsunami in December 2004 (discussed above).

A strong earthquake and subsequent tsunami off the coast of north-eastern Japan was not a surprise; scientists had warned of such a possibility and the Japanese government had made assessments of the possible damage. But M9.0 was one full scale larger than the expected M8 earthquake. However, the culture of prevention, the institutional arrangements fostered over the years through previous experiences of natural disasters in Japan and the application of the latest technologies all contributed to reducing the damage.

Pre-assessment and preparedness against tectonic earthquake and tsunami

The Pacific coast of Tohoku has experienced repeated tsunamis: in 1896, the Meiji-Sanriku Tsunami (M8.3, 22,000 casualties) occurred, followed in 1933 by the Showa-Sanriku Tsunami (M8.1, 3,064 casualties), and in 1960 by the Chile Earthquake Tsunami (M9.5, 142 casualties resulting from a tsunami that began off the coast of Chile). Recent earthquakes that occurred in the area were the June 1978 Miyagi-ken-oki (M7.4, 28 casualties), the 1994 December Sanriku-haruka-oki (M7.6, three casualties), the May 2003 Miyagi-ken-oki (M7.1, no casualties), the September 2003 Tokachi-oki (M8.0, two casualties in Hokkaido), and the August 2005 Miyagi-ken-oki (M7.2, no casualties).

Alerted by these events, in April 2004, the Japanese government had developed legislation for a special act designating 119 municipalities on the Hokkaido and Tohoku Pacific coasts as special zones in which to promote earthquake preparedness. The Central Disaster Management Council published a pre-assessment estimation of seismic ground motion and tsunami models in June 2005. In this pre-assessment, eight types of earthquakes, with evidence of clear repetition, were set as the target earthquakes. The damage pre-assessment for the eight target earthquakes and tsunamis was published in January 2006. It indicated that, in the case of an M8.6 Meiji-Sanriku type, a tsunami will surge to the long coastline ranging from Aomori to Chiba and may result in 2,700 casualties; in the case of an M8.2 scale earthquake off Miyagi coast, 21,000 buildings may collapse. In December 2008, the Earthquake Disaster Reduction Strategic Policy to substantially reduce such damage over 10 years was formulated. Based on this policy, the seismic retrofitting of houses and buildings, construction of shore protection facilities, as well as the mapping and distribution of tsunami hazard maps were promoted. However, the actual magnitude and the source zone of the March 11 earthquake and tsunami were far larger than any of the eight targets, since it was an unexpected multiple conjunction of the target earthquakes. The actual tsunami inundation area was twice as large as the pre-assessed 270km^2.

In March 2005, the Headquarters for Earthquake Research Promotion published an estimate that the probability of earthquake occurrence off the Miyagi coast within the next 30 years would be 99 percent. It was predicted that the city of Sendai, which is the largest city in Tohoku with a population over one million, would experience violent ground motion. Therefore, the city, with the cooperation of the Cabinet Office, organized a large earthquake disaster prevention expo in September 2005 to publicize to local citizens the importance of earthquake preparedness. In April 2008, the city formulated a plan for the promotion of seismic retrofitting in Sendai, and provided a diagnosis service of the earthquake resistance of houses and subsidies for seismic retrofitting.

In the 1995 earthquake in Kobe, the elevated rail tracks of Sanyo Shinkansen and the elevated highway collapsed. Based on this experience, the seismic engineering standard for road bridges was revised in 1996 and 2002. The seismic engineering standard for railways was revised in 1998. Based on this revision, seismic reinforcement began of elevated tracks, bridges, supporting pillars and the tunnels for the Shinkansen and other main artery rail networks.

The effectiveness of seismic enforcement and early warning systems

The tremor caused by this earthquake was far longer, stronger and wider than the 1995 earthquake. However, the casualties through structural collapse were very limited compared to 1995. Most of the damage to houses was from tsunami inundation. The city of Kurihara in Miyagi, located inland, observed the strongest ground motion of JMA seismic intensity 7, but there were no casualties, and not a single house caught fire after collapsing. The city of Sendai observed strong ground motion of seismic intensity 6+ and 6–, with no office building collapsing, and only 1 percent of office buildings suffering partial damage such as gaps in the entrance steps or tilted signboards (CB Richard Ellis Japan 2011). Out of the 1,642 large condominium buildings in Tohoku, not a single building suffered serious structural damage (Condominium Management Companies Association 2011). Moreover, the new base seismic isolation buildings proved their value by substantially decreasing the shaking inside the buildings. The anti-seismic preparations against the M8 earthquake proved to be effective for an M9 earthquake.

The Japanese Shinkansen bullet trains are equipped with early earthquake detection systems. When earthquakes occur, primary pressure (P) waves and secondary shake (S) waves propagate through the earth. P waves travel faster than S waves. However, it is the S waves that cause the physical damage to structures. Seismographs placed along the shoreline and along the rail lines can detect the preliminary tremors of the P waves. Once detected, they will automatically cut the power supply and activate the emergency brakes, slowing down the train before the main shake by the S wave. In the case of the 2004 Niigata-Chuetsu Earthquake, the system worked for the Joetsu Shinkansen, and the passengers were kept safe even though several cars were derailed. Therefore the JR East Company that runs the Joetsu and Tohoku Shinkansen upgraded the system. On March 11, when the earthquake occurred, 27 Shinkansen trains were running; two were running near Sendai at their maximum speed of 270km/h. The system was triggered, power was cut between 9 and 12 seconds before the arrival of the first shake, and the emergency brakes were activated. Some 70 seconds later the main shake came, but since the trains had already slowed down to 100km/h, they were able to stop safely with no derailments and no injuries to the passengers on board. In addition, thanks to the seismic reinforcement of the elevated rail tracks and bridges, none of them collapsed.

Tsunami preparedness education saved the lives of the youth

In line with the Nationwide Movement for Disaster Reduction, the Ministry of Education, Culture, Science and Technology in 2008 initiated a new program to encourage the development of effective disaster education methods and called on universities and research institutions for applications. The city of Kamaishi in Iwate, together with Gunma University, proposed the development of an effective tsunami awareness and evacuation program for students and pupils. Kamaishi had been threatened by the 1896 Meiji-Sanriku and 1933 Showa-Sanriku tsunamis and furthermore was being warned of a possible M8 earthquake and tsunami in the near future. In March 2010, the *Manual of Kamaishi Tsunami Preparedness Education* was published. Based on this manual, all the elementary and junior high schools in Kamaishi were trained, following a proactive program designed by Gunma University, to act immediately and evacuate to safe grounds as the first leaders of evacuation. They were shown the live footage of the 2004 Indian Ocean Tsunami and understood the necessity to be ready for the worst-case scenario.

When the Great East Japan Earthquake and Tsunami hit Kamaishi on March 11, although the inundation in the city of Kamaishi was far broader than what had previously been shown on the Kamaishi tsunami hazard map, the 3,000 pupils and students at the school all evacuated safely to high ground. In the case of Kamaishi Higashi Junior High School, the students took the nearby elementary school pupils in hand and escaped to safer high ground. This is known as the "Miracle of Kamaishi" and demonstrated the effectiveness of tsunami preparedness education programs in saving precious young lives.

Sharing the lessons from the Great East Japan Earthquake and Tsunami, and moving towards the post-2015 Framework for Disaster Risk Reduction

Lessons learned and institutionalized

Japan was prepared for strong M8 class earthquakes and tsunamis of a 30- to 150-year return period. However, the Great East Japan Earthquake and Tsunami were caused by a crustal movement greater than the Jogan Earthquake, 1,100 years before. It is truly regrettable that the latest scientific investigation on tectonics of the Japan Trench was not advanced enough to provide warnings based on satisfactory scientific evidence of the probability of an M9 class earthquake. Nevertheless, structural and non-structural measures, based on the lessons of the successive earthquakes in Japan, have proven to be effective. Furthermore, the lessons and live footage from the 2004 Indian Ocean Tsunami contributed to saving lives. New technologies such as the Early Earthquake Detection System and seismic base isolation have proved to be of great value.

The Central Disaster Management Council immediately commissioned a special Committee for Technical Investigation on Countermeasures for Earthquakes and Tsunamis. Based on the findings of this committee, the Disaster Countermeasures Basic Act was revised twice, in June 2012 and June 2013. One of the pillars of the revision was to institutionalize the inheritance of local disaster lessons and to make the organization of disaster education compulsory for all of the heads of local government organs and managers of important facilities. Furthermore, detailed investigations on the causes of casualties and damage are undertaken by all the relevant governmental agencies and academic institutions.

Sharing the lessons and moving towards the post-2015 framework for disaster risk reduction

The Japanese government was swift in deciding to share lessons with the international community. In May 2011, only two months after the earthquake and tsunami, on the occasion of the Global Platform for Disaster Risk Reduction, the Vice Minister for Disaster Management expressed the Japanese government's desire to host the next UN World Conference on Disaster Reduction in 2015 so as to share the lessons learned. The World Bank, together with the Japanese government, launched a comprehensive study project "Learning from Mega-Disasters" in 2011 to draw lessons for the international community and compiled the detailed "Knowledge Notes" in 2012. The World Bank has organized a series of in-country workshops around the world, to share the findings with national authorities and to seek ways to best adapt the lessons in each national context.

The UN General Assembly at its sixty-seventh session in December 2012 decided to convene the Third World Conference on Disaster Risk Reduction in Japan in early 2015 to review the implementation of the Hyogo Framework for Action and to adopt a post-2015 framework for disaster risk reduction (A/Res/67/209). The UN General Assembly at its sixty-eighth session in December 2013 decided that the Third World Conference will be held in Sendai and agreed that the conference will be convened at the highest possible level (A/Res/68/211). This symbolizes the upgrading of the disaster reduction agenda in the international community when compared to the Second World Conference in 2005, which was to be convened at the senior-official level (A/Res/58/214). The Third World Conference will be held from March 14 to 18, 2015 and is expected to result in a concise, focused, forward-looking and action-oriented outcome document. Study tours to the tsunami-inundated areas will be organized, to share with the international community the live lessons from the gigantic tsunami and the ongoing efforts to "Build Back Better."

Conclusion

Recording the experiences of disasters and the countermeasures taken is the basis of fostering the culture of prevention. Our ancestors have recorded disasters in ancient documents, folklore and stone monuments as a way of passing down the lessons to future generations with the strong wish that their grandchildren will not suffer again. These experiences, when systematically shared over the generations and geographical borders, turn into a powerful tool to reduce disasters. We need to record the scientific observations and multidisciplinary analyses of disasters as well as the effectiveness of the countermeasures employed. Every lesson learned must be recorded and archived, so that the data can be actively referenced by various experts as basic material for formulating policies and programs for disaster risk reduction. A national mechanism for such institutionalization is a necessity and securing its sustainability and progress over the decades is a must, since the lifetime of human beings is far shorter than the recurrence period of extreme natural events. Cultivating and maintaining the awareness of the public to appreciate the value of preventive measures is also a must, since these measures may require additional care and funding. Furthermore, international frameworks for sharing the expertise and cooperation to transfer a country's experience to others must be promoted globally. The promotion of a culture of prevention, including through the mobilization of adequate resources for disaster risk reduction, is an investment for the future affording substantial returns.

Recommendation

Recording the bitter experiences of disasters and the positive effects of counter-measures is the basis of fostering a preventive culture. These experiences, when systematically shared over the generations and across geographical borders, turn into a powerful tool to reduce disasters. The development of national mechanisms for such institutionalization is a necessity and securing its sustainability and progress over the decades is essential. Furthermore, global action is needed to build international cooperation frameworks to share expertise and transfer a country's experiences to others.

Audiences of the recommendation: Communities/citizens, NGOs, private sector, city governments, national governments, donors, international agencies and the United Nations secretariat of the ISDR.

References

Cabinet Office, Government of Japan. n.d. "Bousai Jouhou no Pe-ji" [Disaster Management Information Homepage]. www.bousai.go.jp/kyoiku/kyokun/kyoukunnokeishou/index.html.

CB Richard Ellis Japan. 2011. "Research Report on the Great East Japan Earthquake, Damage to Buildings in Sendai, June 2011." CBRE. Summary available at www.cbre-xgate.jp/stndaln/pdf/article/oj-summer-2011/20110601.pdf.

Condominium Management Companies Association. 2011. "Higashi Nihon Daishinsai Hisai Joukyou Chousa Houkoku" [Report on the Damage by the Great East Japan Earthquake]. April 21. CMCA. www.kanrikyo.or.jp/news/data/hisaihoukoku110519.pdf.

Department of Humanitarian Affairs, United Nations. 1995. "The Great Hanshin-Awaji (Kobe) Earthquake: The Earthquake, On-site Relief and International Response." Geneva: Department of Humanitarian Affairs, United Nations.

Disaster Reduction and Human Renovation Institution. 2014. Homepage at www.dri.ne.jp/english/index.html.

Government of Japan. 1961. "Disaster Countermeasures Basic Act." http://law.e-gov.go.jp/htmldata/S36/S36HO223.html.

—— 2005. "Initiative for Disaster Reduction through ODA." www.mofa.go.jp/mofaj/gaiko/oda/bunya/disaster/pdf/pamph_e.pdf.

Headquarters for Earthquake Research Promotion. 1997. "Active Faults to Be Basically Monitored." www.jishin.go.jp/main/seisaku/hokoku97/p38.gif.

Japan Meteorological Agency. n.d. "Inamura no hi" [Fire on the Rice Sheaves]. www.data.jma.go.jp/svd/eqev/data/tsunami/inamura/p1.html.

Kako, Satoshi and Ogata, Hideki. 1997a. "Hito wo Tasuke Kuni wo Tsukutta Obousan Tachi" [The Priests Who Saved People and Built the Nation]. Tokyo: Japan Construction Training Center.

—— 1997b. "Mizu to Tatakatta Sengoku no Bushou Tachi" [The Feudal Warlords Who Battled Water]. Tokyo: Japan Construction Training Center.

Mitsubishi Jisho Sekkei Inc. 2003. "Project Overview Marunouchi Building." www.mj-sekkei.com/project/marubuil/concept/concept04.html.

Nishikawa, Satoru. 2007. "The Progress of Disaster Management Administration and the Challenges for Disaster Reduction in Japan." IATSS Review 32(2), 6–13.

—— 2010. "From Yokohama Strategy to Hyogo Framework: Sharing the Japanese Experience of Disaster Risk Management." *Asian Journal of Environment and Disaster Management* 2(3), 249–262.

Sangawa, Akira. 2011. *Jishin no Nihonshi* [The Seismic History of Japan]. Tokyo: Chuokoron-Shinsha.

Technical Cooperation Projects of Japan International Cooperation Agency (JICA). 2008. *"Cuaderno de Don Neto: Apuntes sobre terremotos y vivienda segura y saludable"* [Notebook of Mr Neto: Notes on Earthquakes, and Safe and Healthy Houses]. San Salvador.

Toki, Kenzo (ed.). 1993, 1996. "Multi-language Glossary on Disaster Reduction." Tokyo: Japan National Committee for IDNDR.

United Nations. 1994. "Yokohama Strategy and Plan of Action for a Safer World: Guidelines for Natural Disaster Prevention, Preparedness, and Mitigation." World Conference on Natural Disaster Reduction, May 23–27, 1994. www.preventionweb. net/files/8241_doc6841contenido1.pdf.

UN General Assembly. 1987. "Resolution A/RES/42/169: International Decade for Natural Disaster Reduction." Ninety-sixth Plenary Meeting, December 11.

—— 1988. "Resolution A/RES/43/202: International Decade for Natural Disaster Reduction." Eighty-third Plenary Meeting, December 20.

—— 1989. "Resolution A/RES/44/236: International Decade for Natural Disaster Reduction." Eighty-fifth Plenary Meeting, December 22.

—— 1993. "Resolution A/RES/48/188: International Decade for Natural Disaster Reduction." Eighty-sixth Plenary Meeting, December 21.

—— 2000. "Resolution A/RES/54/219: International Decade for Natural Disaster Reduction: Successor Arrangements." Eighty-seventh Plenary Meeting, December 22.

—— 2003. "Resolution A/RES/58/214: International Strategy for Disaster Reduction." Seventy-eighth Plenary Meeting, December 23.

—— 2012. "Resolution: A/RES/67/209: International Strategy for Disaster Reduction." Sixty-first Plenary Meeting, December 21.

—— 2013. "Resolution A/RES/68/211: International Strategy for Disaster Reduction." Seventy-first Plenary Meeting, December 20.

World Conference on Disaster Reduction. 2005a. "Hyogo Framework for Action 2005–2015: Building the Resilience of Nations and Communities to Disasters." www.unisdr. org/2005/wcdr/intergover/official-doc/L-docs/Hyogo-framework-for-action-english.pdf.

—— 2005b. "Common Statement of the Special Session on the Indian Ocean Disaster: Risk Reduction for a Safer Future." www.unisdr.org/wcdr/intergover/official-doc/L-docs/special-session-indian-ocean.pdf.

Part III

Achieving Build Back Better in recovery and reconstruction

7 Recovery and reconstruction

An opportunity for sustainable growth through "Build Back Better"

Ryo Matsumaru and Kimio Takeya

Introduction

In recent years, large-scale disasters have occurred in many parts of the world. Regardless of whether they occur in developed or developing countries, such disasters destroy towns and communities, as well as exacting a high cost in human lives.

Disasters also adversely affect the livelihoods of people, while disrupting regional economies and industry, traditions, culture and the environment. In many cases recovery from large-scale disasters becomes a major priority for affected countries, placing them under a great burden.

According to the secretariat of the International Strategy for Disaster Reduction (ISDR), "recovery" after a disaster is defined as "the restoration, and improvement, where appropriate, of facilities, livelihoods and living conditions of disaster-affected communities, including efforts to reduce disaster risk factors" (United Nations secretariat of the ISDR 2009). In the process of discussion of the Post-Hyogo Framework for Action (HFA), the reduction of disaster risks in recovery processes was considered a crucial element of Build Back Better. However, as disaster recovery is a very complicated process that covers numerous activities and involves many stakeholders, understandings of "recovery" may differ among people who use this term and fluctuate depending on the situations in which this term is used. Furthermore, recovery from disasters varies not only among countries, but also among regions and time periods, relative to the stage of economic development and social conditions in the affected communities. However, through the careful examination of past recovery cases, common features and implications for improving future recovery activities may be determined.

This chapter focuses on the physical safety of societies and nations by attempting to analyze the elements that will make such reconstruction possible. The chapter starts with the specific definition of "Build Back Better" in relation to safety. It then introduces several cases of reconstruction, both in Japan and developing countries, showing the implications that may be derived from such cases. Japan has learned hard lessons following a long series of disasters. These experiences have been useful in disaster risk reduction efforts and may be further applied to future recovery measures. Based on these findings, this chapter discusses how the build back better concept should be incorporated into the recovery process.

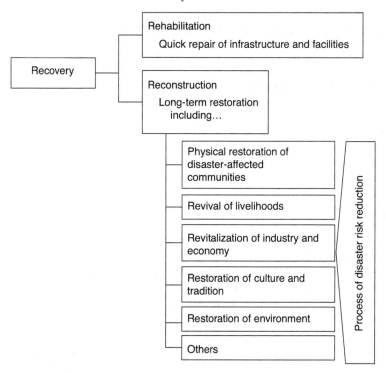

Figure 7.1 Concepts of recovery rehabilitation and reconstruction
Source: Authors.

Build Back Better concept for reconstruction

Two elements of recovery

The definition of "recovery" by the United Nations secretariat of the ISDR does not specifically distinguish different phases in recovery processes. On the other hand, in Japan, recovery processes are normally divided into "rehabilitation" and "reconstruction." The two phases are generally recognized as follows:

- *Rehabilitation*: Rapid repair of infrastructure and facilities to restore economic and social functions of disaster-affected areas (MILT 2010; MAFF 2011). Rehabilitation activities may take several weeks or more than a year depending on the infrastructure and facilities.
- *Reconstruction*: Long-term restoration that includes not only physical improvement of the affected communities but also revival of livelihood, economy and industry, culture and traditions, environment, etc. Also includes a process of risk factor reduction.

The idea for these two phases of recovery is conceptualized as shown in Figure 7.1.

This chapter focuses on the reconstruction phase because the concept of "build back better" comprises much more than simply restoring communities to their pre-disaster condition. Therefore the activities presented here are more likely to be achieved during the reconstruction phase.

Build Back Better in the reconstruction process

The principle of Build Back Better is generally understood as creating more resilient nations and societies than before the disaster through the implementation of well-balanced disaster risk reduction measures, including the physical restoration of infrastructure, revitalization of livelihood and economy/industry, and the restoration of local culture and environment. However, as mentioned above, since large-scale disasters affect a wide range of sectors, reconstruction processes also include a variety of activities. Therefore "good/better reconstruction" will mean different things to different stakeholders depending on the priorities of the individuals or organizations involved. In other words, the idea of build back better also has different implications for each stakeholder.

Meanwhile, disasters tend to reveal the underlying risks related to each of the particular hazards that caused the disaster, whether or not the potential of such risks was recognized beforehand. Therefore, the bottom line of reconstruction should be to address the revealed risks, and hopefully future risks, by giving priorities to investment in risk reduction measures. If disaster risk reduction is not taken into consideration or well planned, reconstruction may lead to the reproduction of the vulnerability of the community or the nation. This consequence should be avoided by any means. This is especially the case when public funds and international assistance are provided for reconstruction purposes. If a community or a nation is repeatedly affected by the same kinds of hazards, funds and assistance are wasted and accountability to donors is not fulfilled. Thus, investment in disaster risk reduction measures to avoid the reproduction of vulnerability may be defined as "build back safer," an indispensable part of Build Back Better (Figure 7.2).

Measures for build back safer include not only physical and structural measures but also non-structural measures such as the installation of early warning systems, and the enforcement of land use regulation.

Implications from past reconstruction processes

Through the review of the past reconstruction cases that are described in the sections below, the following four points were identified as important factors in reconstruction:

1   Different hazards necessitate different approaches to build back safer.
2   Regional characteristics also require different approaches, in the face of trade-offs between safety and the speed of reconstruction.
3   Build Back Better efforts beyond disaster-affected areas are sometimes required when considering the safety of an entire country.

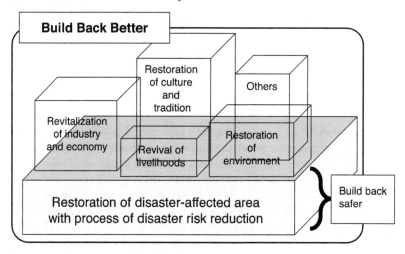

Figure 7.2 The concept of "build back safer" as a component of "Build Back Better"
Source: Authors.

4   International assistance can be a key factor in reconstruction for developing countries.

Build back safer under different hazards

Earthquakes

In the case of earthquake-affected areas, reconstruction will basically take place in the same areas. As the areas may be affected by strong earthquakes again, build back safer is mostly related to reconstruction of buildings. The most fundamental issue is that buildings should be strong enough to withstand tremors during earthquakes. Therefore, in the reconstruction process, buildings have to be rebuilt or renovated/retrofitted based on an upgraded quake-resistance code. In addition, it is also necessary to strengthen resilience through land adjustment measures for such purposes as widening roads, especially in urban areas. It is desirable that those affected by the disaster participate in the discussion process.

As reconstruction takes place in the disaster-affected areas, the revitalization of the livelihood of the disaster victims may also occur in those same areas. In this regard, the period of living in temporary houses should be minimized; otherwise victims may leave the community to seek new livelihoods.

Tsunamis, storm surges and floods

The damage from tsunamis, storm surges and floods has similar characteristics; for example, damage is caused by inundation, topographic conditions have a strong influence over the scale of the damage, and the occurrence of hazards can be predicted to some extent in advance. These hazards can be controlled to a certain extent by constructing structural measures. Therefore, in reconstruction processes, a combination of measures including hazard control, land use regulation and elevation of land surfaces should be implemented in an appropriate manner to prepare for future disasters. The design level of structural measures depends on each area and country's economic condition and strength, which may be called the "civil minimum." However, from a long-term perspective, it is likely that natural phenomena will exceed the design level of the structures, and thus relocation to higher ground may be another option to avoid the recurrence of disasters in the future, especially for the inundation-prone low-lying areas.

Relocation may heavily affect the life of the people who earn incomes dependent on their living locations. In addition, existing communities will not be maintained if relocation does not take place in a well-planned manner. Therefore, measures to compensate people for their loss of livelihood as well as maintaining local communities should be taken together with measures for build back safer.

Sediment disasters (landslides, slope failures)

The extent of damaged areas of sediment disasters is usually rather limited compared with other disasters. In this sense, countermeasures are not likely to be required in the short term. Early revival of the victims' livelihood in the original community by finding the nearest and appropriate living space will be the key for reconstruction.

Regional characteristics: the necessity for different approaches and trade-offs

From the review of past cases, the reconstruction approach varied according to regional characteristics, such as whether the affected community was urban or rural, and differences in the dominant local industries. In terms of reconstruction in urban areas, improving urban functions through investment in risk reduction measures, as well as the rebuilding of affected houses, are priorities. Ensuring that houses are available for urban workers at the earliest possible time is one of the most important aspects in restoring urban services and functions, and delays in reconstruction may lead to compounding negative impacts upon economic and social development. However, a trade-off between rapid housing reconstruction and creation of safer areas has frequently been observed in the case studies provided in the following sections. Creation of safe areas often takes time involving planning, reaching consensus and implementation. If the rapid reconstruction of houses is permitted without due consideration for safety measures, there is the possibility that situations of vulnerability will be reproduced.

On the other hand, in rural areas where the primary industries are dominant, it is also generally agreed that the recovery of livelihoods should be prioritized in reconstruction. In the case of reconstruction in rural areas, another trade-off may be observed between the rapid revival of livelihoods and the creation of safe areas. For people engaged in primary industry, suspension of their work directly affects their income and therefore they need to resume work as quickly as possible. However, if they start working in the same places it may be difficult to implement measures to ensure the safety of the area. Such cases may be observed, for example, in tsunami-affected areas. Where fishermen want to live close to the sea, the elevation of land surfaces may be necessary to protect the area. While it is necessary to implement preventive measures to provide even the most basic level of protection, in some cases, as noted above, it may be a rational decision to lower the protection level to some extent and supplement it with measures such as evacuation roads and early warning systems. This ensures that a minimum safe level can be maintained as well as providing a partial solution to the difficult trade-off situation.

Trade-offs complicate the reconstruction process. Strong leadership by the government is required in establishing earthquake-resistant housing standards or no-building zones and effectively implementing such measures. To minimize the negative impact of these trade-off issues, it is also useful to share a common understanding of risks among stakeholders and to agree on acceptable levels of risk. In other words, the goal is to promote shared responsibility among stakeholders against the risks they are facing. Keeping the memories of disaster risks and handing them on to the next generations is also essential in reducing vulnerability in the future.

Extended reconstruction (reconstruction in a broader context): an effort to the build back better beyond the disaster-affected area

In general, "reconstruction" refers to the reconstruction of disaster-affected areas. Therefore, the idea of "Build Back Better" is normally understood as a concept to be applied to the disaster-affected areas alone (targeted reconstruction). In some cases, however, lessons learned from disaster events and reconstruction processes were applied to other parts of the country through legislation of new laws or dissemination of disaster risk reduction measures and technologies (extended reconstruction). The idea of the two kinds of reconstruction is as follows:

- targeted reconstruction = reconstruction of disaster-affected areas, such as reconstruction of the disaster-affected towns, revival of livelihood, and revitalization of economy and industries;
- extended reconstruction = reconstruction beyond disaster-affected areas, build back better/build back safer as a whole society and nation.

Past experiences indicate that the application of the idea of extended reconstruction has contributed to Build Back Better at the national level. Therefore, in the aftermath of large-scale disasters, the implementation of extended reconstruction should always be considered, as it may reduce disaster risks in the areas that have similar characteristics against disasters. Extended reconstruction includes the improvement and strengthening of institutional arrangements and regulations as well as the implementation of preventive measures.

International assistance, a key for reconstruction in developing countries

International assistance can play a very important role in reconstruction, as resources may be insufficient after disasters – especially in developing countries. International agencies, multilateral development banks, bilateral aid organizations and NGOs have different characteristics and specialties. For example, development banks can provide a relatively large amount of funds for the restoration of infrastructure, while NGOs in general have access to more limited funds and may be specialized in particular fields of humanitarian assistance and reconstruction/development projects, such as livelihood recovery, health care, etc. NGOs have the tendency to move quickly and seek rapid results for the purpose of reporting to donors. It is important to understand the different characteristics and specialties of different actors and to harmonize their efforts.

Many donors and NGOs have recently tried to implement seamless assistance from relief to reconstruction. Their actions towards reconstruction tend to be faster than the recipient governments because they may already have experience in similar activities in other areas/countries. In order to avoid over-involvement of donors and NGOs and to apply appropriate regulations such as the prohibition of uncontrolled reconstruction and land use regulations, the recipient government must have strong leadership and ownership. From the perspective of aid organizations, there should be a consensus to respect such local regulations and needs. In many ways, international assistance can function as a channel for introducing the good practices of Build Back Better to other countries. The knowledge of donors and NGOs has to be introduced to disaster-prone areas with due consideration for local needs.

While international assistance plays a major role in reconstruction, it has also been criticized on the grounds that money from donors has been spent through NGOs and the private enterprises of the donor countries, and thus has had little impact on the revival of local enterprises in the disaster-affected countries themselves.[1] In terms of Build Back Better, the local economy must be revitalized, and therefore careful consideration is necessary to ensure that the money provided through international assistance flows into the local economy.

Lessons learned from reconstruction in Japan

As Japan is a disaster-prone country, it has had rich experience in reconstruction from large-scale disasters. In the process of its reconstruction, Japan learned many lessons that may be applicable for better reconstruction in future and in other countries. In this section, a range of the disaster recovery experiences of Japan will be reviewed. Since this chapter covers two aspects of reconstruction, both "efforts in the disaster-affected areas (targeted reconstruction)" and "efforts to create a better nation and society beyond the disaster-affected area (extended reconstruction)" are the objectives of the review.

Case 1: Great Tokyo fires from the Late Edo Period to the Meiji/Taisho Period (from the mid eighteenth to early twentienth centuries)

The spirit of Build Back Better can be seen even before the modernization of Japan.

Edo, the old name for Tokyo, experienced a number of large-scale fire incidents. In the late Edo Period (mid eighteenth century, before the modernization of Japan), disaster relief and recovery activities became systematic. Food and emergency goods, along with emergency shelters, were provided by public authorities and volunteers. Financial support in the form of tax reductions and employment of disaster victims was also practiced. Furthermore, in the reconstruction of Edo, one of the biggest cities of the world at that time, officers responsible for reconstruction were appointed to improve the physical structure of the city. Measures such as widening roads and the creation of open spaces were adopted to make the city more resistant to large-scale fires (Yasuda 2013; Koshizawa 2012).

Following the modernization of Japan in the late nineteenth and early twentieth centuries, reconstruction after large-scale disasters focused more on improving the physical infrastructure of the city to mitigate the damage from future disasters. In the meantime, laws and regulations, such as the Imperial Decree for Meteorological Observation (1887), the River Act (1896), the Erosion Control Act and Forest Act (1897), the Road Act, the City Planning Act and the Building Standards Act (1919), were enacted and enforced (Koshizawa 2012). These laws provided a legal basis for disaster management activities, such as providing disaster information, measures for reducing risks of natural hazards, and regulating land use including the improvement of urban roads to create societies that were more resilient against disasters.

Case 2: The Great Kanto Earthquake (1923)

Strong leadership and efforts to create a safe capital with upgraded urban infrastructure provided by the opportunity of reconstruction.

Immediately after the earthquake, Shinpei Goto, then the Minister of the Interior, showed strong leadership by preparing a proposal for the reconstruction of Tokyo. To make the city stronger against future disasters, he proposed the upgrading of urban functions by improving the physical structure of the city as well as the establishment of a dedicated agency for reconstruction and the allocation of sufficient amounts of public funds.

Since the plan covered the whole urban area of Tokyo and included areas with little or no damage, the scale of the plan was considered overly ambitious. The plan was met with strong objections and plagued by financial constraints, as well as mistrust of government-led land adjustment measures. The jealousy of

Table 7.1 Summary of the Great Kanto Earthquake (Case 2)

Hazard type	Earthquake (followed by fire) Magnitude: 7.9 (JMA magnitude) Epicenter: Sagami Bay, off the coast of Kanagawa Prefecture
Date	September 1, 1923
Area	Tokyo, Kanagawa, Chiba, Saitama, Shizuoka
Damage	Casualties: more than 105,000 Buildings destroyed: more than 370,000 (due to strong earthquake and subsequent fire)
Related implications	• Build back safer of disaster-affected area of Tokyo

other political leaders forced Mr Goto to scale down his original plan. The plan was ultimately only implemented in the limited areas that were heavily damaged by the earthquake. However, the measures that were implemented, such as the construction and widening of trunk roads and land adjustment in heavily affected residential areas, became the basis of the current urban structures of Tokyo (Koshizawa 2012), by contributing to the building back safer of Tokyo.

Case 3: The Ise-wan Typhoon (1959)

> A turning point for disaster risk management of Japan (or a trigger for paradigm shift for disaster risk reduction of Japan).

Following World War II up until the mid 1950s, Japan suffered a series of large-scale disasters. This was due to the lack of investment in disaster prevention measures during the war period and the active migration of populations to large cities during the process of the post-war recovery. The Ise-wan typhoon was the worst disaster during this period (Takahashi 2012). In the disaster-affected areas, levees and sea-walls were strengthened or improved and land use was regulated to make the areas safe against the same scale of hazards.

Furthermore, the scale of the storm surge became a reference for the design of embankments and dykes along the coast, and those facilities were constructed

Table 7.2 Summary of the Isewan Typhoon (Case 3)

Hazard type	Storm surge Generated by "Ise-wan Typhoon (Vera)"
Date	September 26, 1959
Area	Isewan (Ise Bay) region, close to Nagoya City
Damage	Casualties: approx. 5,000 Affected people: 1.5 million Buildings destroyed: more than 150,000
Related implications	• Build back better/safer of affected area • Extended reconstruction

and improved throughout Japan in the same manner. This is an example of "extended reconstruction."

This disaster has also been recognized as a significant event in the Japanese disaster management system, because the disaster led to the enforcement of a new law, the Disaster Countermeasures Basic Act in 1961. Legislation was passed to establish a comprehensive disaster management system in Japan that included the formulation of a "Basic Disaster Management Plan" (Cabinet Office 2011). This institutional strengthening largely contributed to reducing the damage from subsequent disasters. The disaster management system of Japan was further strengthened through the lessons learned from the following large-scale disasters.

Case 4: The Miyagi-Ken-Oki Earthquake (1978)

> A turning point of policy for earthquake resistance of buildings, key to reconsidering the building code.

This disaster triggered a re-examination of the Building Standards Act. As the damage to buildings, especially to ordinary houses, was enormous, the quake-resistance standards of the Act were re-examined using the seismic force of this earthquake. As a result, the Act was revised in 1981. The revised Act required that buildings be strengthened to withstand level 5 earthquakes based on the Japanese earthquake intensity scale, and should not collapse even at higher intensity levels of 6 or 7 (MILT 2014).

Table 7.3 Summary of the Miyagi-Ken-Oki Earthquake (Case 4)

Hazard type	Earthquake magnitude: 7.4 (JMA magnitude)
	Epicenter: Off the east coast of Miyagi Prefecture
Date	June 12, 1978
Area	Miyagi Prefecture, northern part of Japan
Damage	Casualties: 28
	Injuries: more than 10,000
	Buildings destroyed: approx. 7,400 (by strong shake)
Related implications	• Extended reconstruction

Case 5: The Great Hanshin-Awaji Earthquake

> The first strong earthquake to hit highly urbanized areas. Its impacts were seen in both reconstruction of disaster-affected areas and national-level disaster management.

The concept of "creative reconstruction" was introduced after this disaster in the hope that the reconstruction process would lead to opportunities for the revitalization of the regional economy/industry. In this sense, investment in the restoration of infrastructure was prioritized because it was considered a basis for rapid reconstruction and the growth of the regional economy.

Table 7.4 Summary of the Great Hanshin-Awaji Earthquake (Case 5)

Hazard type	Earthquake magnitude: 7.3 (JMA magnitude), 6.8 (USGS) Epicenter: Southern part of Hyōgo Prefecture
Date	January 17, 1995
Area	Hyogo, Osaka

Damage	Casualties: 6,437
	Buildings destroyed: approx. 150,000, including commercial and office buildings by strong shake and fire
	Infrastructure: 1km collapse (Hanshin Expressway)
	    Destruction of 120 of the 150 quays (Kobe Port)
	    Railway networks incl. Shinkansen, essential utilities such as the water supply, electricity and energy, transportation and logistics and telecommunications that are essential for human life.
	Economic damage: 10 trillion JPY (in April 1995; approximately US\$119 billion at the April 1995 exchange rate)
	    (estimated by the Hyogo Prefecture Government)

Related implications	• Build back safer of the disaster-affected area • Trade-off between reconstruction speed and area's safety for future disasters • Extended reconstruction

Meanwhile, in order to enhance efforts towards build back safer, a land adjustment method that included the re-zoning of irregularly shaped land lots, creating open space and widening and straightening roads was implemented in heavily damaged areas. The residents of the affected areas participated in the discussion but it took time to reach an agreement due to the various interests and opinions of the stakeholders. This led to delays in the reconstruction of individual houses, with the victims forced to stay in temporary accommodation for prolonged periods (Koshizawa 2012; Shiozaki *et al.* 2007). This shows an example of the trade-off between the speed of restoration of houses and the safety of the community.

In terms of extended reconstruction, the Disaster Countermeasures Basic Act and other relevant laws and regulations were revised and/or amended based on the lessons learned from the disaster. Furthermore, revisions of the Basic Disaster Management Plan and improvements in the institutional arrangements were made to meet people's needs and to address the various issues raised by the disaster. This improvement included the enactment of the Act on Support for Reconstructing Livelihoods of Disaster Victims (Cabinet Office 2012).

Case 6: The Great East Japan Earthquake (2011)

Many new challenges in reconstruction.

One month after the disaster, the Japanese government declared an intention to apply the concept of "creative reconstruction" (Cabinet Secretariat 2011).

Table 7.5 Summary of the Great East Japan Earthquake (Case 6)

Hazard type	Earthquake and tsunami Magnitude: 9.0 (Moment Magnitude) Epicenter: Off east coast of Tohoku Region Tsunami: Maximum height of more than 40m (Miyako, Iwate Prefecture)
Date	March 11, 2011
Area	Pacific Coast, from Northern Part to Eastern Part of Honshu Island

Damage	Casualties: 18,506
	Displaced: more than 400,000 (peak time)
	  264,000 (still in temporary living places as of March 2014)
	Buildings destroyed: 400,401
	Infrastructure: Roads, railways, ports and harbors, airport, nuclear power plant, and utilities such as water supply, electricity
	Economic damage: 16,000 trillion JPY (US$157 billion) to 25,000 trillion JPY (US$245 billion)
	  (Estimated by Cabinet Office of Japan)
	  The economic impact extended beyond other areas of Japan to the global economy as the industry of the affected area was a part of the domestic and global supply chain.

Remarks	• Many shortcomings of disaster management measures that had been taken before the disaster were exposed.
	• Meanwhile, there were many positive cases that were proven to be effective, such as:
	  • continuous improvement of the institutions contributed to an effective response and rapid mobilization of disaster relief;
	  • a strengthened building code contributing to a decrease in building damage;
	  • tsunami protection facilities functioned if the tsunami height was lower than the design level, and even in some cases where it was sometimes slightly higher than the design level;
	  • awareness raising, training and education on disaster management contributed to the rapid evacuation.

Related implications	• Build back safer of the disaster-affected area • Trade-off between reconstruction speed and area's safety for future disasters • Extended reconstruction

Three months after the earthquake, the Reconstruction Design Council, established in response to the disaster, strongly recommended that reconstruction be implemented in ways that promoted economic growth. This fact clearly shows that the Japanese government was trying to apply the idea of "Build Back Better" to reconstruction. Although the reconstruction from the disaster is continuing at the time of writing, there are some noteworthy aspects of the reconstruction approach in terms of build back better:

Establishment of the Reconstruction Agency

Since the affected areas were widely spread out and the reconstruction projects covered a wide variety of sectors, a "one-stop" agency was needed for rapid, appropriate coordination and decision-making along with the smooth implementation of reconstruction projects. Therefore, the Reconstruction Agency was established in 2011 and a minister was appointed. This was based on past experiences (e.g. the reconstruction agency for the Great Kanto Earthquake in Japan, and BRR Aceh-Nias for the Indian Ocean Tsunami Disaster in Indonesia).

Introduction of two levels of design standards

In pursuing safety against future tsunami disasters, two levels of design standards were introduced (MILT 2012a, 2012b; Cabinet Secretariat 2013):

- Level 1: Tsunamis that have a high likelihood of recurrence within a certain period (once in several decades to 100 years) have to be addressed by providing structural measures such as breakwaters and coastal levees to protect both residents and assets to avoid repeated damage.
- Level 2: Facilities constructed to prevent Level 1 tsunamis will be insufficient to manage Level 2 tsunamis. These are the largest possible level of tsunami, and are highly likely to cause major damage. The goal here is that damage should be minimized, aiming at the very least at no human losses, by implementing combined measures of structural and non-structural measures, including land use regulation, early warning systems, promoting community awareness and risk sharing through insurance.

Based on this concept, the reconstruction of tsunami-affected areas is being implemented.

Trade-off issues

While more than 3 years have already passed since the disaster, it is hard to say that reconstruction is being implemented smoothly. As for the town planning and physical reconstruction of the affected areas, land adjustment is still in progress, as it is very hard to reach an agreement among the many stakeholders with different interests, especially on the physical redevelopment of safe areas. This delay is forcing the disaster victims to live in temporary accommodation. As was witnessed during the reconstruction of the Great Hanshin-Awaji Earthquake, the issue of trade-offs between the speed of reconstruction and safety of the area has emerged once again.

Lessons learned from the reconstruction in developing countries

In this section, several cases of reconstruction following large-scale disasters in developing countries will be reviewed. While the major points of the review are the same as the cases in Japan, the role of international organizations in providing support has been included in this section.

Case 1: The Indian Ocean Tsunami Disaster (2004)

The Indian Ocean Tsunami caused severe damage to many countries facing the Indian Ocean. Among those countries, the two countries of Indonesia and Sri Lanka are compared here to provide some salient details on build back better.

Table 7.6 Summary of the Indian Ocean Tsunami (Case 1)

Hazard type	Earthquake and tsunami Magnitude: 9.1 (Moment Magnitude) Epicenter: Near the Sunda Trench off the coast of the Indonesian island of Sumatra	
Date	December 26, 2004	
Area	Coastal areas of countries that face the Indian Ocean, including Indonesia, Thailand, Sri Lanka, India, and even some East African countries	
	Indonesia	Sri Lanka
Disaster type	Tsunami: 6 to 12m (Banda Aceh) 15 to 30m (Western coastal area of Sumatra)	Tsunami: 3 to 10m (West Coast) 5 to 15m (East Coast)
Area	1,500km of coastline mainly on the west coast of northern Sumatra Island	About three-quarters of the coastline of the country was affected.
Damage	Casualties: more than 166,000 Displaced: more than 500,000 (peak time) Buildings destroyed: Uncountable Infrastructure: Road, port, utilities Economic damage: 46.5 trillion Rp. (ref. 50.4 trillion Rp. gross regional product of Aceh province)	Casualties: about 37,000 Displaced: 425,620 (peak time) Infrastructure: Roads, ports, utilities
Related implications	• Build back safer of the disaster affected area • Trade-off between reconstruction speed and area's safety for future disasters • Extended reconstruction	• Build back better of the disaster-affected area • Extended reconstruction

Establishment of reconstruction organizations

In Indonesia, the Aceh-based BRR (the Agency for the Rehabilitation and Reconstruction of Aceh and Nias Island) was established as a dedicated implementing agency to handle all reconstruction matters to replace the local government that had lost its capacity to function as a result of the disaster. The agency in general is considered to have functioned effectively in both coordinating and implementing the projects (BRR NAD-Nias 2008). On the other hand, in Sri Lanka, a reconstruction organization, namely the Task Force for Rebuilding the Nation (TAFREN), was established. However, the functions of TAFREN were limited to the reconstruction and relocation of houses, as other reconstruction issues were handled within the ordinary government framework (Matsumaru 2010).

Urban development/physical improvement for build back better

For the city of Banda Aceh, the capital of Aceh province, the Indonesian government first tried to regulate the land use along the coast by applying the buffer zone concept to avoid losses from future disasters. This shows the will of the government to make the city safer than before the tsunami. However, the planning process took time and some displaced people who could not wait until the completion of urban planning returned to their original living place, seeking a rapid revival of their livelihoods. Therefore the original idea was forced to be modified. In addition, in Aceh, a trunk road connecting the towns along the west coast of Aceh province was severely damaged by the tsunami. To avoid repeated damage and to develop a stronger road network capable of withstanding future disasters, some parts of the road were relocated inland (Matsumaru *et al.* 2012).

In Sri Lanka, a buffer zone (or "no-build" zone) was designated to the width of 100m to 200m, depending on the location, to control the rebuilding of houses near the coast and to mitigate the damage of future disasters. However, the necessity of changing urban planning and the introduction of land adjustment measures to make fundamental improvements in the urban structure were not realized because the affected areas in general were limited to the coast. Some villages located near the coast were relocated to new areas, with housing constructed inland and further from the sea. Eventually the buffer zone was relaxed to 35m from the coastline in 2006. Furthermore, the roads along the coast were reconstructed following the same routes as before the tsunami.

Emerging role of NGOs

In Indonesia, many NGOs participated in the reconstruction processes that covered the provision of temporary and permanent houses. Due to the diversity of locations, housing design and construction techniques by different NGOs, there were widespread inequalities in living standards for disaster victims, who were unable to select their living place for themselves (Matsumaru 2010). These diversified approaches sometimes had negative impacts in terms of "Build Back Better" in cases where the NGOs constructed permanent houses in tsunami-affected areas without sufficient preventive measures. In this regard, NGOs needed to be better coordinated by the government in order to avoid detrimental results in relation to build back safer.

Trade-offs or dilemmas between rapid reconstruction and safety of the area

As mentioned above, the Indonesian government aimed to create safe cities by regulating land use. However, the people who could not wait until the completion of urban planning started to return to their places of residence without measures to protect themselves against tsunamis. As this might lead to the future reproduction of vulnerability, the government was forced to take countermeasures such as constructing evacuation roads and towers. This shows the kinds of dilemmas that may occur between speed in reconstruction and the creation of safe areas, while balanced implementation was more difficult.

Improvement of national-level disaster risk management institutions

One common event that occurred after the disaster in the two countries was the establishment of a national agency for disaster management to prepare for future disasters. In Indonesia, the Indonesian National Board for Disaster Management (BNPB) was established in 2008 by expanding the functions of the existing National Disaster Management Coordinating Board (BAKORNAS).

Likewise, as the disaster was the worst ever experienced in Sri Lanka, it had a strong impact on disaster management administration. A paradigm shift occurred from a response-oriented disaster management to a prevention/mitigation-oriented approach. The government showed the necessary will to build a strong society as a whole and enacted a Disaster Management Act, through which it established the Disaster Management Center. Within six months of the disaster, this had become the implementing organization for the formulation of plans and activities related to disaster risk management. In addition, to ensure that people remained aware of the need for disaster risk reduction, the government set the date of the Indian Ocean Tsunami Disaster of December 26 as National Safety Day (Matsumaru 2010).

Case 2: 2005 Kashmir Earthquake (2005, Pakistan-administered Kashmir)

> Good practice in individual housing reconstruction from the build back safer viewpoint.

In this case, the processes of reconstruction of individual houses deserve attention. Many NGOs offered assistance for individual housing reconstruction. However, the government refused permission for NGOs to directly provide houses to disaster victims to avoid the construction of houses with insufficient earthquake resistance. The government was able to keep NGOs under its supervision and only allowed assistance with public building restoration. Disaster victims who wanted financial assistance for rebuilding their houses from the government had to follow technical regulations to avoid severe damage from future disasters. The money from the government was disbursed only after each stage of construction had passed inspection by the government. This would be a

Table 7.7 Summary of the Kashmir Earthquake (Case 2)

Hazard type	Earthquake Magnitude: 7.6 (Moment Magnitude) Epicenter: near Muzaffarabad, Pakistan-administered Kashmir
Date	October 8, 2005
Area	Muzaffarabad Area, Pakistan-administered Kashmir, Northern Pakistan, India
Damage	Casualties: more than 87,300 (Pakistan: 86,000) Injured: more than 75,000 (Pakistan: 69,000) Displaced people: about 4 million Infrastructure: landslides and slope failures cut road networks, isolating some areas Buildings destroyed: more than 32,000 near epicenter
Related implications	• Build back safer of the disaster-affected area • Extended reconstruction

good example of a project that avoided the unregulated reconstruction of private houses and the reproduction of vulnerability. In addition, the Pakistan government established the National Disaster Management Agency (NDMA) in 2007 to cope more efficiently with disasters.

Case 3: Java Earthquake (May 2006, Indonesia)

Good practice of external assistance for reconstruction of strong houses.

Table 7.8 Summary of the Java earthquake (Case 3)

Hazard type	Earthquake Magnitude: 6.3 (Moment Magnitude) Epicenter: South-southwest of Yogyakarta, Indonesia
Date	May 27, 2006
Area	Yogyakarta and Bantul, Central Java, Indonesia
Damage	Casualties: 5,776 Injured: 38,814 Displaced people: 2,310,549 Buildings destroyed: 329,899
Related implications	• Build back better of the disaster-affected area

A huge number of individual houses were damaged in this disaster, and therefore quick rebuilding of earthquake-resistant houses was one of the key issues in reconstruction. Recognizing this, the Indonesian government established a new system for private housing reconstruction with the assistance of JICA. In the new scheme, people who wanted to receive financial assistance to rebuild their houses had to form a union. The union was able to receive financial assistance only when the houses were constructed using at least three key technologies:

(1) the quality of construction materials such as concrete, mortar and foundations; (2) the required size and reinforcement of foundations, columns and beams with a specified maximum span; and (3) the use of structural features such as anchoring, tying, bracing and overlapping. The technologies were introduced through JICA's technical assistance to strengthen brick houses. To accelerate the reconstruction process with this system, 17 additional offices were opened to support and receive the house design and building permission applications and 150 temporary staff members were employed. As a result, about 80 percent of damaged houses in Bantul were rebuilt quickly with higher safety standards against future earthquakes in about one year – remarkable progress compared with other districts. Therefore it may be said that international assistance contributed to both rapid reconstruction and creating a safer environment in the target region.

Case 4: 2011 Thailand Floods, Thailand (2011)

> National priority put on reconstruction from a disaster caused by rapid development with an inadequate consideration of the natural phenomena of flooding.

Table 7.9 Summary of the Thailand Floods (Case 4)

Hazard type	Flood (slow onset)
Date	From August 2011 for three months
Area	Lower Chao Phraya River Basin, about 18,000km^2 of low-lying area
Damage	Total damage: about US$42.5 billion Industrial parks: 7 large industrial parks were submerged
Related implications	• Build back safer of the disaster-affected area • Extended reconstruction

From the 1990s, Thailand experienced rapid economic growth. Urban areas were expanded and many companies, including foreign firms, constructed factories in areas that were affected by the 2011 flood. To address the increasing risks of flooding, the Thai government, together with JICA, formulated a flood control master plan for Chao Phraya River in 1999. However, appropriate measures were not taken because of the low importance placed on the recommendations by the national government and the lack of awareness among the people of the potential flood risk. Several large-scale floods occurred during the 10 years before 2011, but no severe damage was caused.

Following the 2011 flood, the Thai government established the Committee of National Economic Reconstruction and National Strategy of Water Resources under the chair of the Prime Minister. To address flood control and management as a national priority, the Committee undertook intensive discussions and formulated a plan that required the financing of US$10 billion. The important point to mention was that the plan covered not only the Chao Phraya River but also other major river systems around the country. This shows the government's determination to ensure that the country will be better able to manage future floods by mainstreaming disaster management/flood control under the idea of build back better.

Case 5: Typhoon Yolanda (Haiyan), Philippines (2013)

Declaration of "Build Back Better" as government policy for reconstruction immediately after the disaster.

Table 7.10 Summary of Typhoon Yolanda (Case 5)

Hazard type	Storm surge and strong winds generated by category 5 Typhoon "Yolanda (Haiyan)"
Date	November 8, 2013
Area	Leyte and Samar, and other areas in the Visayas
Damages	Casualties: approx. 8,000 Affected people: 1.5 million Buildings destroyed: more than 1.1 million
Related implications	• Build back safer of the disaster-affected area

In recent years, the Philippines has suffered heavily from typhoon/tropical storm disasters, with five major typhoons hitting the country since 2009. Typhoons Ondoy and Pepeng in 2009 hit metropolitan Manila, and typhoons Sendong and Pablo both hit Mindanao in 2011 and 2012. Since many of victims of these tropical storms were living on hazardous flood plains and river courses, the government had already started to implement land use regulations in these disaster-prone areas. Under these circumstances, Typhoon Yolanda (Haiyan) hit the Visayas Region and caused devastating damage.

When the government announced the reconstruction concept based on a proposal developed through discussion with JICA, "Build Back Better" was clearly stated as a principle. Under this concept, land use regulations, namely "no dwelling" zones, control zones and safe zones, have been introduced as part of the physical reconstruction. With regard to the revival of livelihood, high value-added agricultural products and fisheries are being introduced to increase the income of the primary industry workers who were most affected by this disaster.

Conclusion

In this chapter, through the review and discussions on the past reconstruction cases, several common characteristics and universal elements of reconstruction were identified. As a conclusion, the following could represent an ideal reconstruction from the viewpoint of Build Back Better. Reconstruction aims to create stronger and more resilient nations and societies against disasters compared to the situations before the disaster. This is made possible through the implementation of disaster risk reduction measures in conjunction with a well-balanced implementation of restoration and the revitalization of the economy/industry, livelihood, local culture, history and environment. Required safety levels for urbanized areas may be higher than in rural areas because it is more likely that there will be economically expensive assets in urban areas.

To raise safety levels of disaster-affected areas, structural measures such as flood control dykes as well as the reinforcement of roads and bridges are necessary. On the other hand, there is always the possibility that the actual force of the hazard will exceed the design capacity of structural measures. Therefore, structural measures should always be reinforced by non-structural measures. In fact, the higher the target level of protection by structural measures, the more non-structural measures will be necessary to complement the structural measures. In addition, when public funds or international assistance are provided for reconstruction, it becomes necessary to make prevention and mitigation measures the highest priority to avoid repeated vulnerability and inefficient investment. Reconstruction further includes activities to expand the effects of the lessons learned from the disaster-affected area to wider areas to create safer societies as a whole against natural disasters.

It is often the case that it is only after large-scale disasters when many people start to pay attention to affected areas and a large amount of money is spent on response and recovery. Although pre-disaster investment is desirable, if it is not done, post-disaster investment may be the only opportunity to improve the vulnerable area, especially in developing countries. Therefore, the process of Build Back Better, and especially the process of build back safer, should be the central part of reconstruction processes. Disasters disrupt the economic and social functions of affected areas. Prolonged reconstruction processes will hinder the recovery of economic and social activities. In this regard, in the areas where disasters are foreseen, pre-disaster recovery planning, namely a plan for reconstruction prepared before disasters strike, is recommended as a preparedness measure. It has often been observed that disasters usually affect the most vulnerable parts of society. As a result, problems such as poverty, income disparity and depopulation may be exacerbated, further reinforcing vulnerability. To escape from this vicious cycle, recovery from disasters and economic and social development should be promoted concurrently.

Recommendation

Reconstruction from disasters should be implemented with a clear strategy of reducing the vulnerability of disaster-affected areas and communities. The "Build Back Better" approach has to include a "build back safer" approach, as the essential keys to breaking the negative spiral of disaster and poverty and achieving sustainable development. Competing needs such as the speed of recovery of livelihood need to be addressed in a balanced manner so that safety is not compromised.

Audiences of the recommendation: NGOs, national governments, donors, international agencies and the United Nations secretariat of the ISDR.

Acknowledgment

Tables that show summaries of disasters were prepared based on the information of the Cabinet Office of Japan, Japan Meteorological Agency, National Police Agency of Japan, Fire and Disaster Management Agency of Japan, Asian Disaster Reduction Center, United States Geological Survey, World Health Organization, Center for Research on the Epidemiology of Disasters, and other official sources.

Note

1 "Haiti Earthquake: Where Is US Aid Money Going? Get the Data." The Guardian Datablog, January 10, 2014. www.theguardian.com/global-development/datablog/2014/jan/10/haiti-earthquake-us-aid-funding-data.

References

BRR NAD-Nias. 2008. "Enriching the Construction of Recovery: Annual Report 2007." BRR NAD-NIAS.

Cabinet Office. 2005. *Bousai Hakusho* [White Paper for Disaster Management]. Tokyo: Cabinet Office of Japan.

—— 2011. "Disaster Management in Japan." Tokyo: Cabinet Office of Japan. www.bousai.go.jp/1info/pdf/saigaipanf_e.pdf.

—— 2012. *Bousai Hakusho* [White Paper for Disaster Management]. Tokyo: Cabinet Office of Japan.

Cabinet Secretariat. 2011. "Higashinihon-Daisinsai Fukkou Kousou Kaigi no Kaisai nit suite" [About the Holding of the Reconstruction Design Council in Response to the Great East Japan Earthquake]. Tokyo: Cabinet Secretariat of Japan. www.cas.go.jp/jp/fukkou/pdf/setti.pdf.

—— 2013. "Shiryou 4-2" [Materials for the 2nd Meeting of National Resilience Committee]. Tokyo: Cabinet Secretariat of Japan. www.cas.go.jp/jp/seisaku/resilience/dai2/siryou4.pdf.

Emergency Survey Team for the Niigata Prefecture Chuetsu Earthquake. 2005. "Chuetsu Jishin Higai Chousa Houkoku" [Report on the Damage Survey for the Niigata Prefectural Chuetsu Earthquake 2005]. Tokyo: Japan Society of Civil Engineers.

Koshizawa, Akira. 2012. *Daisaigai to Fukku/Fukko Keikaku* [Disaster and Recovery Plan]. Tokyo: Iwanami Shoten.

MAFF (Ministry of Agriculture, Forestry and Fisheries). 2011. "Sumiyakana Fukkyu ni Mukete" [Toward Smooth Implementation of Rehabilitation]. Tokyo: MAFF. www.maff.go.jp/j/nousin/bousai/bousai_saigai/b_hukkyuu/pdf/panfu.pdf.

Matsumaru, Ryo. 2010. "Influence of Social Characteristics on the Reconstruction Process after the Indian Ocean Tsunami Disaster" (Doctoral Thesis). Yokohama: Yokohama National University.

Matsumaru, Ryo, Nagami, Kozo and Takeya, Kimio. 2012. "Reconstruction of the Aceh Region following the 2004 Indian Ocean Tsunami Disaster: A Transportation Perspective." *IATSS Research* 36(1), 11–19.

MILT (Ministry of Land, Infrastructure, Transport and Tourism). 2010. "Saigai Fukkyuu Jigyou ni Tsuite" [Regarding the Works Toward Disaster Rehabilitation]. Tokyo: MILT. www.mlit.go.jp/river/hourei_tsutatsu/bousai/saigai/hukkyuu/doc.pdf.

——— 2012a. "Sekkei Tsunami (Tsunami Level 1) no Suii no Settei Houhou" [How to Set the Design Water Level for Tsunami Level 1]. Tokyo: MILT. www.mlit.go.jp/river/ shinngikai_blog/kaigantsunamitaisaku/dai02kai/dai02kai_siryou3.pdf.

——— 2012b. "Tsunami Shinsui Soutei no Tebiki" [Guidelines for Setting Estimated Inundation Areas of Tsunamis]. Tokyo: MILT. www.mlit.go.jp/river/shishin_guideline/ bousai/saigai/tsunami/shinsui_settei.pdf.

——— 2014. "Kenchiku Kijunhou no Taishinkijun no Gaiyou" [Summary of Quake-Resistance Standards of the Building Standards Act of Japan]. Tokyo: MILT. www. mlit.go.jp/common/000188539.pdf.

Shiozaki, Yoshimitsu, Nishikawa, Eiichi and Deguchi, Shun-ichi. 2007. *Saigai Fukkou no Gaido* [A Guide for Human Recovery from Natural Disaster]. Kyoto: Creates Kamogawa.

Takahashi, Yutaka. 2012. "Kawa to Kokudo no Kiki" [Crisis on Rivers and National Land]. Tokyo: Iwanami Shoten.

USGS. 2005. "Magnitude 7.6 – PAKISTAN, US Geological Survey." http://earthquake. usgs.gov/earthquakes/eqinthenews/2005/usdyae/#summary.

United Nations secretariat of the International Strategy for Disaster Reduction (ISDR). 2009. "UNISDR Terminology on Disaster Risk Reduction." Geneva: United Nations. www.unisdr.org/files/7817_UNISDRTerminologyEnglish.pdf.

Yasuda, Masahiko. 2013. *Saigai Fukko no Nihonshi* [History of Disaster Recovery of Japan]. Tokyo: Yoshikawa Kobunkan.

8 Lessons from promoting "Build Back Better" in the post-tsunami recovery of Aceh

Kuntoro Mangkusubroto

Introduction

On December 26, 2004, a devastating earthquake and subsequent huge tsunami struck Indonesia's western-most point in the Province of Aceh. The total death toll from both disasters was estimated to be about 180,000 people. This represented 4 percent of the population in the Province of Aceh. In some of the coastal districts of Aceh, up to 35 percent of the population was lost. Beyond the loss of life, half a million people lost their homes and livelihoods, thousands of kilometers of roads were destroyed, thousands of hectares of rice and other agricultural fields were ruined, and even critical public records needed to affirm land and other property rights were lost.

In addition to the devastation caused by this set of disasters, the people of Aceh had suffered for more than a generation as a result of an ongoing secessionist insurgency. Indeed, at the time of the tsunami, the Province of Aceh was under martial law.

In the immediate post-tsunami period, a new set of dynamics began to emerge. These related, first, to the enormous scale of the generous support offered by the global community to the victims of this disaster. The second and related critical dynamic was the scale of the resources that were mobilized by non-governmental organizations independently of their host-donor governments. This resulted in the arrival of a large number of NGOs in Aceh and the Islands of Nias (part of the neighboring Province of North Sumatra also gravely affected by these disasters) to support rehabilitation and reconstruction efforts.

All of these complicating factors, including the unfortunate state of the communities of Aceh even prior to the devastation caused by the earthquake and the tsunami, underlined very strongly the importance of doing more than merely returning to some kind of status quo ante. In this regard, the concept of "building back better" was highly appropriate and became a major inspiration for policymakers. It also offered hope to the affected communities that it was possible to achieve a better future.

When considering what constitutes "build back better," the most common pictures that come to mind include the following:

- access to better technology;
- better familiarity with building standards;
- better community preparedness for future disasters;
- better understanding of mechanisms for stakeholder engagement;
- suffering from fewer losses through various forms of corruption, and so on.

These kinds of achievements, however, do not appear out of thin air. Where the operational environment is not conducive, even great ideas and technologies will fail to take hold. This means that it is critical to examine the governing environment to see whether it is capable of enabling or actually disabling the potential for build back better approaches to be applied.

The Indonesian government established the Agency for the Rehabilitation and Reconstruction of the Regions and Communities of the Province of the Nanggroe Aceh Darussalam and the Nias Islands, Province of North Sumatra (hereafter referred to as BRR) to lead the rehabilitation and reconstruction effort. The "build back better" approach provided an effective opportunity for the whole rehabilitation and reconstruction program to incorporate various technical and technological approaches, leaving Aceh and its people in a much better state than before the tsunami. The experience of BRR demonstrates that appropriate governance arrangements comprise enablers that permit, each of which can contribute to building back better. It is for this reason that the chapter focuses on the enablers deployed by BRR to direct the reconstruction program rather than particular policies or technologies such as better escape routes during a tsunami or ways of improving standards for housing construction.

This chapter, therefore, outlines the policies and approaches applied by the Indonesian government in managing reconstruction in the wake of the earthquake and tsunami, with a particular focus on why the build back better approach was adopted by the government. In doing so, the chapter seeks to answer the questions of "why" certain approaches were made, not just "what" impacts occurred as a result of the decisions taken. In this regard, the chapter focuses "upstream" to review the policies and institutional designs that permitted the people of Aceh to pursue a better future than would have been possible using standard operating procedures and business-as-usual approaches to rehabilitation and reconstruction (R&R).

The immediate aftermath

The first official response from within Indonesia was to identify the extent of the disaster. As is normal under such circumstances initial reports varied. Most underestimated the scale, with lines of communication disrupted for people in the areas most affected. Conflicting stories and even rumors spread quickly. However, as the quality and geographic basis of information began to improve, so did the realization that this was a mega-disaster and well beyond the magnitude of other disasters that earlier Indonesian governments had needed to confront.

Within a couple of days, the scale of the disaster became quite clear not just to leaders in Jakarta but across the world. By this stage, unprecedented offers of support began to pour in, both in terms of financial support and the provision of logistics and human resources.

An early and critical decision taken by the government was to open the region of Aceh to international offers of help. Within days, international help, including various forms of logistic support from the military of foreign countries, had arrived. They were able to work with Indonesian officials and local communities to launch initial response activities such as dealing with the deceased and injured as well as the homeless and others in need. This decision to open the region of Aceh, despite being under martial law, was received very favorably by the international community as a statement that Indonesia was willing and able to work in close partnership with others and was prepared to make difficult decisions, including opening an area that had hitherto been under martial law to military officers and soldiers from foreign countries.

For the government, inaugurated just two months before the tsunami, there was a very rational recognition that, in spite of the political/security circumstances of Aceh, there was no way that a "business-as-usual" approach was feasible. The scale of the disaster would test any country's capacity to support the needs of the victims. Finally, given the enormous international media coverage of the disaster, and particularly given the extent to which this disaster had also affected tourist destinations in neighboring countries, a "no-comment" option by the Indonesian authorities to developments in its own affected areas was simply not viable.

While initial emergency relief programs were being launched on the ground, a process was initiated to consider the steps necessary for the rehabilitation and reconstruction phases. This included identifying what had been lost and what would need to be replaced. At the same time, there was a strong recognition that existing institutional and administrative arrangements for managing disasters were simply inadequate to bring the numerous agencies, sectors and levels of administration together into a coherent program. The existing arrangements consisted of an initial emergency management phase led by the Coordinating Minister for Public Welfare. This arrangement lasted for 90 days. Subsequently, programs of rehabilitation and reconstruction were to be implemented through established government agencies at national and subnational levels with no specially empowered agency to facilitate substantive coordination or break through any of the bottlenecks that would inevitably have arisen. Furthermore, the situation had left the province with very weak government, especially in those districts most affected by the tsunami, and this added additional requirements to the prospective management of the rehabilitation and reconstruction phase.

Negotiating a blueprint for reconstruction

As the planning technocrats began sifting through the emerging data, crafting policies to guide reconstruction and designing programs for reconstruction, communities in Aceh, especially those living near the sea, began to rally against one proposal, namely the proposal to establish a wide buffer zone along the coastline within which people could not live. This was a similar policy to that proposed in Thailand and Sri Lanka, two other countries seriously affected by the tsunami. In the case of Aceh, the communities argued against these buffer zones, stating that their lives were based around the sea and they "could not live in the mountains." Initially, the planning technocrats sought to ensure that the buffer zones would remain part of the reconstruction plan.

In response, the Acting Governor of Aceh called for a public consultation process on issues affecting the community, in which officials would present their proposals and then answer concerns by members of the community. The subsequent flood of complaints and questions from regular citizens, who, because of the long-term conflict were unaccustomed to open and direct opposition to proposals from Jakarta, resulted in changes to one key policy proposal at the time. By the time of the final plans, it had been decided that the buffer zones would not be applied. Rather, escape hills, roads and buildings would be incorporated as key components of the program for disaster preparedness.

The value of this exercise was also to demonstrate that modern and democratic approaches to engagement between officials and citizens were able to resolve issues and indeed incorporate the strongly held preferences of citizens. There was also a view that, at this point in history, with renewed efforts to find a peaceful resolution to the long-term insurgency, there was much to be gained by incorporating the views and preferences of affected citizens, rather than trying to force a top-down-driven reconstruction agenda. All of this was conducted before BRR was established.

Once the body had been created, the head of the BRR Executing Agency spoke to all the different parties involved in the long-term conflict. It was necessary to demonstrate to the people of Aceh that discussions between all parties were being held, as this assisted in legitimizing the decisions that would impact upon the people of Aceh. The program for R&R developed by the planning officials became the blueprint for R&R. However, it was adjusted frequently to take into account rapidly changing developments on the ground as well as evolving aspirations of affected communities and opportunities presented by the resources that had been mobilized.

Creating a powerful and dedicated agency

As the planners continued their work towards creating the reconstruction blueprint, others were working to develop the institutional arrangements that would guide the reconstruction efforts.

Key imperatives in developing a new agency included the following considerations:

- To reduce the potential for inter-agency and inter-ministerial "turf battles" to create delays and stumbling-blocks, the new agency would have

to be empowered with strong authority to command the reconstruction
program.

- In order to receive input at the highest levels to endorse new policies, the
  agency would need to be established at ministerial level.
- To reduce concerns about corruption in Indonesia, the agency would have to
  be structured to ensure the clear and transparent execution of its mandate.
- To effectively manage the complexities of program implementation on the
  ground and the ongoing separatist sentiments towards Jakarta, the agency
  would need to be based in Aceh.
- To be aware of pre-existing sensitivities among the various communities
  in Aceh, the agency would need to operate on the basis of demonstrable
  participation and engagement with communities.

On each of these issues there were, of course, strong debates within and among
agencies and leaders. On many occasions, objections to endorsing the proposed
changes reflected a combination of conservative attitudes such as "we have never
done it this way before so why change?" as well as turf control arguments such as
"we are the experts on this issue." It was even suggested that an agency head at
ministerial level could not possibly be located in a province: "How could she or
he attend ministerial meetings?"

In seeking to deal with each of the above imperatives a number of breakthroughs
were achieved, including the following:

- Parliament passed a law, initially as a government regulation in lieu of a law,
  to establish an agency dedicated to the rehabilitation and reconstruction of
  Aceh and the Nias Islands, BRR.[1] In doing so the agency was empowered to
  lead all efforts, including the direction of other agencies in the implementation of rehabilitation and reconstruction. This would also mean that BRR
  would become the "go-to" agency for any partners and communities engaged
  in rehabilitation and reconstruction efforts.
- To ensure effective collaboration at the highest levels of government, the
  head of the agency was established at ministerial level, thus permitting
  full access to cabinet-level policymaking and ensuring that inter-agency
  engagements could not be held hostage to bureaucratic proceduralism.
- A number of initiatives were conducted both through the provision of legal
  instruments and, more importantly, at the level of implementation to ensure
  that the potential for corruption to subvert the rehabilitation and reconstruction efforts could be minimalized. This issue will be discussed in greater
  detail below.
- It was also decided that the agency, while it was a national government
  ministerial-level agency, would be based in Banda Aceh, the capital city of
  Aceh.
- As part of the efforts to ensure that the agency could be both an effective executing agency but also open to various stakeholders, BRR consisted of three
  top-level components: the Steering Council (which consisted of several

ministers and leaders of various community stakeholders), the Supervisory Council (which consisted of various respected citizens and activists) and the Executing Agency. Henceforth, unless otherwise specifically noted, reference to BRR will be used to refer to the Executing Agency of BRR. This was the component responsible for leading and being accountable for the day-to-day programmatic implementation of the actual rehabilitation and reconstruction efforts on the ground. This three-component approach established an overall umbrella for BRR to reach various constituents while also allowing the Executing Agency to operate on a professional basis. The only deviation to this principle was established in the wake of the peace agreement with the Acehnese insurgents, when the BRR Executing Agency was tasked with providing opportunities for former combatants to play a role in the rehabilitation and reconstruction program.[2]

- In addition to the above, a clear distinction was drawn between BRR's "coordinating" and "implementing" roles. This distinction was important considering the inevitable atmosphere of competing interests. While BRR maintained an emphasis on coordination, its implementing role proved to be an essential element by enabling gaps to be filled that, in turn, assisted in avoiding an unbalanced allocation of resources. In this regard BRR could provide an enabling environment to assist the vast range of donors and implementing partners to be able to implement their projects smoothly in the field while also being ready to fill in any gaps by conducting certain reconstruction activities directly. This would not always be an easy balance to achieve.

Figure 8.1 provides a summary view of the BRR "engine" designed and operated to manage the government's rehabilitation and reconstruction program.

Facing critical challenges: corruption

In addition to the other challenges facing Aceh, one final problem at the time of the tsunami was the recent arrest for corruption of the then Governor of the province. While hardly alone in facing challenges of corruption across Indonesia, the problems of high-level corruption, combined with the deleterious impact of violent conflict on the social fabric of Acehnese society, constituted critical dynamics that needed to be considered by policymakers in overseeing the huge reconstruction effort.

As noted above, the Indonesian government deemed that corruption constituted one of the gravest risks to the whole rehabilitation and reconstruction program. Identifying corruption as a key risk and not just a "good governance" program reframed quite starkly the ways in which the government dealt with this issue. For example, in designing any of its programs, and indeed even in the very design of the agency, the need to focus on potential corruption vulnerabilities had to be a central consideration, rather than being "quarantined" as a discrete set of good governance initiatives.

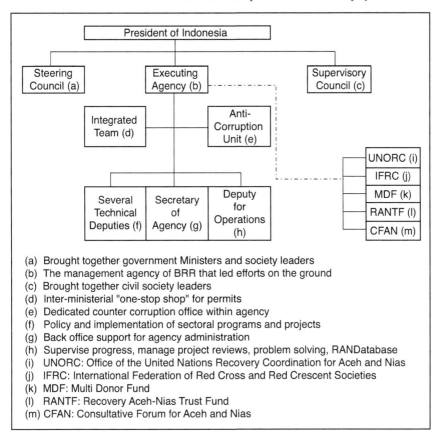

(a) Brought together government Ministers and society leaders
(b) The management agency of BRR that led efforts on the ground
(c) Brought together civil society leaders
(d) Inter-ministerial "one-stop shop" for permits
(e) Dedicated counter corruption office within agency
(f) Policy and implementation of sectoral programs and projects
(g) Back office support for agency administration
(h) Supervise progress, manage project reviews, problem solving, RANDatabase
(i) UNORC: Office of the United Nations Recovery Coordination for Aceh and Nias
(j) IFRC: International Federation of Red Cross and Red Crescent Societies
(k) MDF: Multi Donor Fund
(l) RANTF: Recovery Aceh-Nias Trust Fund
(m) CFAN: Consultative Forum for Aceh and Nias

Figure 8.1 Summary of organizational structure of BRR
Source: Author.

This risk of corruption was deemed to exist at a number of levels. At its most basic, corruption represents an inefficient and unjust allocation of resources. This often means that victims who should receive support do not. At another level corruption, or even the perception of corruption, can drive away support as donors seek to delay, divert or cancel pledges. They may also add further layers of controls and oversight to their programs – sometimes to the extent that their programs become bogged down administratively and implementation is very slow. Each of these potential developments weakens the capacity of any program to build back better. The emergence of corruption also has a negative impact on the social fabric of a society and encourages poor performance and lack of accountability – certainly not the kinds of practices that leave a community better off.

The approach used by BRR to face the corruption challenge was multifaceted, although it contained a strong focus on prevention. The process began by stating to all communities from the outset that corrupt practices had no place in the reconstruction program. This was soon followed up with the development of a special integrity pact signed by every member of staff of BRR (not just those engaged in procurement). Firm declarations and the signing of pledges, however, are insufficient. Institutional backup of these declarations was required. To this end BRR established a dedicated Anti-Corruption Unit (SAK), the first such unit established within any ministry in Indonesia. The head of the SAK reported directly to the head of BRR and was also given freedom to communicate and work directly with law enforcement agencies, most notably the nation's prestigious Corruption Eradication Commission (KPK). The work of the Unit was quite extensive and included the following:

- receipt and processing of any complaint lodged with it, including by anonymous sources, as well as from other staff within BRR;
- conducting various kinds of investigations to assess complaints with a view to identifying what, if any, breaches had occurred;
- submitting the results of any case in which potential corruption was revealed, including all added information generated through the Unit's investigations, to the KPK;
- reviewing regulations and providing advice on integrity enhancement and corruption proofing to other parts of BRR as well as to rehabilitation and reconstruction partners, including international partners;
- conducting public information campaigns and specific information campaigns with various stakeholders on the threats of corruption;
- providing regular updates to the media on progress in the Unit's work, including statistics on the kinds of cases being brought to the Unit and what was being done with these complaints.

In addition to a range of internal control systems, BRR lobbied to encourage key anti-corruption and audit agencies to beef up their operations in Aceh. This included having the country's supreme audit agency establish a dedicated office in Banda Aceh as well as the KPK establishing an office based in the main university in Banda Aceh. This was the first branch established by the KPK outside Jakarta.

In terms of operational relationships designed to reduce the potential for corruption, BRR requested that the Ministry of Finance establish a specially dedicated Treasury Office.[3] This special Treasury Office was dedicated to focusing only on the BRR account, thus allowing staff a more clear understanding of the programs and projects for which they had to make payments. In addition, this office had to provide full and online disclosure of all submitted payments requests while they were being processed and finalized. This permitted anyone to see where payments were and prevented blockages and delays (deliberate or otherwise) that may have impeded efficiency and removed a pathway towards corrupt practices. This innovative system represented a breakthrough and set new standards for disclosure and transparency in financial administration. By the end of the BRR program there were no complaints from any business leaders (who in Indonesia are generally very quick to complain) about delays or possible corruption/extortion efforts from this dedicated Treasury Office.

One further critical integrity and corruption prevention approach used by BRR was to provide its staff with competitive and streamlined remuneration. This meant paying salaries at levels that were competitive with the private sector and donors. This also meant "simplifying" remuneration packages by removing the ubiquitous plethora of top-ups, annuities and stipends that pad out civil servants' salaries elsewhere. The search for these various top-ups traditionally constitutes a major distraction in productivity as well as blurring the boundaries between legitimate income and inappropriate or even corrupt practices. An additional and important outcome from this process was that the agency did not suffer from any "head-hunting" losses of staff to donors and other agencies. Undermining the capacity of host government agencies can be a common problem in the aftermath of a disaster.[4] Equally important, the application of a single "all-in" system of remuneration meant that it was possible to legitimately connect the tasks undertaken by staff with productivity outcomes. Thus a third aspect to BRR's work on integrity was to make use of productivity contracts.

The critical lesson from the work by BRR on countering corruption is that basic pledges and strong statements must be backed up with appropriate investments to enforce these standards. Too often in situations of major disasters or related circumstances there is a tendency to be somewhat permissive of corruption, even falling back on tired old clichés like "corruption greases the wheels." In the case of BRR the view adopted was that "corruption is not grease to turn the wheels of the system. It is a spanner in the works." Each of these reforms reduced the potential for inappropriate and quality-sapping policies and practices from subverting the reconstruction agenda. This helped ensure that better proposals based on merit, rather than on less noble interests, were able to influence policy and practice.

Facing critical challenges: coordination

A common misconception is that issues related to coordination between programs in a complex situation of this nature can be solved by simply conducting a series of regular meetings. In the context of BRR, coordination was conceptualized and applied in a far more comprehensive manner. A number of key factors helped lead BRR to execute its responsibilities for coordination in this way. The first issue again related to the scale of resources mobilized by international partners together with the number of partner agencies that sought to support rehabilitation and reconstruction efforts. Another issue was that BRR was established more than three months after the tsunami. Indeed, Indonesia's then emergency response agency had actually completed its standard three-month operation, thus leaving a gap in national-level and on-the-ground leadership. This meant that many other agencies had already established a presence and had begun to implement various projects. It was therefore imperative that BRR be able to quickly ascertain who was doing what, where, how and when, etc.

A key consideration inside BRR was that the agency should not be a hindrance or burden that would hold up the programs and projects of agencies whose work was already underway. At the same time some programmatic order had to be established across Aceh to ensure that standards of reconstruction performances were met as well as other critical development considerations such as ensuring that certain areas and communities were not overlooked or that others were not being flooded with support in addition to ensuring that support across sectors was effectively connected and coherent.

The comprehensive approach to coordination undertaken by BRR consisted of five key areas. An outline of each is presented below.

Endorsement of concept note (projects)

To provide some coherence and to build up a clear picture of the who, what, when, where, and how of actors and projects across Aceh, BRR established a process under which every program and project had to pass through a concept note review. This meant that every agency undertaking any project had to pass their projects through a review. The term "concept note" referred to a very basic project document. BRR decided that, certainly in the beginning, there would be no need for detailed project documentation.

This was done for the prime reason that BRR's own capacities were still quite modest and thus its capacity to record, sift and interpret vast amounts of data in detailed project documents was simply not there. Demanding this kind of detail from rehabilitation and reconstruction partners would have wasted essential time while overwhelming BRR's capacity. The approach adopted, by contrast, was to seek clarity on basic issues from each project proponent. In addition, the notion of sequencing reconstruction was an essential part of planning, considering the enormity of the work required. The information required in the concept note included the following:

- In what sector/s of work will the project be undertaken?
- Where will the project be undertaken?
- What is the estimated cost (funding requirements) of the project?
- Who is/are the donor/s of the project?
- What kinds of consultations with affected communities were conducted to endorse these activities?
- What kinds of integrity and anti-corruption approaches have been incorporated into the project?
- What key performance indicators (KPI) can be used to measure effectiveness?

Recording and monitoring the various KPIs greatly assisted BRR's capacity to report to the public the progress being made. It should be noted, nonetheless, that establishing common KPIs for hundreds of organizations is not straightforward and their maintenance remained a challenge throughout the reconstruction program. To provide transparency to this project review process, BRR always ensured that outside stakeholders were participants in the reviews. This very open approach was adopted as part of efforts by BRR to build public trust in its work as well as to strengthen the basis and quality of these reviews.

Some agencies, especially the very biggest and the very smallest project proponents, were initially reticent about putting their projects through the review process. However, within a short period of time virtually all had decided to submit to the process. Among the reasons for the take-up of engagement was that, first, the process was quite easy and not too onerous for these organizations, and, second, project endorsement by BRR provided many benefits in terms of project security and government support.

Creating the map of rehabilitation and reconstruction (R&R) implementation

Having developed a database of projects endorsed by BRR, the next step in the overall R&R coordination program was to locate each project on an online map. The system developed, as an extension of the pre-existing donor assisted database, was the Recovery Aceh Nias Database or RANDatabase.

BRR decided to integrate the concept note review process into the RANDatabase. This meant that each project manager was given access to the RANDatabase to upload all the basic information. They were responsible for maintaining and updating information on the sector/s in which the project/s were being implemented, the geographic locations, the value of the project and the status of implementation. Certain basic data (essentially targets that had been agreed between BRR and the project management) were "frozen" once uploaded. They could only be adjusted by agreement with the BRR officials responsible for the relevant sector. Other data, once uploaded, could be adjusted by the project managers at will. Transparency was promoted by providing local communities and community activists with access to the information to ensure that it was accurate.

At the same time project donors could also view the state of progress of the project/s they were funding. BRR was also able to view progress and identify any projects experiencing difficulty or delays. In addition, BRR was able to view overall progress and ensure fair and effective coverage of activities across the region. With specific respect to that common problem in regions whose communities are suffering from trauma, namely mutual mistrust, the transparency of the data projected provided a basis for demonstrating the fairness of project coverage across regions.

The Integrated Team

One of the most important tools for R&R coordination created by BRR was the Integrated Team. At its core it was a "one-stop" shop for processing a wide variety of government permits covering immigration, taxation and customs, forestry, police and the registration of organizations that were new to Indonesia and focused only on R&R activities in Aceh and Nias. The Integrated Team consisted of officials from their home agencies seconded to process the permits and licenses that were within the purview of the BRR program. All members of the Integrated Team from the head of the Team down worked in an open plan structure that further facilitated and accelerated the processing of necessary permits and licenses across ministries and agencies. More fundamentally, the Integrated Team provided people and organizations whose projects had been endorsed and registered with BRR with the opportunity to avail themselves of all of these support services. People and organizations that were not recognized or registered were not able to seek this support from the Integrated Team. In this regard the Integrated Team offered a very valuable service of support to implementing partners while also providing a strong incentive for all implementing agencies trying to operate outside the wider program to connect and coordinate their projects within the wider BRR-led R&R program.

Another positive factor provided by the Integrated Team approach was that it enabled implementing partners to operate with integrity. For example, organizations that were new to Indonesia (and only in Indonesia to support R&R in Aceh and Nias) normally had no official legal status in the country. Under normal circumstances such agencies, as in any country, have to operate in a legal gray zone with restricted legal status (e.g., ineligibility to open bank accounts, etc.). All too often such organizations end up having to engage in unorthodox or even questionable operational and administrative activities that may also leave them vulnerable legally as well as exposed to criticism about their organizational ethics.

Given BRR's determination that this R&R program would not be subverted by corruption, this also meant providing an environment in which its partner agencies could operate with integrity. One key task of the Integrated Team was to provide legal status to agencies engaged in agreed R&R activities. This allowed these organizations to engage in normal contracting and financial transactions in a transparent and accountable manner.

BRR operations support

Ostensibly, the core function of BRR's operations support was to pull together parties and groups facing a particular problem and then scoping out an effective answer. The BRR operations team, led by the Chief Operations Officer (a deputy to the Head of the BRR Executing Agency), provided more direct support to implementing partners as they undertook their activities in the field. On many occasions, issues such as logistical shortages or bottlenecks and, at times, even overlapping efforts by other groups emerged. On other occasions there were regulatory or other administrative issues that were complicating or even obstructing progress.

Among the key tasks of BRR's Deputy of Operations was to assist all implementing partners in overcoming these kinds of issues. When problems arose for these partners they had a port of call in BRR to seek answers. On many occasions, problems could be addressed by bringing the various stakeholders and officials together and negotiating answers to remove the obstacles. Addressing these problems often required bringing in new groups with particular capacity to advise or indeed to provide the necessary support; for example, to provide additional logistics support in certain areas. At other times, addressing the problems on the ground required raising the consultative arrangements to higher levels, even including the Cabinet, in order to find ways to redress regulatory problems that were obstructing the implementation of various aspects of the R&R program.

However, organizations seeking to undertake projects or activities that had not been processed through the concept note review process were unable to secure much support from BRR. Indeed, in any dispute with other agencies undertaking recognized activities in similar areas, these other organizations soon found that they had little support to address their problems.

A final aspect of coordination at the level of operations was the decision to establish regional offices across Aceh. These offices acted as focal points for program delivery and provided project proponents with more specialized support mechanisms where local knowledge and engagement of local stakeholders could be made more accessible. Furthermore, a more effective reporting facility was initiated through these offices, enabling BRR to better address potential or emerging gaps in the R&R program. These offices were developed only after the institutional and operational capacities of BRR were already well established.

Networks of coordination

One further form of coordination undertaken consisted of the more conventional method of bringing groups of R&R actors together to discuss current issues and identify broader general developments and trends as well as highlight existing or potential problems. Given that the number of implementation partners to the program numbered over 1,000 organizations – national and international – the notion of sitting all parties in a room to "coordinate" respective programs was, of course, impossible. Instead the approach to coordination at this level consisted of a number of separate but interrelated processes. A number of examples of these networks of coordination are outlined below.

Coordination with the United Nations organizations

Among the most important set of R&R implementation partners were the various agencies of the United Nations. To promote effective inter-agency cooperation and synergies as well as to link closely the work of the UN agencies with BRR's work and priorities, BRR worked with the UN to establish the Office of the United Nations Recovery Coordinator for Aceh and Nias (UNORC). The way in which this Office operated once established represented a great example of the much-vaunted "One UN" concept in action. The head of UNORC played a critical role in communicating with other UN agencies as well as providing invaluable feedback to BRR on developments affecting activities of the UN as well as offering advice on opportunities on how to more effectively engage with the UN system both in Indonesia and globally.

International Federation of the Red Cross and Red Crescent Societies (IFRC)

One of the most outstanding dynamics of the R&R program in Aceh and Nias, as noted in the introduction, was that non-governmental organizations represented huge sources of funding mobilized independently of their host governments. Indeed, the non-governmental sector mobilized more resources than the bilateral donors. As an example, the various national members of the IFRC alone contributed over US$1 billion in support of the R&R efforts. The various national members of the IFRC coordinated efforts closely, and at the leadership level of IFRC representation there were very regular meetings and exchanges with leadership in BRR and also in coordination with other "peak" coordination bodies such as UNORC.

Multi Donor Fund and RAN Trust Fund

While some bilateral donors opted to implement programs and projects themselves, a number of others agreed to pool their resources in a trust fund managed by the World Bank known as the Multi Donor Fund (MDF). The MDF was aligned also with the government's State Budget.

In addition to this fund a number of other donors asked BRR to establish its own trust fund and expend their resources through this funding mechanism directly. The mechanism concerned was the Recovery Aceh Nias Trust Fund (RANTF). These trust fund modalities provided a platform not only for coordination but also for integration of efforts among the R&R partners.

Consultative Forum for Aceh and Nias (CFAN)

There were an enormous number of partners in the R&R program. They worked across a wide geographic area and operated in a wide variety of sectors in which R&R was required. As a result of these factors it is feasible that stakeholders may have had an excellent view of their own activities but a very poor understanding of the wider dynamics and trends affecting the overall program, and thus, with time, the effects of their own project/s within the overall program. BRR believed there were great benefits to be derived if all stakeholders had the opportunity to meet directly outside the normal work environment and also to provide information to all stakeholders about the wide canvas of developments relating to the program. This provided each stakeholder with a sense of where they were located within the whole program and what progress was being made or what problems were then facing the R&R program together with potential issues to watch.

In addition to people and organizations engaged fully with the program, BRR also saw great value in providing a forum for people and organizations for whom this R&R program represented only part of their wider range of responsibilities. This included people such as MPs, journalists, ambassadors and NGO activists. At a more fundamental policy level BRR also saw the need to strengthen its systems of accountability to the public regarding what it was doing and how the overall program of R&R was progressing.

The mechanism BRR chose to use to address these issues was the Consultative Forum for Aceh and Nias (CFAN). CFAN was more than a huge event bringing stakeholders together twice a year. The lead-up to the event included various working groups that discussed and promoted issues of wider concern to stakeholders. This helped inform the agenda for the big event. The nature of the event also allowed easy access between people on the ground and senior policymakers, particularly those in Jakarta, who are not easily available to those living in the regions affected.

Conclusion

In summary, the essential elements outlined above consisted of the following components:

- to establish, from its design stage, a powerful agency able to pull various components of government together;
- to establish, uphold and support partners to maintain high standards of integrity in order to prevent corruption;
- to develop comprehensive means to ensure effective coordination of the overall R&R program;
- to provide mechanisms to ensure accountability, transparency and public participation in the conduct and oversight of the program. These were mandated within the law that created BRR and were institutionalized as BRR went into operation.

A fair question to ask is how these factors relate to "building back better." As noted in the introduction these factors are best seen as enablers. In short, the existence of these institutional arrangements, together with the pursuit of these principles/policies, allowed issues to be discussed before they became uncontrollable problems. They also offered space for people to raise issues and provided technical means to identify existing and potential problems that could affect the programs. In essence they provided for an operating environment in which better reconstruction policies and technologies, etc. could be sourced, endorsed and applied.

One critical performance indicator of any rehabilitation and reconstruction program is the capacity to transform pledges into completed projects on the ground. On many occasions the incapacity to transfer pledges into action in other post-disaster or post-conflict locations is caused by an array of obstacles and bottlenecks that become intractable and can reach a point where resources are never spent. These problems represent a major danger to any reconstruction program. In the case of the programs in Aceh and Nias, the transfer from pledge to completed activities had reached 93 percent by the time BRR concluded its mandate in April 2009. This was and remains a record. It was all the more impressive given that the scale of support offered by so many organizations was already very generous. This was all made possible through establishing the institutional arrangements. This meant that all partners requiring answers and support to address whatever problems emerged in the field were met with a government partner that was empowered to actually deliver and to support them in overcoming those problems. This dramatically reduced the amount of time lost in implementation.

A second danger to these kinds of post-disaster or post-conflict situations is that corruption or even perceptions of corruption can emerge. For agencies accountable for the expenditure of funds they hold under trust, be it from taxpayers or from other forms of personal donation, the last thing they ever want to do is to try to explain how they "lost" these funds to corruption. As a rule they respond programmatically to fears of corruption (or perceptions of it) by adding more layers of control and imposing other restrictions upon the use of the funds or ultimately simply never using those funds. With such a high transformation of pledge to action this was clearly a problem avoided in Aceh. A related issue that helped provide a level of comfort and trust to partners was that arrangements were set in place that offered donors a variety of options for disbursing their funds. This helped donors (bilateral, multilateral or NGO) find a modality that suited their needs and preferences while ensuring that the overall program was enriched with the resources needed to implement R&R projects. BRR aggressively maintained a firm integrity system, including the use of the kinds of arrangements described above, as well as firm action to uphold these standards, coupled with efforts to help other agencies operate with integrity. This meant that despite the scale of the program and the number of partners, the issue of corruption, or even perceptions of it, never came to threaten or subvert the program.

In relation to the issue of the physical security of R&R programs, BRR adopted the approach of transparency and active engagement with stakeholders without discrimination on the basis of political orientation. This meant that it was possible to retain sufficient trust with various factions to ensure that R&R projects and programs were, by and large, saved from the kinds of threats that often undermine programs in other post-conflict regions.

A number of the policies employed here created virtuous cycles. For example, the presentation of all progress on all projects through the RANDatabase allowed BRR to note when and where certain areas were being neglected. Some of these areas were widely considered to have been especially affected by the conflict. To have continued to leave these areas untouched would have opened up the possibility for some new and unhelpful political dynamics to enter the rehabilitation and reconstruction program and also undermined the emerging post-conflict developments.

Many may consider the concept of build back better to be connected specifically to factors like using the best or most appropriate policies, standards or technologies. However, in many respects the capacity to select those policies is very closely connected to the environment in which the decisions are made. In the case of the rehabilitation and reconstruction program in Aceh and Nias, the

Indonesian government critically decided at the outset that success in any goal of building back better would be determined by creating an enabling environment in which build back better approaches could be more effectively promoted.

Recommendation

To guarantee "building back better" as a priority for reconstruction, there should be an initial focus on ensuring that the governing arrangements for the reconstruction program are founded on high levels of integrity, accountability, transparency and responsiveness. Furthermore, clarity is needed in recovery management to resolve conflicts of interests. This includes an empowered state agency, capable of making informed decisions on reconstruction. This environment enables technical decisions on specifications to be made that produce better reconstruction results.

Audiences of the recommendation: National governments and donors.

Notes

1 Perpu 2/2005 subsequently transformed into Law 10/2005 on the BRR. The full translation of the name of BRR was "The Agency for the Rehabilitation and Reconstruction of the Regions and Livelihoods of the Communities of the Province of Aceh Abode of Peace and the Islands of Nias, Province of North Sumatra."
2 MoU Helsinki Article 1.3.9: "GAM will nominate representatives to participate fully at all levels in the commission established to conduct the post-tsunami reconstruction (BRR)."
3 The Directorate General for Treasury, under the Ministry of Finance, is responsible for, among other things, making payments to payees and other vendors of the government.
4 Professor Ashraf Ghani, Chancellor of Kabul University, Afghanistan, lamented that "Within six months of starting my job as Finance Minister, my best people had been stolen by international aid organizations who could offer them forty to a hundred times the salary we could." Ghani, Ashraf, Lockhart, Clare and Carnahan, Michael. (2005). "Closing the Sovereignty Gap: An Approach to State-Building." Working Paper 253. Overseas Development Institute, London. www.odi.org.uk/Publications/working_papers/wp253.pdf.

Part IV

Increasing the roles of stakeholders

9 Community empowerment and good governance

The way forward for DRM in developing countries

Muhammad Saidur Rahman

Introduction

The impact of hazards in the developing countries is disproportionately high compared to those in the Western world. To give a concrete example: the 1991 cyclone in Bangladesh, with wind speeds of 240km per hour, killed over 138,000 people, whereas just one year later Hurricane Andrew in Florida, USA, with an even higher wind velocity (270km per hour), caused only 15 human casualties. Therefore it is not only the fury or intensity of any hazard that is responsible for the loss of life and property; there are other factors such as poor physical infrastructure, high vulnerability, low capacity and, most important of all, a poor state of governance.

Even after the adoption of the Hyogo Framework for Action (HFA) at the Second United Nations World Conference on Disaster Reduction in Kobe in 2005, declarations made at several sessions of the Global Platform for Disaster Risk Reduction and the Asian Ministerial Conferences on Disaster Risk Reduction, and following billions of dollars having been spent in the name of disaster management, hardly any significant impact on the lives and livelihood of people in vulnerable communities has been made. It has been observed that in the developing countries, the same communities are affected every time disasters strike their locality.

The major areas of financial investment for disaster management have been post-disaster emergency relief and rehabilitation operations, physical infrastructure development, procurement of equipment and machinery, as well as capacity development for practitioners (Kellett and Caravani 2013). A large amount of money also goes on hiring very highly paid "consultants." We must understand that the "trickle-down" theory has hardly been successful in developing countries and cannot be expected to be so in the future. Unfortunately, until now only minimal investment has gone towards reaching a real solution: sustainable poverty reduction and risk reduction for disadvantaged communities, led by those communities themselves.

Disaster managers are rarely affected by any disaster – rather, disasters create opportunities for them. In any developing country, it is the poor and disadvantaged communities which are always affected by disasters, not the rich and powerful ones. If we want to reduce the risk for vulnerable communities, we have got to understand their problems. Their basic problem is not disasters per se, but poverty. There is an urgent need to appreciate that many poor people in developing countries have no other option but to live in high disaster risk areas. They are obliged to work in such areas just to earn a living, while all the time they are being heavily exploited economically, socially and politically.

Disasters should not be seen in isolation. Any effort aimed at sustained disaster risk reduction must address the root causes of poverty. It must contribute to the establishment of good governance in the economic, social and political spheres. The focus should be on the empowerment of the communities at risk. There should never be a purely top-down approach; all problems should be tackled simultaneously at national and grassroots levels. The communities should be capacitated so that they themselves can identify and prioritize their risks, plan for mitigation and treat the risk factors, because only they know where the shoe pinches. Ultimately, using human rights principles and good governance tools, they should be empowered enough to have direct access to and control over the public resources allocated for them. This is the only solution to breaking the vicious cycle of poverty and disasters.

Three case studies from Bangladesh are presented in this chapter. The first one examines a permanent organization of volunteers who disseminate cyclone early warnings. This highlights the value of investing in community people over the long term. The efficacy of the "People, Private and Public Partnership" (4P) approach is showcased in the second study. The final case study deals with the "bottom-up and top-down" approach, showing how, using public resources, disadvantaged communities can be empowered through the establishment and practice of good governance and social accountability in public service agencies, in order to reduce their vulnerability in the long term.

Case Study 1 – Volunteerism in disaster management: an example from Bangladesh

The number 500,000 is not just a meaningless statistic (Ghosh 2011); it is the approximate number of human lives that were lost during the worst hydrometeorological disaster in the recorded history of the world.[1] The cyclone struck the coastal belt and the offshore islands of Bangladesh on November 12, 1970. The root cause for this colossal loss of lives is the failure on the part of the then public authorities to warn the people at risk in advance and evacuate them to safe places (the present territory of Bangladesh was at that time a part of Pakistan called East Pakistan; the country earned its independence through a war of liberation in 1971). That disaster highlighted the urgent need to establish an effective national cyclone management system, focusing in particular on the dissemination of early warnings.

Bangladesh, due to its geographical location, is subject to a number of natural hazards such as cyclones, floods, tidal surges, riverbank erosion and more. The funnel-shaped coastline facing the Bay of Bengal makes the country highly vulnerable to cyclones. On average, Bangladesh is affected by at least one severe cyclone every 3 years. The most recent ones have been Sidr (2007), Aila (2009) and Mahasen (2013).

Natural hazards affect people unevenly. Due to their poor socioeconomic conditions, disadvantaged communities are worst affected and suffer the most. Poverty is the key element that compels people to live in areas with a high disaster risk, and at the same time makes them more vulnerable, reducing their ability to bounce back. As Edwin Louis Cole once said, "You don't drown by falling in the water; you drown by staying there."[2]

The impact of any natural hazard can be significantly reduced through structural and non-structural measures. The first one requires billions of dollars for investment in physical infrastructure development, namely the provision of embankments, dykes, reinforced concrete shelters, cyclone-resistant houses, raised roads, etc. Resource-constrained developing countries like Bangladesh should employ a combination of both structural and non-structural measures. Maximum attention should be paid to non-structural measures including early warning dissemination, family- and community-level preparedness and so on. One of the best examples of successful investment in people and use of non-structural measures is Bangladesh's widely acclaimed Cyclone Preparedness Programme (CPP). This has managed to ignite and sustain the fire of volunteerism in tens of thousands of poor and middle-class people living in disaster-prone areas. It clearly demonstrates how investment in people can be highly effective in the field of disaster management, having a sustained and long-term effect, especially in a low-income country like Bangladesh.

Following the devastating cyclone of 1970, the United Nations mandated the International Federation of Red Cross and Red Crescent Societies (previously known as the League of Red Cross Societies) to establish and run the cyclone early warning system in Bangladesh. LORCS started the program in 24 high cyclone risk subdistricts. The program involved approximately 20,000 volunteers, ten from each of the villages under the program area. The volunteers are usually respected men and women, aged between 18 and 60, and engaged in different professions (e.g., farming, teaching, small business, etc.) in normal times. In 1973, having appreciated the effectiveness of the Cyclone Preparedness Programme in saving human lives, the Government of Bangladesh took over responsibility for covering all the recurring expenses of the program. Today, CPP has a volunteer base 50,000 strong (comprising 15 volunteers in every village: ten male and five female) and covers all of the 13 districts in the coastal area. While the program is very much Red Cross in nature, it is administered jointly by the government and the National Red Crescent Society.

The essence of the CPP is its spirit of volunteerism. During the emergency phase just before the storm, when the sky is covered with dark clouds of uncertainty, the volunteers disseminate early warnings to the communities at risk and encourage families to move to safer places. Quite often they risk their own lives to save the lives of their fellow villagers. In addition to giving out warning messages, the volunteers are responsible for evacuating people to shelters, conducting search-and-rescue operations, providing first aid to the injured and supporting other agencies during the rollout of post-disaster response operations. During the time between emergencies, the volunteers are given extensive training in different aspects of disaster management so as to ensure a high level of performance in times of crisis. The CPP also conducts massive public awareness programs, including disaster simulations centering on the cyclone shelters.

As soon as a depression is known to have formed in the Bay of Bengal, warnings of possible cyclones are generated by the Bangladesh Meteorological Department and transmitted to the headquarters of CPP. The CPP head office passes the message on to all its field-level officers by single sideband and HF radio. In turn the warnings are conveyed to the village-level volunteer teams through the volunteer team leader at the union, the lowest administrative level. The village volunteers keep track of the movement of the cyclone through the special weather bulletins broadcast continuously by state-owned radio and television. When the danger warnings are announced, the volunteers disseminate the warning to each and every household at risk, by hoisting flags in prominent places, sounding sirens and making announcements by megaphone, or through face-to-face contact. When major danger signals are being given out at the height of the hazard, volunteers help vulnerable elements of the population (such as the aged, children, disabled people, pregnant and lactating mothers) to evacuate to purpose-built cyclone shelters. Immediately after the cyclone has moved on and the surge of seawater has receded, the volunteers conduct intensive search-and-rescue operations to recover missing people and those who are trapped or wounded. In post-disaster response operations, particularly during the emergency survival phase, the contribution of volunteers is enormous. In circumstances likely to cause trauma and panic, the presence of volunteers, with their discipline and positive spirit, instills courage, patience and hope in the remainder of the population.

The Government of Bangladesh has recognized and institutionalized the roles and responsibilities of the CPP in its Standing Orders on Disasters and this has given added value to the program. The structure and management of the CPP, an organization of volunteers, has been acclaimed all over the world, and is being replicated in various cyclone-prone countries. The CPP plays an important and crucial part in strengthening the disaster management system of Bangladesh. "The statistics speak an impressive language. In 1970, half a million vanished in a super-cyclone. In the 1991 cyclone, around 139,000 people lost their lives. In 2007, 3363 people died. Lastly, in cyclone Mahasen only 17 people succumbed." This reduction in the casualty figures, from the BDRCS website, is a testament to the noble and effective work of the CPP (Bangladesh Red Crescent Society 2014).

"It's good to be blessed. It's better to be a blessing" (Jerry Smith).[3] The volunteers of the Cyclone Preparedness Programme are indeed a blessing to over 11 million people living in high cyclone risk areas. In the devastating cyclone of 1991, 23 CPP volunteers were killed while discharging their duties in the course of a real-time emergency operation. Since its establishment in 1972, the CPP has not only survived through four turbulent decades but also expanded its area of operation and increased the number of volunteers. Today 50,000 volunteers are giving their time for free – a remarkable statistic in a low-income country like Bangladesh. At the heart of the program's success and sustainability lies the dedication, commitment and spirit of service of the volunteers. In return they get immense satisfaction and a huge amount of recognition and appreciation from the communities they serve.

Although there has been some erosion in values due to the present market economy and competition from NGOs offering attractive pocket money or wages, the commitment and dedication of CPP's volunteers remain exemplary. For people to help one another in times of crisis is part of the tradition and culture in this part of the world. The Cyclone Preparedness Programme has endured for 42 years, and hopefully will continue for many more years to come. It remains a perfect example of the benefit of investing in people and inculcating the spirit of volunteerism in their hearts.

Case Study 2 – Sustained livelihood for disaster vulnerability reduction: the 4P approach

Bangladesh, often referred to as a "supermarket of disasters," has put in place an effective system and structure for disaster management. Starting with the National Disaster Management Council headed by the Prime Minister, down to the lowest level of local government, there are a number of committees at different levels charged with responsibilities for various aspects of disaster management including risk reduction, preparedness and dealing with the aftermath of a disaster. Ever since Bangladesh achieved independence in 1971, there has been a ministry dedicated to disaster management. The country is well equipped with the relevant legislative framework, policy guidelines, standing orders, and several other instruments and tools for disaster management. One such tool is the widely used and replicated set of Community Risk Assessment (CRA) guidelines. The case study presented below will show how CRA findings have been incorporated into the Local Disaster Action Plan (LDAP) and led to the adoption of the "People, Private and Public Partnership (4P)" approach towards alleviation of poverty, which has made a major contribution to the reduction in disaster vulnerability.

Morrelganj is a remote subdistrict in the south-western coastal area of Bangladesh. Adjacent to the Bay of Bengal and the vast mangrove forest of the Sundarbans, it is prone to cyclones, tidal surges and the impacts of climate change. Due to a high level of salinity in the soil, crops can be cultivated only once a year, during the monsoon season. The only source of drinking water in the area is open-air ponds. Currently, 44 percent of the population live below the poverty line. Disasters often have an adverse effect on the livelihood of the people of this area, which results in an increased vulnerability to subsequent disasters. Despite comprehending the precariousness of their situation, people continue to live in vulnerable areas as they have few other options – they live there just to earn a living. Disaster management initiatives often ignore the fact that greater focus should be given to building the capacity of the poor through creating more livelihood options. It may easily be assumed that people will spend more on disaster risk reduction to save their lives and property when they have sufficient savings. However, it will be the lowest priority for them as day-to-day survival must take precedence.

A national non-governmental organization, the Bangladesh Disaster Preparedness Centre (BDPC), is implementing an integrated disaster management project in Morrelganj entitled "Community-Based DRR and CCA Fortified Livelihood Initiatives through Good Governance." It aims to reduce the disaster risk by alleviating poverty through the empowerment of vulnerable communities. Among various activities planned and implemented, a community risk assessment (CRA) was conducted in the village of Amorbunia by the local communities themselves. As per the standard grammar of CRA, it comprised focus group discussions (FGDs), social mapping (identifying vulnerabilities and resources), preparation of seasonal calendars, hazard ranking, and finally the development of a Risk Reduction Action Plan (RRAP). The CRA highlighted the lack of sustained employment and year-round means of livelihood as the main cause for the people's low level of capacity and high level of vulnerability to climate-induced hazards. Inadequate supply of water for human and animal consumption as well as for the irrigation of paddy fields was flagged as the immediate problem to be addressed. The exercise identified a derelict canal, silted up to the level of the adjacent paddy fields, as a potential source of water. As required in any CRA, the community people prepared an RRAP focusing on the excavation of the approximately 3,000-foot-long canal.

Initially, this gigantic project appeared to be an almost impossible task for a poor community. Right from the planning stage, the CRA and its findings were shared with the entire community in order to develop a sense of ownership. The RRAP was then discussed with the local disaster management committees and elected leaders of the local government institutions. Through the neighborhood office of the lowest tier of civil administration, an application for matching financial support was submitted to the national-level Comprehensive Disaster Management Programme (CDMP) of the Government of Bangladesh. From the planning stage onward, a series of consultations, meetings and advocacy initiatives were conducted to ensure the continued involvement of all the concerned agencies. The process is summarized in Figure 9.1. The project at last bore fruit when the Amorbunia Canal (2,700 feet long, 30 feet wide and 10 feet deep) was dug manually during the months of March to June 2012 with the contribution of the following stakeholder organizations at a total financial cost of US$20,000.

1   *Local community*: The people played the key role in planning, implementing and supervising the project. They effectively contributed voluntary labor by digging the canal at a rate of pay 50 percent lower than the existing government rate.
2   *Civil society*: Although BDPC's financial contribution amounted to only 19 percent of the total cost, its role in anchoring the entire project and mobilizing support at the national level was crucially important.

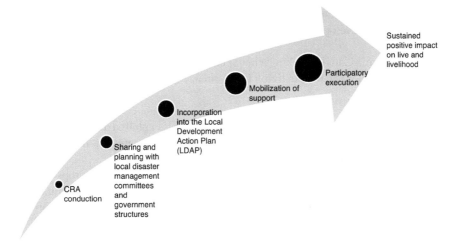

Figure 9.1 The chronological steps of excavation of Amorbunia Canal
Source: Author.

3 *Local government*: The organs of local government (at grassroots level, the Union Parishad and at subdistrict level, the Upazila Parishad) conducted a Food for Work Programme (FFW) through which 19 percent of the total cost was covered

4 *Central government*: CDMP is a US$79 million project of the Government of Bangladesh, funded by various multilateral and bilateral development partners. It made a financial contribution equivalent to 62 percent of the total cost.

Once the excavation of the canal was completed (see Figures 9.2 and 9.3), the real program for the improvement of livelihood of the poor people in the area, ultimately leading to a reduction in their disaster vulnerability, began with the support of the public service agencies as follows:

- The Department of Forestry of the Government of Bangladesh supplied 10,000 saplings of different shrubs and trees free of charge, for planting on the sides of the earthen road that had been constructed alongside the canal using excavated earth.
- The Department of Fisheries supplied 45 kilograms of fish fry, once again free of charge, to help start up a pisciculture program.
- The Department of Agricultural Extension, part of the Ministry of Agriculture, conducted several capacity-building programmes for small and marginal farmers in the area.
- The Livestock Department arranged a vaccination program for cattle and poultry.

- Various NGOs are making their own contributions by operating socio-economic development programs.

The Amorbunia Canal is making a major contribution to the improvement of life and livelihood for the people living in the area. Some aspects worth mentioning are as follows:

- The huge water reservoir created by the project is exploited as a reliable year-round source of water for both human and cattle consumption. It is also used for irrigation of crops in the dry season.
- For the first time, the farmers are able to produce two paddy crops a year instead of only one, and also grow vegetables in the dry season. The number of farmers engaged in paddy cultivation has tripled since the excavation of the canal.
- Seasonal unemployment was a major problem in the area contributing to increased poverty and high disaster vulnerability. Production of two crops and the vegetable gardening have created and secured a steady employment for landless laborers and this has reduced their seasonal migration to cities.
- The income levels of farmers and landless laborers have been increasing significantly.
- The services of various public service agencies have started flowing down to the people in need.
- A significant enhancement of the local environment has been achieved, and this has also helped to maintain biodiversity.
- People now have a greater level of confidence in their ability to access public resources, and awareness of their right to do so.

Thanks to the factors mentioned above, the people's vulnerability to disaster has been reduced significantly.

"Climate related impacts will continue to grow due to both development and climate drivers" (IPCC 2013). Therefore, long-term preparation for disaster resilience is imperative to protect the lives and livelihoods of millions of households in the coastal region of Bangladesh. This is not a task that can be accomplished by the government alone.

The project discussed above was a People, Private and Public Partnership (4P) approach in the truest sense of the term: it aimed at the betterment of lives and livelihoods for a disadvantaged coastal community. Now there is a felt need to scale up such initiatives to ensure sustained empowerment of all vulnerable communities, leading to the alleviation of poverty and reduction of their disaster vulnerabilities.

Case Study 3 – Disaster management and good governance

Disasters are not natural, but the result of failure on the part of public authorities to deliver proper development services. Billions of dollars are given to Third

Figure 9.2 Amorbunia Canal, before re-excavation
Source: Photo credit – Naimul Islam Moon, BDPC.

Figure 9.3 Amorbunia Canal, after re-excavation
Source: Photo credit – Naimul Islam Moon, BDPC.

World governments every year by multilateral and bilateral development agencies as development aid and soft loans (Kellett and Caravani 2013). Unfortunately, such a huge transfer of wealth has resulted in hardly any significant positive impacts either in terms of socioeconomic development or reduction of disaster risk for the people in the lowest economic strata of society. Rather, it has been widening the gap between rich and poor, the haves and the have nots, the powerful and the powerless. The "trickle-down" theory of development aid has proved, in most cases, to be a failure in practice.

The root cause of disaster vulnerability among people living in disaster risk areas is poverty. People living below the poverty line are at much greater risk than others, and they are more inescapably affected by disasters. Disaster management agencies merely offer them relief and temporary support with rehabilitation. The poor remain trapped in a vicious cycle of poverty and disaster. Each disaster pushes them further down and helps to perpetuate their poverty.

It is ultimately the responsibility of the government of a country, not of civil society organizations, to protect the lives and livelihoods of its people against disasters and ensure continued development. In countries where democracy is not being practiced in the truest sense of the term, public service agencies tend not to be responsive to the needs of their citizens. The situation is even worse in countries that have a legacy of colonial rule. Good governance and social accountability are often alien to the culture of public administration in such countries. At the same time, many people living in developing countries are unaware of their constitutional rights, entitlements and privileges. Nor are they aware of their potential power as a political class. This lack of awareness limits their ability to establish their rights and gain access to public resources, to change their lives and livelihoods for the better.

Conscious of the factors outlined above, the Bangladesh Disaster Preparedness Centre is trying in its own humble way to introduce the concept of good governance and social accountability in disaster risk management, by focusing on empowerment of the communities living in high disaster risk areas, engagement with service-providing agencies and the creation of a congenial environment for constructive interaction between the two stakeholder groups. The activities supported by BDPC projects in high flood and cyclone risk areas include but are not limited to the following:

- formation of right-based groups with 40 chronically poor people, 20 males and 20 females, in every village in the project areas;
- selection of two volunteers per village, who are trusted and respected by their local community, as Change Agents;
- formation of volunteer advocacy groups of 20 members in each of the subdistricts of the project areas with the socially respected and powerful ones;
- intensive training of the group members and Change Agents in various aspects of social accountability and good governance (e.g., constitutional

rights, human rights, right to information (RTI), public hearing meeting (PHM), community scorecard (CSC), etc.);

- orientation and training in disaster management, focusing in particular on the reduction of vulnerability and enhancement of capacity;
- strategic planning, involving methods of gaining access to public resources;
- interaction of the groups with service providers, including both local- and national-level government service-providing agencies.

In each project, intensive efforts are put into serious engagement with those public service-providing agencies that are directly relevant to the lives and livelihoods of the poor: for example, the Departments of Agriculture, Livestock, Health, Education, Disaster Management, etc. Responsible officers of the departments are given orientation and training in good governance and social accountability tools, especially in how to ensure the delivery of services at the lowest level. Direct linkages between service providers and service recipients are made and facilitated through various activities of the project.

Internationally accepted and nationally approved social accountability tools, especially designed and developed for project beneficiaries, are used and promoted. These include public hearing meetings, community scorecards, participatory selection process, citizens' charter (CC) and right to information (RTI). Some of the tools are briefly described below.

Public hearing meeting (PHM)

A public hearing, as the name suggests, is a unique tool that creates a platform for the public to interact directly with service providers. It is often the case that the people in a community are deprived of their rights, and the services they receive from service providers are below standard, failing to meet their needs and expectations. The public hearing platform creates a scope for open discussions, where service recipients can raise questions with the service providers. For their part, the service providers can explain the problems and limitations they face in providing their services. The objectives of this tool are to improve the quality of services, to make service providers more accountable for their actions and to build a bond between the two stakeholder groups: recipients and providers. This tool also gives ordinary people a chance to raise their voices and change the mindset of the service providers. PHMs are playing a crucial role in establishing good governance at a local level.

Community scorecard (CSC)

The community scorecard is another interesting tool that is used to measure the level of satisfaction of communities regarding the services given by the service providers. This tool also helps the group to later appraise their own performance, enabling them to address their shortcomings. The objective of this tool is to identify gaps and upgrade the quality of services. Once scores have been given, an

Table 9.1 Sample of an action plan based on scorecard results

Sl*	Indicator	Score by service providers	Score by public	Recommendation	Planning	Timeline	Responsible person/ organization
1	Timely delivery of fertilizer	80	30	**Service recipient** – Increase the amount of fertilizer – Ensure fair price in the market – On time delivery of fertilizers **Service provider** – Coordinate with associated departments to increase the allocation of fertilizers – Display the price list of the fertilizers in front of the stores	– Apply to the associated department to increase the allocation and ensure timely delivery of fertilizer. – Hang the price list of the fertilizers in front of the stores	Starting from January 2013	Subdistrict Executive Officer and Agriculture Officer

Source: Author.

Note: *Serial number.

interface meeting is held where the two parties confront each other and discuss the reasons behind the scores. On the basis of the scorecard results, an action plan is developed in which commitments and responsibilities are laid out so as to facilitate an improvement in the delivery and quality of services. CSC has been successful in enhancing transparency, accountability and responsiveness in service providers, ensuring consumers' access to public resources.

Participatory selection process (PSP)

The participatory selection process (PSP) is a procedure that involves the engagement of the local community in selecting beneficiaries for welfare benefits such as a vulnerable group development (VGD) card or the various welfare allowances (for elderly, widowed or disabled persons) provided by the Government of Bangladesh under its Social Safety Net Programme. This process is carried out in public, and the service providers select the beneficiaries. The poorest among the poor are selected by the applicants themselves in front of the entire community. PSP ensures accountability and transparency in the process of service delivery.

The social accountability tools adopted in the project have been a huge success and have brought about some remarkable results, among which are the following:

- It has built awareness among the members of the rights-based groups and boosted their confidence that their voice can make a difference. They are playing active roles in claiming services.
- The Change Agents are acting as a catalyst in establishing rights of the community. They are taking part in different awareness-building activities.
- Advocacy groups are lobbying with the government service providers to solve the problems identified by the rights-based groups.
- Service providers are becoming accountable and aware of their responsibilities. Agricultural officers are conducting capacity-building activities and also ensuring transparency in the delivery of services, such as making sure that the dealers are selling the fertilizers at government-fixed rates. Livestock officers are conducting vaccination campaigns for cattle and poultry. Education officers are responding to the need to ensure quality education.

The projects in which the non-governmental organization BDPC is acting purely as a catalyst are having considerable success in improving the delivery of public services to the people in need. Positive efforts are now being made in Bangladesh, in both public and civil society institutions, to replicate this model and roll out similar initiatives at the national level in such a way as to fully cover the social, economic and political spheres. These programs are playing very important roles in the betterment of the lives and livelihoods of the poor community, and have a long-term impact upon poverty alleviation, which ultimately leads to reduction of vulnerability to disasters.

Conclusion

These stories from Bangladesh, a country perennially prone to disasters, reaffirm the truth that socio-political empowerment of vulnerable communities and practice of good governance in the public sector will not only ensure a reduction in climate-induced disaster risks, but also sustain social and political growth and stability in developing countries. At present the political, economic and disaster management systems in many Third World countries are neither aimed at the poor nor orientated towards poverty reduction, and hence cannot realistically be expected to promote democracy, economic stability or risk reduction.

Now is the time when we have to come out of the box and think up new ideas. In the world today, resources are not a problem, but the mindset of leaders most certainly is. The need to understand and appreciate the danger of poverty and the potential power of poor communities once liberated from their disadvantages has never been more urgent. We must start to take a holistic approach to disaster risk management, based on the needs and priorities of disadvantaged communities. Encouragement, support and resources must be channeled towards those initiatives and programs that are planned, led and executed by the communities themselves. Only then can we expect a better world in the future.

Recommendation

Poor communities in the developing world are trapped in the vicious cycle of poverty and disaster. As such, any effort aiming at sustained community resilience must address the root causes of poverty through a combination of bottom-up and top-down approaches. The disadvantaged communities must be empowered to have access to and control over the public resources to change their lives for the better. The service-providing agencies must adhere to the principles of good governance in delivering the services to the people in need.

Audiences of the recommendation: Communities/citizens, NGOs, city governments, national governments, donors, international agencies, the United Nations secretariat of the ISDR.

Notes

1 The 35 Deadliest Tropical Cyclones in World History (Deadliest World Tropical Cyclones). www.wunderground.com/hurricane/deadlyworld.asp.
2 www.brainyquote.com/quotes/quotes/e/edwinlouis170162.html.
3 www.quotesdonkey.com/217-help-quotes/15569-its-good-to-be-blessed/.

References

Bangladeshi Red Crescent Society. 2014. In Between Cyclones: Cyclone Preparedness Program. Last updated May 8, 2014. www.bdrcs.org/news/between-cyclones.

Ghosh, Palash. 2011. Hurricane Watch: 1970 Cyclone in Bangladesh Killed 500,000 (International Business Times). www.ibtimes.com/ hurricane-watch-1970-cyclone-bangladesh-killed-500000-302837.

IPCC. 2013. *Climate Change 2013: The Physical Science Basis. Summary for Policy Makers.* Working Group I Contribution to the IPCC Fifth Assessment Report.

Kellett, Jan and Caravani, Alice. 2013. Financing Disaster Risk Reduction: A 20 Year Story of International Aid. www.odi.org.uk/sites/odi.org.uk/files/odi-assets/publications-opinion-files/8574.pdf.

World Food Program. Bangladesh Poverty Map 2005. www.foodsecurityatlas.org/bgd/country/food-security-at-a-glance.

10 The role of the private sector in disaster risk management following catastrophic events

Hitoshi Baba and Toshiyuki Shimano

Introduction

Following a disaster, rapid regeneration of local industry as part of the rehabilitation and reconstruction phases is essential in the reconstruction of people's living environments and the normalization of socioeconomic activities. Any impacts of disasters upon the industrial sector are likely to have significant effects on the local economy, causing loss of employment and population outflow in particular, and resulting in impacts that may spread throughout the country. Therefore, raising local economic resilience to disasters is an important issue not only for local governments but also for nations. The Great East Japan Earthquake and Tsunami in 2011, for example, put an incredible strain on the national economy and also had global impacts throughout the supply chains of industry. The disaster severely disrupted the supply of Japanese-made vehicle parts to automobile assembly plants, forcing Toyota, GM and major automotive manufacturers around the world to shut down production for a lengthy period of time (Ando and Kimura 2012). The 2011 Flood of Chao Phraya River in Thailand again was a further reminder of the risks of business disruptions, with impacts upon national, regional and global economies through their supply chains (Komori *et al.* 2012).

Studies have shown that preventive investments in risk reduction and emergency preparedness are extremely cost-effective and can greatly reduce the impact of natural hazards (Jha and Stanton-Geddes 2013). Considering the recent increases in economic damage caused by disasters and recognizing the importance of the private sector as an actor and partner in disaster management, the Global Platform for Disaster Risk Reduction (2013), organized by the United Nations, concluded that it is essential to promote economic resilience and foster new opportunities for public–private partnerships as part of overall improved risk governance. It also highlighted agendas including the efforts of the private sector to progressively align risk reduction efforts and develop business practices that promote resilience. The most significant contribution by the private sector for economic resilience has been the development of business continuity plan/planning (BCP) or the business continuity management (BCM) system (BCMS). A BCMS refers to any effort that aims to achieve business continuity by engaging in whatever is considered necessary to protect a company's production, information, equipment and employees. The BCP or BCM systems are standardized as ISO22301 (ISO 2012) and disseminated through many business enterprises around the world.

However, many business enterprises have shown little interest in taking action towards disaster preparedness. BCPs or BCMS have not yet been formulated or implemented in the majority of local enterprises in many of the industry-agglomerated areas that are located in areas vulnerable to disasters. At the same time, those enterprises are still interconnected through the global supply chain. When a major disaster occurs, the damage may extend to roads, power supplies and other infrastructure. Disruption of these common resources often results in bottlenecks for effective business continuity across widespread areas. Therefore, the efforts of individual companies, even if BCPs are prepared, may be insufficient to achieve the desired level of business continuity. In order to minimize economic impacts or losses, particularly in cases of large-scale disasters that disrupt fundamental infrastructure across extensive areas, it is important to carry out risk assessments at a proper scale and to develop scenario-based contingency plans for regional damage mitigation. In addition, it is vital to have integrated resource management and strategic recovery plans that could support each enterprise's BCM actions in coordination with the public sector's activities.

Some studies have suggested that further research on area-wide management of business continuity is required. Warren (2010) found that a significant number of public sector authorities are not preparing integrated disaster management plans or BCPs. He noted that further research is necessary into the impact of disasters on assets, and the role of public sector management of certain areas in assessing the risks, as well as strategies to prepare coordination frameworks and to mitigate against the effects of natural disasters and severe catastrophic events.

In conjunction with recent economic growth, particularly in ASEAN countries, there has been a rapid development of industrial agglomerated areas. As explained below, these industry agglomerations are mostly located in coastal areas for transportation convenience and industry integration effectiveness. But at the same time these locations are vulnerable to natural disasters as well as to the increasing risk of catastrophe. This has led to an understanding of the necessity of area-wide business continuity management.

Based on this, JICA developed the new concept of Area Business Continuity Plans (Area BCPs) and Area Business Continuity Management (Area BCM) to improve continuity in the local economy in times of disaster. The feasibility of the concept was tested and confirmed in a study entitled "Natural Disaster Risk Assessment and Area Business Continuity Plan Formulation for Industrial Agglomerated Areas in the ASEAN Region," which JICA launched in February 2013 in collaboration with the ASEAN Coordination Centre for Humanitarian Assistance (AHA Centre) (Baba *et al.* 2013). Area BCP/BCM refers to the efforts of an area that aim to prevent economic stagnation of the targeted area regardless of the circumstances. To achieve this goal, cooperation between the private sector, national government, municipalities, operators of infrastructure and utilities in the area is necessary. Area BCM also requires a process of scientific assessment, as a part of the management cycle, in order to develop a common understanding of risks and impacts in the area which should be based on a multi-hazard, multi-scenario and probabilistic analysis. The initiative intends to strengthen the resilience of local economies, as well as regional and ultimately global economies.

This chapter aims to introduce the concept of Area BCP/BCM, provide case studies of its application in industry agglomerated areas of ASEAN, and examine the prospects of the private sector's role as a proactive actor of disaster management in local economies. Utilization of the Area BCP/BCM approach will provide a new opportunity for building economic resilience to disaster.

"Area BCP" and "Area BCM": new opportunities for improving economic resilience

Before introducing the new concepts of the Area BCP and Area BCM, it is worth re-examining the existing BCP or BCM approaches, which are internationally recognized as important systems for sustaining business continuation of a single business entity following a disaster. The limitations of these systems will then be underscored by considering how common business resources, which all the businesses in industry area may depend on, can be vulnerable to disruptions. This section, therefore, provides an argumentative basis for introducing the new concepts of Area BCPs and Area BCM.

Existing BCP/BCM approaches as disaster management systems for single entities

Once a natural disaster has hampered or damaged a business, it is self-evident that a certain amount of time will be required for that business to recover and to return to a level of production sufficient for trading to take place. The recovery process may be disrupted due to the loss and lack of business resources such as personnel, machinery, electricity, gas and water. Other indirect effects may include increased expenses, lack of demand, short-term loss of market share, travel difficulties, involvement in recovery operations, loss of production efficiency, loss of supplies, and withdrawal of licenses, as well as loss of quality accreditation or approved standards. For many businesses, these impacts can be catastrophic.

A business continuity plan, or BCP, is a documented plan that describes methods and means to continue or quickly re-establish "core businesses" (high-priority business operations) in an emergency situation, as well as preparatory actions by each subjective enterprise (Figure 10.1). BCP describes tactics to minimize the above-mentioned loss and lack of business resources in an emergency (Ministry of Economy, Trade and Industry, Japan, 2012). A BCM, on the other hand, is a framework for identifying an organization's risk of exposure to internal and external threats. The goal of a BCM is to provide the organization with the ability to effectively respond to threats such as natural disasters or data breaches and protect the business interests of the organization.

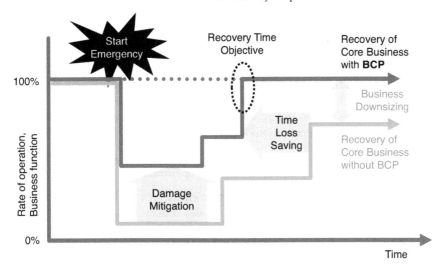

Figure 10.1 Concept of Business Continuity Plan (BCP)
Source: Author (H. Baba, original).

According to ISO 22301, a BCM system emphasizes the importance of the following:

• understanding continuity and preparedness needs, as well as the necessity to establish BCM policies and objectives;
• implementing and operating controls and measures for managing an organization's overall continuity risks;
• monitoring and reviewing the performance and effectiveness of the business continuity management system;
• continual improvement based on objective measurements.

A BCP or BCM is however designed to be a single organization's internal document and framework. It simply seeks to protect an organization's profits from the risk of exposure to internal and external threats. The purpose of the system in private companies, as mentioned in the standard guides, may be considered as being 'competitive' with other companies, rather than 'cooperative' in the locality where the company operates. Another limitation of the BCP/BCM is that the assumption of the threats is rather more vague than scientific. It normally starts from considering how to mitigate the "business impact" caused by any unspecified threat of disaster, accident, power or energy disruption, lifeline service failure, terror or cyber-attacks, etc. The process is nebulous, because organizations seldom have the ability to analyze the threat or hazard, or to assess its area-wide impacts. The prospect of a severe accident, such as total devastation of the power network in a wide area for a long period following a large-scale disaster, for example, is normally beyond the scope of analysis.

The limitations of conventional BCPs or BCM systems were really self-evident following the Great East Japan Earthquake and the flood of the Chao Phraya River in Thailand (Okada 2011). Some prearranged BCPs/BCMs in private enterprises helped them survive to some extent but overall, the plans failed to provide a sufficient basis for the continuation of business or quick recovery from damage (Sato and Bessho 2011). This was due mainly to the disruption of area-wide installed common resources such as energy, water, transportation and communications that are essential for business operations (Special Study Team 2011).

Internal and external resources for business operations

When a large-scale flood strikes, inundating entire areas, it has the potential to cause major damage to factories. In that case, companies and industrial parks must repair and replace damaged machinery to restart operations. However, their business cannot be re-established solely through a company's efforts. For a company to continue its business, the restoration of public infrastructure such as power supplies, water supplies, roads, ports and airports is essential.

Analyzing the causes of operation cessation in recent large-scale disaster cases, the elements of business resources that are crucial for production and distribution may be classified into internal and external ones (Table 10.1). Internal resources, such as a company's buildings, facilities, parts and raw materials, are under the control of each enterprise. External resources, on the other hand, such as energy, water and transportation infrastructures, are normally managed by the public sector and are not under the control of private enterprises. External resources are also distributed not only for business purposes but also for securing community life. Therefore, following emergencies, limitations on the allocation of those resources may be imposed. In such cases, collaborative efforts may be required between the private sector, public sector and the local community.

The absence of some external resources may result in common bottlenecks for effective business continuity across a wide area following a disaster. Disruption of transportation systems, for example, could force all companies to halt the

Table 10.1 Internal and external resources

	Human	Component	Finance	Information
Internal resources	Managers, workers, employees	Buildings and facilities, equipment, parts and raw materials, fuels	Money account system, assets	Computer systems, operation data, archives
External resources	Public officers and workers	Energy (electricity, gas), water (supply, sanitation and sewerage), transportation (road and rail, ports, airports, etc.)	Banking Transaction system	Internet, telephone and fax, communication systems

Source: Author (H. Baba, original).

delivery of products and parts. It may also lead to situations where workers and staff become stranded in the place they were when the event occurred. If the recovery process is lengthy, and they are unable to commute back home, the area may suffer difficulties resulting from lack of food, water, accommodation and a safe environment for the workers. However, if area-wide measures for stranded people have been prepared by the public sector or by some major enterprises, they can effectively solve the problem through area-wide coordination.

Concept of "Area BCP" and "Area BCM"

The term "Area BCP" has been derived from "Area Command," an organizational structure designated under the National Incident Management System (NIMS) of the Federal Emergency Management Agency (FEMA) in the United States (Waugh 2009). Area command is used to oversee the management of multiple incidents or a major incident that requires multiple incident command systems (ICS) or management teams to establish critical resource-use priorities between various incidents and to coordinate disaster management actions. ICS is a subcomponent of the NIMS, as established by the US Department of Homeland Security in 2004. It was designed to give standard response and operation procedures to reduce the problems and potential for miscommunication during incidents.

The Area BCP designates a framework for the direction of coordinated damage mitigation measures and recovery actions of stakeholders, including individual enterprises, industrial area managers, local authorities and administrators of the relevant infrastructure in order to enable business continuation of the industrial area as a whole (Figure 10.2).

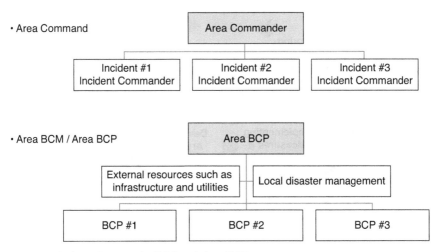

Figure 10.2 Area Command of ICS and Area BCP

Source: Author (H. Baba, original).

Since the term and concept of the "Area Command" has already been adopted by many countries, including the US, and following the spatial scope of emergency management that "area" indicates, our definition of the new concept uses the same term to designate a framework and direction of area-wide disaster management as above. Similar to the Area Command in terms of management scale, the Area BCP coordinates multiple BCPs by different enterprises in the affected area. As a point of comparison, management of external resources and relevant coordinated actions of disaster management should be conducted under the coordination of the Area BCP.

The Area BCM then is defined as a cyclical process of understanding risks and impacts, determining common strategies for risk management, developing the Area BCP, implementing the planned actions and monitoring to continuously improve the Area BCM System, in coordination with stakeholders, in order to improve the capacity of the effective business continuity of the area (Figure 10.3).

Area BCM and local disaster management (ICS)

An ICS is based on a changeable, scalable response organization providing a common hierarchy within which people can work together effectively. These people may be drawn from multiple agencies that do not routinely work together.

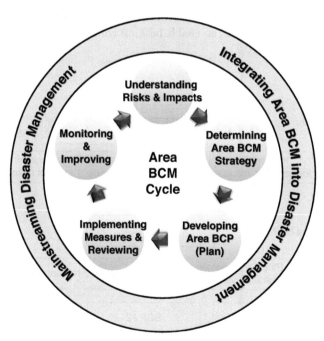

Figure 10.3 Area BCM Cycle
Source: JICA study team (2013).

Similarly, the scale of the Area BCM system must be dynamic so that it can expand or be reduced in response to the scale of disaster impacts and the operational situation. In practice, it is difficult to predetermine the size of an area with a changing and uncertain disaster occurrence. As with Area Command, the affected area size and levels of emergency depend on the magnitude of the disaster. Therefore, the coordination structure of Area BCM should be organized in such a way as to expand as needed based on the prospective damage, the availability of critical resources and changing hazards. Coordination hubs should be established with the most important and authoritative positions of local and national government as well as the management organization of an industrial cluster. In this command structure, the "multi-stakeholder risk management system", which is one aspect of the Area BCM, may normally involve serious conflicts of interests among stakeholders. Therefore, preparation of a conflict management policy is also necessary.

The maximum size of the coordination of an Area BCM should not exceed the scale of local disaster management (ICS) that will be required to oversee not only business continuity but also work for the benefit of the whole society (Figure 10.4). The geographical scope of a particular Area BCP, however, depends on local conditions or the size of a stakeholder's coordination area, so that an industrial park, an industrial agglomerated area or even a nation can be its scope.

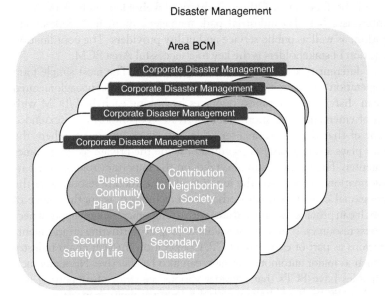

Figure 10.4 Corporate disaster management, Area BCM and local disaster management
Source: Author (T. Shimano, original).

Interactive functions of BCP/BCM and Area BCP/Area BCM

While the BCP is designed to prevent the company's core business from being suspended in emergency circumstances, the aim of an Area BCP/BCM is to secure the critical external resources that are essential in supporting business operations in and around the industrial agglomerated area. Through the process of an Area BCM, which will be discussed below, the existing disaster management capacity of each enterprise or organization, including documented BCP, formulated BCMS or any disaster relevant system, will be examined in order to analyze the vulnerability of the area. Through a process of reviewing and coordinating all the stakeholder's BCPs, Area BCPs can contribute to measures to address the issues revealed, as well as clarify the roles of the various stakeholders. Area BCP/BCMs promote an area-sensitive standardized coordinated management system as well as bolstering resilient businesses by enhancing the relationships between them. In this sense, the functions of the BCP/BCM and the Area BCP/BCM may be interactively coordinated. The plan of activities of both systems should be reflected in each other when reviewed.

Table 10.2 explains the relations between individual BCP/BCM and Area BCP/Area BCM, and provides a plan for local disaster management.

Cooperation of stakeholders in Area BCM

The Area BCM, as defined, requires participation from both the private and public sectors, the members of which are involved in various kinds of businesses or services in the focus area. Other important stakeholders include not only private enterprises but also industrial park managers, municipal workers and administration, as well as public service and utility providers. The coordination and cooperation of stakeholders is the key to a successful Area BCM.

There are different types of cooperation (Figure 10.5). The most simple form entails cooperation between multiple enterprises in an industry-agglomerated area that can share critical business resources by linking each BCP/BCM with any system of emergency operation. Public–private cooperation is an extended arrangement of shared roles in area-sensitive disaster management, where the public sector plays a role mainly as coordinator while the private sector becomes the implementer. The public sector also takes on the important role of distributing risk information and securing the function of infrastructure resources for the area. Interregional cooperation with other areas of industry is another mode of cooperation. It can provide the affected area with a temporary backup supply of necessary business resources. It may be beneficial to prepare partnering arrangements between regions as part of each Area BCP. Cooperation through chain industry networks, such as major automotive groups, can also be effective. Normally such major companies have BCPs that consider various scenarios of supporting line companies. Area BCPs should link up with this industry chain cooperation.

In the case of the Great East Japan Earthquake, where supply chains were negatively affected even far outside the disaster area, there was significant disruption

Table 10.2 BCP/BCM, Area BCP/Area BCM, local disaster management

	BCP/BCM	Area BCP/Area BCM	Local disaster management
Objectives	To protect enterprise from losing customers, market share and corporate value due to disruption of core business	To minimize economic damage or losses of an industrial agglomerated area as a whole by coordinating efforts of stakeholders to secure common business resources (critical external resources in particular)	To reduce disaster risks or damage through systematic efforts of effective measures by national and local organizations, and awareness of and responses to disasters by community and residents
Plan	Documented procedures that guide organizations to respond, resume and recover to a predefined level of operation following the disruption	Documented framework for coordination of damage mitigation measures and recovery actions of stakeholders, including individual enterprises, industrial area managers, local authorities and administrators of the infrastructure in order to enable business continuation in the industrial area as a whole	Document prepared by an authority, sector, organization or enterprise that sets out goals and specific objectives for reducing disaster risks together with related actions to accomplish these objectives (2009 UNISDR Terminology on DRR)
Coordination	Separately by: private enterprises, national and local authorities, emergency responders, infrastructure and utility operators	Local authority where the industry agglomeration area is located. National disaster management authority and that of industry and economic sectors. Management organization of an industrial cluster.	National and local authorities, sector, organization or enterprise, operator of infrastructure and utilities, community and others

Source: Author (H. Baba, original).

of production parts delivery (Saito 2012). Ota (2011), however, found that supply chain cooperation could provide an effective alternative, as businesses could quickly establish replacement delivery networks of essential parts or resources for production and operation. In order to benefit from this approach, we argue that it is also better to prepare or strengthen alternative supply chain networks in advance.

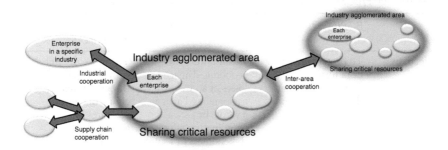

Figure 10.5 Different means of cooperation under Area BCM
Source: Author (H. Baba, original).

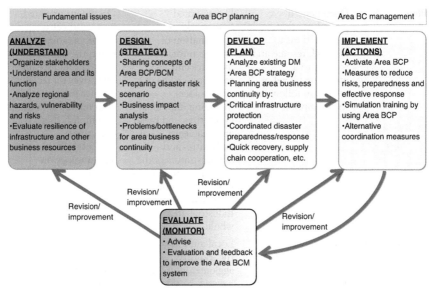

Figure 10.6 Process of the Area BCM
Source: Author (T. Shimano, original).

We also found that, in restoration and reconstruction activities, cooperation between the affected community and neighboring enterprises in the region, or assistance from outside the affected areas, was an effective practice in order to generate private sector participation in disaster management. Local governments should promote support for this with a wider scope of BCPs in order to enhance cooperation (Kagiya and Isouchi 2009).

The Area BCM process

As defined above, the Area BCM must be conducted as part of a continuous cycle of improving the capacity of local resilience in the economy to disasters on an area-wide scale. To meet this, the management process must be designed in a way that incorporates fundamental issues, Area BCP formulation and management concerns, as Figure 10.6 illustrates.

The first step of developing an Area BCM is that private companies, local governments, infrastructure and utility operators should sit down together. The size of the area should be determined based on the interest of organized stake-holders, who should have a common understanding of the potential weaknesses of the area in times of disaster. In the process meetings, the stakeholders should work to identify possible bottlenecks that may lead to the disruption of business, and generate measures that will lead to a plan for business continuity of the area. Measures that are implemented may then be monitored and evaluated for better management of business continuity. The following steps are the central components of the Area BCM process.

Analyzing and understanding the risks and impacts

In order to create a common understanding of disaster risks and impacts among all parties involved in the Area BCM process, it is essential to have a scientific analysis of probable hazards, existing vulnerabilities and the resulting risks to business interruption. Ideally, the analysis should be based on a multi-hazard (natural, Natecs, man-made), multi-scenario and probabilistic methodology. This would include the potential hazards based on an assessment of the probabilities of their occurring.

In order to prepare for risk scenarios in the target area, it is necessary to evaluate the disaster resilience of infrastructure and business resources as well as the current state of supply chains. The vulnerability and resilience of the elements related to the business continuity of the area may be assessed.

Determining the Area BCM strategy

The result of the above simulation and evaluation should be followed by a business impact analysis on an area-wide scale as well as within each of the participating organizations. Discussion of the impacts will then expose the problems and bottlenecks of the area. Creation of risk scenarios can provide the basis for discussing the risk management strategies, plans and measures by stakeholders as part of the next step. Through this process, as a regulated system of risk management, cooperation between various stakeholders is expected to strengthen.

Developing the Area BCP

This part of the process consists of analyzing existing measures as well as the private sector BCPs for use in natural disasters, working to establish a strategy for Area BCP/BCM, and then formulating a plan for cooperation. The plan should include promoting infrastructure development to increase resilience, coordinate disaster responses and establish procedures for monitoring the Area BCM activities to provide feedback.

In this process, all parties should have opportunities to select single or mixed measures considering the balanced combination of *tactics*: (1) strengthening existing area-wide capacity for risk reduction and damage mitigation through infrastructure improvement, for example; (2) preparing alternative measures, such as second lines of transportation, networking of power distribution and groundwater extraction facilities; and (3) making temporary backup systems, such as emergency batteries and temporary accommodation facilities.

The parties should also discuss *schemes* (or practical methods) of implementing those measures, such as: (1) cooperation with other stakeholders to share essential resources for business continuation in the area, by controlling or adjusting the logistics flow on the congested transportation, for example; (2) making new investment for area-wide resilient development, by constructing common facilities for accommodation cum emergency operation, for example; and (3) transferring the risk, by mutual insurance or public compensation, for example.

Implementing the planned measures

This part of the process includes developing preparedness for planned measures, simulation-based training, coordination activities and actual responses to any emergency. This is linked with the BCP/BCM of each single entity and thus every BCP should be redesigned if necessary to coordinate with the Area BCP. The Area BCM does not always require costly investment by the private and public sectors but can start from small efforts. At the very least, it may include activities such as information sharing and promotion of disaster risk reduction actions to the extent that this is possible.

Monitoring and feedback

Evaluation and feedback of the process are always important. In the Area BCM, monitoring should be designed to provide advisory feedback on all the steps of the Area BCM cycle through discussions among the stakeholders. A variety of scenarios based on differential hazards should also be targeted in the continuous process of Area BCM development.

Applying the Area BCM: a case study

This section introduces a case study of three pilot areas among ASEAN nations that were selected for the JICA project on the application of the Area BCP/BCM.

Industry agglomeration in ASEAN nations

Triggered by direct investment, especially in the electricity and/or electronics industries, industrial agglomerated areas in many countries in Asia have made successful contributions to national development. The increasing inflows of foreign capital accompanied by high technologies has driven developers and local governments of industrial areas to further attract foreign-affiliated firms by providing special measures, such as establishing export-processing zones (JMC 2000).

Industrial agglomeration generally tends to occur along coastal or riverine zones, which are convenient for physical distribution. The formation of industrial clusters in cities is also linked to the progress of urbanization, along with the concentration of workers, as one outcome of the increasing production (METI 2010). In ASEAN, the supply chain networks of these industrial clusters are also expanding within the region as ASEAN constantly develops, which further accelerates industrial agglomeration in and around recently developing cities. These newly developed locations, however, tend to be vulnerable to floods, typhoons, storm surges and other natural hazards. Earthquakes, tsunamis and volcanic hazards are also significant in some Asian nations along the Pacific Rim.

One indicator of these vulnerabilities was the 2011 flood in Thailand, which caused extensive damage over a wide range of areas, from the capital city of Bangkok to the north. Flooding over long periods of time caused heavy losses in the industrial sector. The seven industrial estates near Ayutthaya Province, where a number of enterprises including Japanese firms are located, were ravaged for more than a month by the flood starting in October 2011. The destruction of Ayutthaya province had a severe impact upon the global economy through supply chains, especially in the automotive and electronics industries. According to J.P. Morgan (2011), the event set back global industrial production by around 2.5 percent. Its aftermath continued for a long period of time – for months or years in the case of some of the companies and products (METI 2012).

Nowadays, areas of industry agglomeration in other ASEAN countries show vulnerability to the increasing incidence of disasters, such as floods, typhoons/ cyclones, earthquake, tsunamis and others. In fact, East Asia is experiencing rapid industrialization and urbanization (Jha *et al.* 2012). Cities are becoming disaster hotspots (Dilley *et al.* 2005). Large numbers of people and most areas where economic activity occurs are vulnerable to natural disasters, as Figure 10.7 shows.

Considering the situation, JICA selected Indonesia, the Philippines and Vietnam, all of which are high-risk countries within the ASEAN region, as countries for piloting the Area BCP/BCM formulation. In each country, Bekasi– Karawang industrial area, Cavite–Laguna–Metro Manila and Hai Phong industrial area, respectively, are specified as the target areas since they are highly agglomerated by various industries as well as exposed to the increasing risk of disasters, such as earthquakes, floods, tsunamis and typhoons/cyclones.

Probabilistic hazard analysis

Through the practical implementation of the pilot project, a standard method of Area BCP formulation was developed that may be applied in many industry

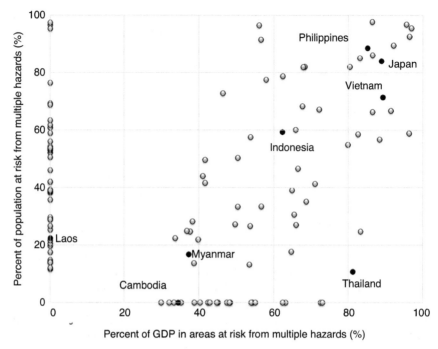

Figure 10.7 Percentage of population (vertical axes) and percentage of GDP (horizontal axes) at risk from multiple hazards

Source: Adapted by the authors from Dilley *et al.* (2005).

agglomerated areas, particularly in developing countries where technical disadvantages may be found. To facilitate this purpose, the elements and methods employed in hazard analysis should not be unnecessarily sophisticated or highly technical. Situations where basic data for analysis are lacking and there are limitations on financial capacity should also be considered.

Based on the above conditions, the elements (i.e., tools and software) of probabilistic hazard analysis applied in the pilot project were selected from widely used, easily handled and generally applicable elements, as shown in Table 10.3.

Identified dominant hazards

The project identified the dominant hazard in the industrial agglomerated area using probabilistic analysis of multiple hazards (Figure 10.8). Floods and earthquakes are the top two hazards in the Bekasi–Karawang area while earthquakes in Cavite–Laguna–Metro Manila, and typhoons and storm surges in Hai Phong are considered the dominant hazard types.

Table 10.3 Software tools, models and data for disaster simulation

Earthquake	Tsunami	Flood	Storm surge
Earthquake hazard analysis: – EZ-FRISK and GSHAP for earthquake source model – NEHRP ground classification and amplification parameter of Building Seismic Safety Council (2009) – Data used in previous JICA studies – Existing geological maps	Numerical simulation of tsunami propagation and run-up: – TSUNAMI-N1, N2, N3 by Imamura *et al.* (2006) – bathymetry data from GEBCO 08 Grid data (30") Previous studies by: – Vu and Nguyen (2008) – Okal *et al.* (2011) – Nguyen (2011)	Indonesia: – Run-off model by IFAS – Inundation model by iRIC Philippines: – Run-off model by MIKE-11 – Inundation model by MIKE-FLOOD Vietnam: – Inland flooding by MIKE-21	Storm surge simulation: – Princeton Ocean Model (Mellor *et al.* 2004) – The Typhoon Model of 2D wind and air pressure (Myers 1954) – Bathymetry from GEBCO 08 – Elevation from ASTER GDEM and observed tide level

Source: JICA Study Team (2013).

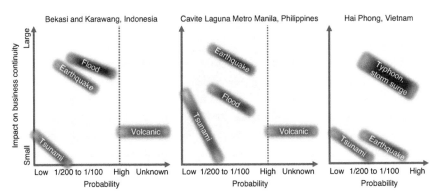

Figure 10.8 Dominant natural hazards and probabilities in the pilot areas
Source: JICA study team (2013).

Business impact scenarios

Figures 10.9 and 10.10 show simulation results of the flood in the Bekasi–Karawang industrial area in Indonesia. In this case, some cities and sections of road networks, including the central highway and two electrical substations, are inundated by flooding. The industrial parks, however, are not directly hit by the flooding. Inundation depths at the most severely affected parts, such as the highway near the local city of Suryacipta, exceed 4m for more than two weeks.

Based on the projected hazard and vulnerability analysis, the basic scenario was created as follows.

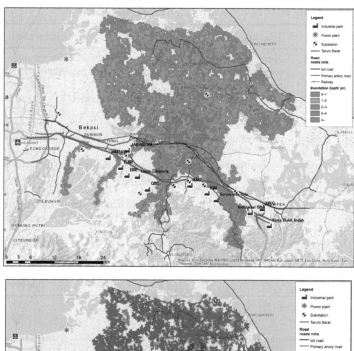

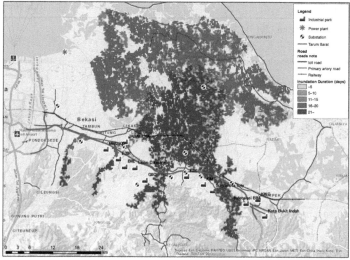

Figures 10.9 and 10.10 Simulated flood inundation (top) and duration (bottom) in Bekasi–Karawang industry area, Indonesia. Simulation software: IFAS for run-off analysis and iRIC for inundation analysis. Rainfall data: 3B42RT three hours of interval data are enlarged to the scale of ground-based rainfall data. Elevation data: GTOPO 30, ASTER GDEM, grid size: 200m. Boundary condition: five hydrographs calculated with run-off model are given as upper boundary conditions. Assume that Jatiluhur dam is filled and run-off inflow from catchment is released with no control. Return period: 200 years. This map is intended to be used for disaster scenario creation. It is not a forecast of future hazards (analytical condition).

Source: JICA study team (2013).

1 Buildings in industrial park

- Karawang City and surrounding area are inundated for more than two weeks.
- Industrial parks, however, are not inundated, and facilities are not damaged.

2 Electric power and lifelines

- Two substations in Karawang City are inundated to over 2m in depth and cease operations for two weeks.
- Some base stations of telephones and mobile phones cease operations because of the shortage of electrical power.

3 Transportation infrastructure

- Freeway (Jakarta–Cikampek Toll Road) is closed both in the west and east of KIIC for more than two weeks.
- Primary Road in Karawang City is closed for more than two weeks.

4 Workers in the industrial parks

- Many employees are absent because of the inundation of their houses.
- The traffic conditions become worse, inducing the workers to stay at home.

Since the Jakarta Port is the only shipping point used in this area to export/import products and parts, disruption of the transportation route to/from the port for days and weeks, as above, is assumed to hamper the production in factories that are located on the eastern side of the inundation area. In addition, other factories may be forced to reduce their operations because of workers' absence or inability to commute.

Figures 10.11 and 10.12 show the simulation results of an earthquake in Cavite–Laguna–Metro Manila in the Philippines, which supposedly has a probability of once in 200 years, and the area at risk is 8–9 on the Modified Mercalli Intensity scale (MMI). The figure also indicates the high potential area of liquefaction along Manila Bay.

Based on the projected hazard and vulnerability analysis, business impacts were considered based on the following scenarios:

1 Buildings in industrial parks

- Ten percent of the buildings suffer moderate damage. Repair is necessary.
- Some of ceiling panels and illuminators fall down. Part racks topple.
- Non-anchored machinery moves.
- Transformers topple.

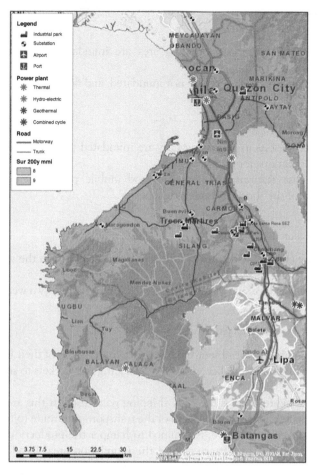

Figures 10.11 and 10.12 Simulated earthquake intensity (above) and liquefaction
        potential (opposite). Cavite, Laguna and Metro Manila,
        Philippines.
Supposed probability: once in 200 years.
Earthquake source model: GSHAP and EZ-FRISK.
Surface amplification is evaluated by NEHRP ground classification.

Source: JICA study team (2013).

2 Electric power and lifelines

- The electricity substation stops operations for one week. Capacity recovers
  to 50 percent one month w and it takes three months for full recovery.
- Wired phones and mobile phones become congested because of the shortage
  of electric power.
- Wells and water tanks cease operating for several days. Capacity recovers to
  50 percent after one week and it takes one month for full recovery.

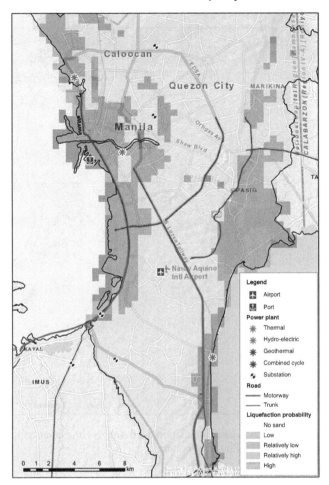

3 Transportation infrastructure

- The expressway between Manila and Cavite is closed for two weeks because of the liquefaction. After temporary restoration work, limited traffic becomes possible.
- Traffic capacity of the Expressway between Manila and Laguna is limited in some sections. It takes one week for 50 percent recovery and two weeks for full recovery.
- Most piers of Manila Port are unable to be used for several months because of the liquefaction. Several piers become usable after temporary restoration work.
- In the container terminal, gantry cranes are severely damaged. It will take six months to recover 50 percent of the capacity for cargo handling.

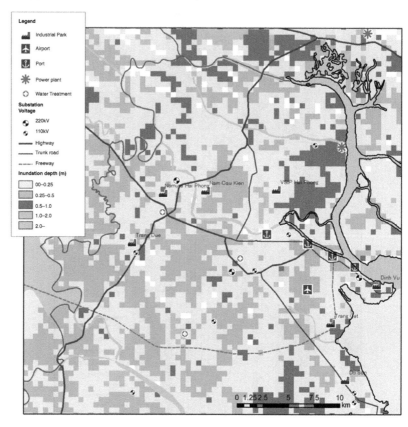

Figures 10.13 and 10.14 Simulated inundation depth (above) and duration (opposite). Hai Phong, Vietnam.
Supposed probability: once in 200 years.
Run-off analysis model: IFAS, MIKE-11.
Inundation model: iRIC, MIKF-FLOOD.
Elevation data: ASTER, SRTM.

Source: JICA Study Team (2013).

4 Workers in the industrial parks

- Some employees are absent because 10 percent of their houses are heavily damaged, with a further 20 percent suffering moderate structure damage.
- The traffic conditions become worse and employees arrive late at the factory.

Figures 10.13 and 10.14 show simulated results of the storm surge and rainfall event in Hai Phong, which is supposed to occur in high tide conditions under

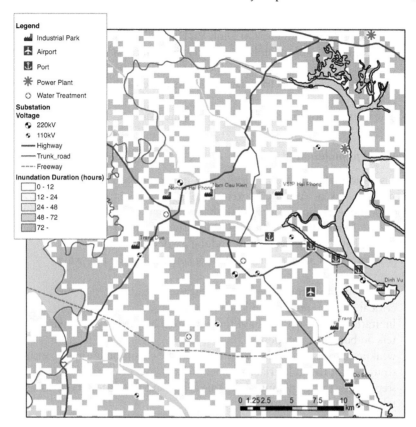

the worst-case typhoon track. Expected rainfall is 565mm/day, the probability of which is approximately 0.5 to 1.0 percent.

The map indicates that in the prospective areas, some parts of the industrial area will be inundated to 1m depth and this will continue for several days. In terms of water depth it may not seem like a severe disaster, but if analyzed considering the vulnerability of external resources necessary for business continuation, we may assume the following impact scenario:

- Buildings of factories in industrial parks along the coast suffer inundation by the storm surge.
- Hai Phong Power Plant is inundated to 0.5 to 1m depth. Electric power to Hai Phong area is limited.
- The 220kV substation in Dinh Vu is severely damaged by seawater.
- The 110kV substation near the coast suffers damage from seawater.
- Some base stations of telephone/mobile phones cease operations due to the power shortage.

- Dinh Vu Port is affected by the storm surge.
- Cargo-handling equipment of Dinh Vu Port is damaged by seawater.
- The container yard in Dinh Vu area ceases operations.
- Some of the roads in the city are closed for several days.
- Some employees of factories are absent because of the inundation of their houses.
- The traffic conditions in Hai Phong become worse.

Area BCP formulation

The discussions of participants for the pilot project in each area under the established framework of Area BCM were facilitated by the study team. A series of meetings and workshops were held to share information and improve knowledge needed to formulate the Area BCP. Sessions were structured to promote interaction between the consultant and the participants.

The information and knowledge sharing consisted of the following:

- hazards affecting the industrial agglomerated area;
- critical business resources in disaster situations;
- limitations of existing BCPs at the individual business level. Impact of disasters on business operations;
- weaknesses or bottlenecks in the area and the effects on business continuity;
- strategies for the industrial agglomerated area as a whole; and
- steps necessary for planning an Area BCM and the necessary actions to be taken by both private and public parties.

Some findings from this case study are as follows:

- Some parties started trying to establish their own BCPs after realizing the importance of preparing a BCP.
- The entity that takes the initiative towards developing an Area BCM and leads the discussion differs according to country and local conditions. In the three areas, the prefecture level of government in Indonesia, the municipality (People's Commission) in Vietnam, and an authority overseeing the economic sector (Philippines Economic Zone Authority) in the Philippines took the lead.
- Discussions relating to the Area BCM framework may help to promote public sector plans, particularly in terms of infrastructure development.

Benefits of Area BCMs

The Area BCM process unifies the efforts of stakeholders of the area, directs them towards a common goal, and allows the area to achieve recovery and reconstruction quickly, efficiently and effectively. The range of measures, for example, the method selected, can help to encourage each business continuity manager to consider how to secure available business resources. They also develop ways of cooperating through enhanced communication with other partners by sharing information among related parties in the area, as well as the clients of each enterprise. Furthermore, these considerations can promote expanded coordination with other industrial agglomerated areas and other strategically critical areas. Coordination through the supply chain is also enhanced by preparing an alternative supply chain network.

Each organization's efforts were enhanced due to the increase in responsibility following the development and coordination of the Area BCM. Even companies that currently have no BCP/BCM may still start developing their own BCP/BCMs. Moreover, cross-industry cooperation resulting from Area BCP/BCMs can further promote cooperation among industries in a supply chain. It automatically distributes the concept of the Area BCMs to other areas. Another benefit of Area BCP/BCMs is that they can give private companies the incentive to prepare plans for each stage of the disaster management cycle (prevention and mitigation, preparedness and response, restoration and rehabilitation), rather than following the usual tendency to prepare only the plans for a response due to their financial constraints and lack of experience. Private parties will be involved more deeply in planning structural measures of risk reduction on an area-wide scale, for example. In disaster risk reduction, it is understood that some extent of redundancy in measures and functions is important in order to establish backup measures and alternative actions effectively. The combination of different schemes under the Area BCM, consisting of sharing resources, investing in measures to minimize the effects of disasters while transferring risks, will add more redundancy to the area's resilience. The public sector is also encouraged to invest in developing a more robust infrastructure. Since the regeneration of local jobs, the reconstruction of people's living environments and the normalization of socioeconomic activities are essential for the earliest rehabilitation of the locality, it is important for both public and private parties to increase their capacities in the area surrounding disasters. Linking individual efforts of companies and public organizations, opportunities under the Area BCM can enhance strategic operations in normal businesses to avoid unexpected business risks and eventually contribute to disaster prevention as well as sustainable growth for all concerned parties.

Although it is premature to evaluate the total benefit of the Area BCM, the enhancement of resiliency may encourage other enterprises to transfer their operations to the target area, where disaster risks are rather low compared to the other areas. The increased resilience of the area would also be reflected in the asset value as an investment environment, which could reduce the disaster insurance costs of local enterprises. If a cost reduction follows, it will attract more investment to the industry area.

Enhanced continuity of the business in the area as a result could foster the local economy and employment, which may have a huge impact upon the nation. Enhanced continuity of business in the area could result in fostering a vital economy, which may then bring substantial benefits to the nation. The process of Area

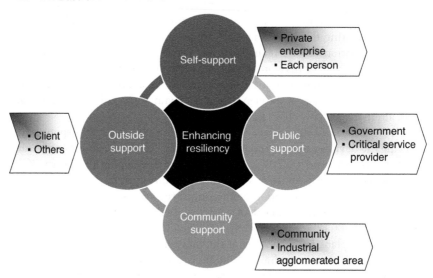

Figure 10.15 Connectivity among the stakeholders in disaster management

Source: Author (T. Shimano, original).

BCP/BCM prompts all the engaged parties to be aware of the connections (Figure 10.15) to other members and helps the private sector to prepare well-balanced and standardized plans for all the stages in the disaster management cycle.

Conclusion

Economic losses as a result of disasters – particularly of catastrophic disasters in industry agglomerated areas – have extensive economic impacts for nations and for the global economy. As noted earlier, loss of employment and population outflow from the area can also have irreversible social impacts. The private sector can play a significant role in promoting resilient continuation of area business and early regeneration of local industry. In addition, the public sector needs to pay attention to industrial agglomeration areas in order to avoid catastrophic impacts upon the national economy by developing strategies for area-wide disaster management and involving the private sector in the system of management.

To encourage contributions by both private and public sectors, the preparation of area-wide coordinated systems of disaster risk reduction such as Area BCP/BCM, as introduced in this chapter, is becoming an increasingly important means of enhancing area resiliency to disasters or other threats of business disruption. The Area BCM enables all the stakeholders of private and public sectors to create mutual links and connectivity to avoid unexpected risks of losing assets and benefits. Two important questions here concern who will first take the leading initiative of the Area BCM in the area of industry agglomeration. And who will need to do what?

As the case study has revealed, the entity that takes the initiative in developing the Area BCM and leads the discussion of strategies and actions may differ according to country and local conditions. In some cases, local government will be the leader. In recent years, authorities in the industrial and economic fields have become more interested in taking on initiatives and developing the concepts of area-wide resilience to disasters. While the private sector is definitely a part of the area-wide framework, it is not usually at the center of the management system. However, it is not an easy task for private enterprises to implement the scientific risk and impact analysis, which is based on an area-wide, multi-hazard, multi-scenario and probabilistic methodology, as mentioned above. Since this comprises one of the essential steps of the Area BCM, some public organizations should take the central role of implementing the Area BCM.

However, the role of the private sector remains important. First, participation of all key stakeholders in the Area BCM system is essential to ensuring effective coordination. Private–public cooperation will provide the basis for generating the Area BCM process. Moreover, the private sector, as an actor in implementing disaster management plans in the actual location, should be able to provide coordination between the entities in the areas concerned and those in the external regions through interregional networks, industrial chains and supply chain cooperation.

Second, it needs to be recognized that general management in private organizations may not take the process as seriously as they should, asking BCP managers to write or say anything to make the auditors go away (Wallace and Lawrence 2010). Conversely, after participating in an Area BCM process, private enterprises then have the responsibility of linking their own BCPs to the Area BCP. For example, to share the risk information, all parties would need to disclose information related to common business resources, current disaster management capacities and any hazardous materials that may affect the area. This will effectively be reflected in the Area BCP formulation. The individual BCP will then be reviewed interactively by each private enterprise with serious concerns. Constant dialogue and simulation exercises can also be effective in revealing the risks and difficulties that each stakeholder faces. It enables them to prepare a well-balanced and coordinated initial response capacity for catastrophic disasters with effective and efficient use of existing resources.

Learning from recent large-scale disasters that disrupted external resources, which were essential for each enterprise's business continuity, the private sector as a group of enterprises should also encourage the public sector to strengthen the external resource's resilience to disaster through a framework of area-wide cooperation. Since the industrial function of any specified area depends on critical common resources and infrastructure, including those outside the area, the concerned private enterprises should create a capacity as a coordination framework with the public sector, including local and national governments, to secure the local economy.

The first application of such a framework, the Area BCP/BCM in industrial agglomerated areas, has been introduced in ASEAN. Since the concept of Area

BCP/BCMs is still new, the experienced members of the private sector are expected to disseminate the lessons and knowledge of Area BCP/BCMs in other industry agglomerating areas and nations. In addition, this concept of area-wide resiliency will be applicable not only to industry agglomeration but also to urbanization. To foster sustainable urban development, together with the vital economic growth of each locality, private and public cooperation needs to be strengthened through the new opportunities presented by coordinated risk management.

The recent efforts of the private sector indicate what may be achieved and what challenges remain. The private sector can promote disaster resilience by developing BCPs and establishing BCM systems, as well as strengthening supply chain networks to ensure backup of business operations. The concept of shared resource management is also becoming better understood. In some companies, the BCM plans have included concepts of corporate social responsibility (CSR) in emergency events, by incorporating plans for helping affected people. However, there is still more progress to be made. Area-wide disaster management with the significant participation of stakeholders is one area where further progress is necessary in order to scale up the coordination system of resilient society. In this, the private sector can provide one key to success.

Recommendation

Area-wide disaster management with significant participation of both private and public sectors is an essential DRM framework to promote economic resilience. This approach will support the continuation of businesses following disasters and the early regeneration of local industry. It should include the coordination of all stakeholders in understanding risks, formulating strategies, implementing measures and continually improving the cyclical process of area-wide DRM. To achieve this objective it is proposed that Area Based Business Continuity Management and Planning (BCM/BCP) be scaled up into a cross-sector coordination framework of disaster risk management to ensure the continuity of area-wide businesses.

Audiences of the recommendation: Private sector, national governments, donors and the United Nations secretariat of the ISDR.

References

Ando, M. and Kimura, F. 2012. "How Did the Japanese Exports Respond to Two Crises in the International Production Networks? The Global Financial Crisis and the Great East Japan Earthquake." *Asian Economic Journal* 26(3), 261–287.

Baba, H., Adachi, I., Takabayashi, H., Nagatomo, N., Nakasone, S., Matsumoto, H. and Shimano, T. 2013. "Introductory Study on Disaster Risk Assessment and Area Business Continuity Planning in Industry Agglomerated Areas in the ASEAN." *IDRiM Journal* 3(2), 184–195.

Building Seismic Safety Council. 2009. "NEHRP Recommended Seismic Provisions for New Buildings and Other Structures." FEMA P-750/2009 Edition. Washington, DC: Federal Emergency Management Agency.

Dilley, Maxx, Chen, Robert S., Deichmann, Uwe, Lerner-Lam, Arthur, L., Arnold, M. with J. Agwe, P. Buys, O. Kjekstad, B. Lyon and G. Yetman. 2005. *Natural Disaster Hotspots: A Global Risk Analysis*. Washington, DC: The International Bank for Reconstruction and Development, the World Bank and Columbia University.

Global Platform for Disaster Risk Reduction. 2013. "Chair's Summary: Resilient People, Resilient Planet." Fourth Session of the Global Platform for Disaster Risk Reduction, Geneva, May 21–23.

Imamura, Fumihiko, Yalciner, Ahmet Cevdet and Ozyurt, Gulizar. 2006. "Tsunami Modelling Manual." UNESCO IOC International Training Course on Tsunami Numerical Modelling. www.tsunami.civil.tohoku.ac.jp/hokusai3/J/projects/manual-ver-3.1.pdf.

ISO. 2012. "Societal Security – Business Continuity Management Systems – Requirements." ISO 22301:2012. Geneva: International Organization for Standardization (ISO). www.iso.org/iso/catalogue_detail?csnumber=50038.

Japan Machinery Center for Trade and Investment (JMC). 2000. "Proposal about the Japanese Company for Contributing to Symbiotic Development of the Electricity and the Electron/IT Industry in Asia, and the Role of the Japanese Government" [in Japanese]. www.jmcti.org/kaigai/doc/kaigai082000ap.pdf.

Jha, Abhas K. and Stanton-Geddes, Zuzana (eds). 2013. *Strong, Safe, and Resilient: A Strategic Policy Guide for Disaster Risk Management in East Asia and the Pacific*. Washington, DC: The World Bank. www.gfdrr.org/strongsaferesilient.

Jha, Abhas K., Bloch, Robin and Lamond, Jessica. 2012. *Cities and Flooding: A Guide to Integrated Urban Flood Risk Management for the 21st Century*. Washington, DC: International Bank for Reconstruction and Development and The World Bank. www.gfdrr.org/gfdrr/urbanfloods.

J.P. Morgan. 2011. "Global Data Watch." Economic Research, November 11. www.adr.com/Home/LoadPDF?CMSID=2c3de19feb2943fd982284c56c16b176.

Kagiya, Hajime and Isouchi, Chikako. 2009. "Research of Regional Contribution and Cooperation in Business Continuity Plan." *Proceedings of the Annual Conference of the Institute of Social Safety Science* 25, 61–64.

Komori, D., Nakamura, S., Kiguchi, M., Nishijima, A., Yamazaki, D., Suzuki, S. and Oki, T. 2012. "Characteristics of the 2011 Chao Phraya River Flood in Central Thailand." *Hydrological Research Letters* 6, 41–46.

Mellor, George L. 2004. "Users Guide for a Three-Dimensional, Primitive Equation, Numerical Ocean Model." Program in Atmospheric and Ocean Sciences, Princeton University, Princeton, NJ.

Ministry of Economy, Trade and Industry (METI). 2010. "White Paper on International Economy and Trade 2010." Ministry of Economy, Trade and Industry, Japan. www.meti.go.jp/english/report/data/gIT2010maine.html.

—— 2012a. "White Paper on International Economy and Trade 2012." Tokyo: METI. www.meti.go.jp/english/report/data/gIT2012maine.html.

—— 2012b. "Guidelines on Formulating and Implementing BCPs for Small and Medium Enterprises." Tokyo: METI. www.meti.go.jp/english/press/2012/0427_05.html.

Myers, V.A. 1954. "Characteristics of U.S. Hurricanes Pertinent to Levee Design for Lake Okeechobee, Florida." *Hydro-Meteorological Report* 32. Weather Bureau, US Department of Commerce.

Nguyen, Hong Phuong, Phuong, Vu Ha and Truyen, Pham Tre. 2013. "Simulation of a Worst Case Tsunami Scenario from the Manila Trench to Vietnam." The Joint Symposium of Seismic Hazard Assessment, Sendai, Japan, June 17–19.

Okada, Norio. 2011. "Integrated Disaster Management in Japan and Lessons from the March 11 Events." High-Level Roundtable on the Financial Management of Earthquakes, Paris, June 23–24, 2011, OECD Headquarters. www.oecd.org/dataoecd/1/24/48440903.pdf.

Okal, Emile A., Synolakis, Costas E. and Kalligeris, Nikos. 2011. "Tsunami Simulations for Regional Sources in the South China and Adjoining Seas." *Pure and Applied Geophysics* 168, 1153–1173.

Ota, Saburo. 2011. "An Empirical Study of Bankruptcy and Turnaround in Post-March 11 Northeastern Japan: Corporate Risk Management for Natural Disasters." *Management Journal* 4, 23–44.

Saito, Yukiko Umeno. 2012. "Impact of East Japan Earthquake Disaster on Companies in Non-Affected Areas – The Structure of Inter-Company Network of Supply Chain and its Implication." *Japan Statistical Society* 42(1), 135–144.

Sato, Koji and Bessho, Yusuke. 2011. "Regional Disaster Measures and Business Continuity Plan for Logistics." *Proceedings of the Annual Conference of the Institute of Social Safety Science* 28(5), 27–30.

Special Study Team for Earthquake and Tsunami Countermeasures Learning from the Great East Japan Earthquake. 2011. "Interview Survey Results of Evacuation Actions in the Great East Japan Earthquake." Central Disaster Management Council. Seventh meeting on the Great East Japan Earthquake, August 16, 2011. Distribution Papers No. 1. www.bousai.go.jp/jishin/chubou/higashinihon/7/1.pdf.

Vu, Thanh Ca and Nguyen, Dinh Xuyen. 2008. "Tsunami Risk Along Vietnamese Coast." *Journal of Water Resources and Environmental Engineering* 23, 24–33.

Wallace, Michael and Webber, Lawrence. 2010. *The Disaster Recovery Handbook: A Step-by-Step Plan to Ensure Business Continuity and Protect Vital Operations, Facilities, and Assets*, 2nd edition. New York: Amacom.

Warren, Clive M.J. 2010. "The Role of Public Sector Asset Managers in Responding to Climate Change: Disaster and Business Continuity Planning." *Property Management* 28(4), 245–256.

Waugh, W.L. Jr. 2009. "Mechanisms for Collaboration in Emergency Management: ICS, NIMS, and the Problem with Command and Control." In *The Collaborative Public Manager: New Ideas for the Twenty-First Century*, edited by Rosemary O'Leary and Lisa Blomgren Bingham. Washington, DC: Georgetown University Press, 157–175.

11 Disaster risk governance and the principles of good governance

Angelika Planitz

Introduction

The governance arrangements made by countries provide the overall environment for disaster risk management (DRM) by shaping the way in which societies reach their decisions and implement their affairs. This includes decisions that guide investments and policy agendas aimed at reducing and mitigating the impacts of natural hazards as well as those aimed at implementing adaptive measures to address the uncertainties associated with global climate change.

Processes of human development and disaster risk are closely interlinked. Rapid economic and urban development can lead to growing concentrations of people and economic assets in areas that are prone to natural hazards, such as earthquakes, droughts, floods and storms. If the exposure of people and assets to natural hazards grows faster than the ability to strengthen risk-reducing capacities, the risk of disasters increases. Hence, exposure by itself does not necessarily lead to high risk, as long as vulnerabilities are reduced. Ultimately, it is social, economic and political processes that determine how exposure and vulnerability to hazards change over time.

Climate change is another factor that increasingly contributes to growing disaster risk levels, and it is a good example of how anthropogenic factors are changing the nature of hazards. No longer can hazards be perceived as constant and purely natural phenomena. Natural and anthropogenic hazards that occur in conditions of exposure and vulnerability may result in disasters. Disasters and their catastrophic impacts, therefore, are not "natural". They are triggered by human acts of omission and commission (World Bank and United Nations 2010).

Every disaster is unique, exposing actions by individuals and governments that led to its catastrophic impact. Had these actions incorporated disaster risk reduction measures from the outset, the very same hazard that caused the disaster may have resulted in fewer deaths and less damage. Societies with strong disaster risk governance arrangements have a greater ability to manage risks, and hence have been able to make good progress in substantively reducing their disaster losses and impacts. Disaster risk governance is therefore at the heart of resilience building by ingraining risk reduction into a country's institutional, political and financial systems. For the purpose of this chapter, "disaster risk governance" refers to the way in which the public authorities, civil servants, media, the private sector and civil society coordinate at the community, national and regional levels in order to manage and reduce disaster and climate-related risks. This means ensuring that sufficient levels of capacity and resources are made available to prevent, prepare for, manage and recover from disasters. It also entails mechanisms, institutions and processes for citizens to articulate their interests, exercise their legal rights and obligations, and mediate their differences (UNDP 2013a).

This chapter aims to provide an overview of how the concept of disaster risk governance has evolved. The chapter will also examine the advantages of applying core governance principles for achieving sustainable disaster risk reduction outcomes. It will conclude by offering forward-looking recommendations on how disaster risk governance can be strengthened.

Evolution of disaster risk governance

From the early 2000s onward, disaster risk governance was framed as strengthening institutional and legislative systems (ILS) for disaster risk management. This term encompassed a whole range of issues, including the organizational structures, processes, strategies, policies, laws and regulations, resources and procedures that governed how a country managed disasters and disaster risk. It also acknowledged the interplay of multiple stakeholders, such as the state, civil society and the private sector, as well as their formal and informal interactions. Noteworthy in this discussion is that the support aimed at developing dedicated ILS for DRM that operated within a country's governance context. In addition to strengthening the merely technical capacities for DRM, ILS also recognized that effectively reducing disaster risk would require a number of soft management skills, such as leadership, planning, organization, communication and control (UNDP 2007). The five core elements comprising ILS were identified as:

- legal and regulatory frameworks
- policy and planning
- organizational aspects
- resources and capacities
- partnerships (domestic and international).

This outlook eventually evolved following a major review of UNDP's contribution to ILS for DRM in its program countries, commissioned in 2004/2005 (UNDP 2007). The report identified governance as an important determining factor of the potential success of DRM and called for greater linkages between disaster prevention and recovery on the one hand, and democratic governance on the other. This included embedding DRM into public administration reform, decentralization, and governing institutions, as well as anti-corruption and civil society programs. Combining disaster risk reduction (DRR) and governance was a new concept that first gained wider prominence through the UNDP flagship publication *Reducing Disaster Risk: A Challenge for Development* (UNDP 2004; Lassa 2010). However, except for a few isolated examples, practical attempts at mainstreaming DRM into democratic governance programs were hampered by fears of overburdening already complex and often sensitive programs.

Building on democratic governance work also meant incorporating the principles of good governance into DRM efforts, namely: equity and inclusiveness, participation, transparency, accountability, rule of law, effectiveness and efficiency, responsiveness and consensus orientation. This notion was embraced more readily, since DRM in disaster-prone countries was seen as a potential opportunity to deepen the application of these principles, especially in post-disaster recovery operations. In practice, however, this turned out to be a challenging undertaking, especially in fragile countries characterized by overall weak governance systems. In particular, the issue of equity in DRM and the related question of who are the winners and losers in decisions regarding available risk management options have not been pursued vigorously enough, presumably due to their apparent political implications. It is important to note in this context that it was precisely the less tangible aspects of "good governance" that eventually determined the long-term success of a program intervention, rather than the tangible outputs, such as policy documents, laws, plans or an institutional organogram. In summary, ILS for DRM was, by definition, understood to be part of the wider governance system, and that there was an interdependence that could be either supportive or unsupportive. The predominant nomenclature used in UNDP following the findings of the ILS report was "governance for DRM," emphasizing the governance context in which ILS for DRM operated.

With DRM embedded in UNDP's crisis prevention and recovery practice, this eventually paved the way to investigate the interface between disasters and conflicts more closely. A 2011 study of comparative experiences in countries suffering from both disasters and conflicts (UNDP 2011) concluded that there was a need to create programmatic approaches that were more sensitive to this interrelationship. It warned that solutions which single-mindedly dealt with disaster risks would be unlikely to achieve the desired results. In a worst-case scenario, these could even aggravate or contribute to conflict or tensions. The realization grew that risks formed an interlinked system that was not only determined by financial and economic instability, food insecurity, disasters and climate change but also that many global and regionalized factors contributed to conflicts and violence. These included disease and epidemics, environmental degradation, extreme poverty, and the radicalization of politics. While full operationalization of these findings in programmatic approaches is still at a nascent stage, there have been some promising examples of UNDP programs that address the disaster–conflict interface, such as in Myanmar and Indonesia. The focus on multifaceted risk management has now been firmly embedded in UNDP's Strategic Plan 2014 to 2017 (UNDP 2013b). Certainly, the international discourse on climate change and its magnifying impact on disaster risk has also contributed to an examination of a broader spectrum of risks (United Nations secretariat of the ISDR 2009; IPCC 2012).

With this growing emphasis on multifaceted risk, the terminology changed once again to the now popular "risk governance" or "disaster risk governance", which places risk and how risk is governed at the center of attention. This is a much broader approach in comparison with "governance for DRM" and the more narrowly defined ILS for DRM. While the ILS for DRM approach treated DRM as a sector in its own right and focused predominantly on the dedicated institutional, legislative, policy and planning arrangements for DRM, "disaster risk governance", in comparison, takes the wider governance framework as the starting point for effective risk management, along with its ability to manage an interlocked system of risk. Development and political stakeholders that have previously been perceived as participants in a multi-stakeholder DRM approach, such as ministries of planning and finance or parliamentarians, are now recognized as protagonists that need to take the lead in the management of risks inherent to the development process.

The growing complexity and interconnectedness of issues in disaster risk governance require much more flexible solutions that are context specific. Blueprints and simple rollouts will not be sufficient. Instead, analytical capacity coupled with a thorough understanding of the local context is essential, as well as an ability to connect across different disciplines and to engage and partner with non-traditional stakeholders in DRM (UNDP 2014) While these requirements easily resonate with the comparative advantages of development agencies that work across sectors and stakeholders utilizing a partnership approach, it must be recognized that this new method of interdisciplinary work is expected to demand considerable investments in time and resources. Particularly in high-risk and fragile contexts, state and institution building is a long-term undertaking that may span several decades.

The DRM community, however, is still expected to transform societies and achieve disaster resilience in much shorter time frames. The duration of any typical DRM program spans on average 3 to 5 years, sometimes 8 years when a second phase extension is granted. This is clearly reminiscent of the origins of DRM in emergency management, where short-term interventions of a few months to 1 or 2 years at best are the rule. Also required is a much more serious and long overdue engagement with the political economy of disaster risk management.

Governance principles in disaster risk reduction and recovery

The importance of the principles of "good governance" in achieving sustainable disaster risk reduction (DRR) outcomes have already been mentioned above. In general terms, good governance (UNDP 2010) refers to the process of how a society reaches its decisions and implements its affairs, for example, by ensuring full participation, equity, responsiveness and so forth. This may be unachievable in full, and in reality only a few countries have come close to implementing all the principles of good governance. Nevertheless, good governance has become a requirement for accessing international aid from many donor agencies, as well as

UN and international financial organizations. Importantly, good governance is not a judgment on any particular government system. Elements of good governance may be found in monarchies, democracies, and even authoritarian regimes – depending on how governance principles such as responsiveness or rule of law are managed.

Many poor and less developed countries encounter considerable difficulties in working towards good governance due to capacity and resource constraints as well as being in situations of conflict or transition. This has paved the way for the more flexible concept of "good enough governance" (Grindle 2004, 2007). It takes account of the prevailing conditions and capacities of a country and opens the door to strive towards incremental improvements in governance when new opportunities arise. This implies that development advances are necessary for strengthening governance. This notion is also reflected in research on development and governance, which has shown that good governance is dependent on development rather than the other way around (UNDP 2014). This presents an interesting point of reflection for the DRM community, as it has typically argued that good governance is a prerequisite for advancing DRR (United Nations secretariat of the ISDR and UNDP 2004) – in itself a development advance. There are concrete examples of how DRR has contributed to strengthening governance. In India, for example, as part of the recovery operations following the earthquakes in Maharashtra (1993) and Gujarat (2001), housing records were digitized and land titles that were traditionally only recorded under the name of the male head of household for the first time also included the female head of household. Eventually this practice was institutionalized, and transformed the general practice of social housing in these states.

Drawing from this background on the concepts of "good" or "good enough governance", each governance principle will be discussed in greater detail below to illustrate how their application can influence the success or failure of a DRM intervention. While they will be presented in sequence, it should be noted that the principles are closely interlinked and reinforce each other.

The importance of *accountability* for DRM has been increasingly debated in recent years (United Nations secretariat of the ISDR 2011). The basis for any accountability framework is an agreement on the mandates, roles and responsibilities of the organizations and stakeholders involved in DRM. It is not surprising that the DRM community laments an inherent lack of accountability of DRM systems when looking at how some national DRM plans assign roles and responsibilities. Vague formulations or the assignment of functions to whole groups of stakeholders are all too common, resulting in overlaps and gaps. This leaves organizations and individuals with an option to withdraw themselves from their responsibilities or to shift them to someone else, making it nearly impossible to hold organizations or individuals accountable for their deeds or their failure to act. Even when mandates and roles are clearly spelled out, the bottleneck may be a lack of awareness or training of stakeholders regarding their roles. Hence, any initiative to strengthen accountability for disaster risk reduction must start with clarifying roles and responsibilities. This is not a new concern in DRM at all, but one that – probably due to its operational connotation and origin in emergency management – has been sidelined by the more noticeable policy work, such as integrating DRR into national development strategies. Agreement on assigned roles and responsibilities may require some negotiation in cases of competition over roles, or the reluctance to engage in certain functions that are seen to be complex or less rewarding. However, it is not unusual to see some players or government authorities claim accountability – and eventually get the praise – for DRM interventions. This happens more frequently in highly visible post-disaster humanitarian or recovery contexts, as seen in the Colombian and South African cases presented by Williams (2011). While in principle a good practice, the motive is one of political calculations.

There is also a need to devise clear lines of accountability. Three main lines may be distinguished (Transparency Accountability Initiative 2014). First, upward accountability to higher levels of government may be accomplished by reporting on the use of funds or implementation of work plans. This is the usual and most widespread form of accountability, as it is a prerequisite for maintaining a continued flow of funds and support for DRM programs. Second is downward accountability to the lower echelons of government and the recipients of DRM interventions at the community level. This line of accountability is less developed, especially in weak overall governance contexts. Post-disaster recovery processes, however, can provide unique opportunities for downward accountability, for example, by establishing information kiosks or similar mechanisms for the affected populations that provide updates on the progress and planned steps in implementing the recovery plan or program. This has been particularly successful in India and Indonesia following the Indian Ocean Tsunami and in Iran after the Bam Earthquake. The third line of accountability refers to the capacity of government institutions to examine abuses by other public agencies and branches of government, or the requirement for agencies to report sideways.

Any accountability framework also needs to address the issue of who will take responsibility for the generation of risk (United Nations secretariat of the ISDR 2011). Stakeholders, whether government or non-government parties, who make investment or development decisions that lead to increased risks need to be answerable for their actions. This is still a less common feature of known accountability frameworks for DRM, obviously due to the challenges in establishing such accountability. The risk generation process is seldom one-dimensional, as there are several contributing factors and stakeholders involved. Take the example of building a new residence on a known flood plain. Who is ultimately accountable? The public works department for not having updated the building code? The home owner who has circumvented the inspection process? The building inspector who has accepted a bribe? Or the department of lands for having declared a particular plot a residential area? Assigning responsibility in these cases is not an easy task. The issue also raises the question of legal liability, although its usefulness in DRM is still under debate (IFRC and UNDP 2014). Accountability also needs to be established in terms of evaluating the achievements in reducing disaster risk.

This requires establishing of baselines and involving communities in monitoring risk levels and progress in implementing DRM and recovery measures.

Accountability and *transparency* can be mutually reinforcing. Together they enable citizens to have a say about DRM issues that matter to them, as well as providing a chance to influence decision-making and hold those making decisions to account (Williams 2011). Simply making information available on disaster risks and existing disaster reduction and recovery initiatives, however, is not sufficient to achieve transparency. Information that is too technical or not tailored to the needs of the public may be counterproductive and breed opacity rather than transparency. Information should be presented in plain and readily comprehensible language and formats appropriate for different stakeholders and audiences. It should retain the detail and disaggregation necessary for analysis, evaluation and participation. This is easier said than done, since exposing risk information may curtail economic benefits, for example, when the value of properties or industries decreases after new information on hazard risks is disclosed or in the aftermath of a disaster event. The latter has happened in Thailand, where the lucrative car manufacturing industry is located on a major flood plain that suffered serious flood impacts in 2011 (Vaidya and Rao 2011). Debates on the trade-off between short-term economic gains and medium- to long-term risks of placing productive assets in high-risk zones, and the implications for all parties involved, need to be exposed so that decisions on risk-taking and avoidance become a conscious and transparent process. Information should also be made available in sufficient time to permit analysis, evaluation and engagement by relevant stakeholders (Transparency Accountability Initiative 2014), especially when disseminating early warning messages in situations where minutes do matter.

Effectiveness and efficiency are governance principles that are closely linked to accountability, demanding the best use of scarce resources to achieve risk reduction outcomes. A crucial step towards achieving effectiveness and efficiency in DRM is the risk identification process that helps determine the priority risks to which scarce DRM resources, time and capacities should be allocated. Depending on the problem at hand, the risk identification process will offer a menu of risk reduction or mitigation options to choose from, and ideally the most effective and efficient option should proceed. Cost–benefit analysis and similar methodologies are useful instruments that can be applied to support the decision-making process. Currently, however, neither risk identification nor cost–benefit capacities are well developed in most countries (Benson and Twigg 2004; Venton 2007).

The role of legal and regulatory frameworks in DRM is well acknowledged as a means to ensure that disaster risk reduction is a national and local priority (World Conference on Disaster Reduction 2005). DRM legal frameworks encompass not only dedicated DRM laws, such as a national disaster management bill, they also cover the broader body of meta[1] and sector laws, even though there are still great variations in the extent to which these truly integrate disaster risk concerns (IFRC and UNDP 2014). The reflection of disaster risk considerations in sector law is important so that disaster risk can be regulated where it is generated. However, experience has shown that laws alone cannot guarantee success unless they are supported by a strong *rule of law*. Following the rule of law and implementing DRM laws and regulations are the responsibility of all DRM stakeholders. How well this is observed is primarily influenced by the prevailing culture of compliance or non-compliance. While a weak rule of law is often linked to contexts of fragility, low capacity and low human development, documented examples may also be found in countries with high human development (Israely 2009).

Another frequently mentioned constraint when it comes to the implementation of DRM laws is a lack of resources, especially at the local level (Williams 2011; IFRC and UNDP 2014). Although resources may certainly be an issue, there is a growing understanding that the legislative provisions themselves may be to blame, namely when they are not adapted to the realities on the ground and demand high levels of safety standards that are impossible to achieve (UNDP 2007; Venton 2007). In these situations, laws are often bypassed through corruptive practices or simply non-compliance. Hence, in order to attain rule of law in DRM it is crucial to design the best possible law given prevailing resources and capacities; in other words, a "good enough law" may be what a particular country needs in order to progress to the next level of compliance and DRR. Problems of enforcement may also occur in the case of legislative provisions that overlap, contradict each other or leave gaps, as they provide loopholes that impede smooth implementation.

The call for more *participation* in DRM has a long history, aiming to involve a variety of stakeholders (Maskrey 1989; GNDR 2011), including communities, local government, the private sector, NGOs, academia and media, as well as population groups such as women, children, people with disabilities, the elderly and the at-risk or vulnerable populations to name just a few. Participation is also one of the drivers of effective DRM monitored under the Hyogo Framework for Action 2005–2015 (World Conference on Disaster Reduction 2005), based on the assumption that it ensures the appropriate identification and address of diverse DRM needs. Active involvement in decision-making and implementation has made a difference in many places around the globe, resulting in greater ownership, collective action, and control over the decisions that affect the lives of at-risk populations, and ultimately the long-term sustainability of DRM initiatives (Gero *et al.* 2011; Shaw 2012). Participation in DRM has many faces, the most obvious being community-based disaster risk management, decentralizing DRM to the local level, multi-stakeholder platforms, or the more recent concept of network governance. Yet, meaningful participation cannot be simply taken for granted and, more often than not, falls well short of expectations. The reasons are plentiful: power relations that work against a genuine intention to involve some groups or stakeholders; limited capacities to follow through with participatory tools and processes; short project durations that do not allow for comprehensive participatory consultations; weakness of civil society; or the complexity of involving a wide spectrum of institutions and people. In particular, decentralization, a much-praised panacea for strengthening the interface between communities and local government in DRM, has been re-evaluated in recent years. The potential for improving DRR through decentralization often could not be realized because of low levels of citizen awareness of DRR, funding constraints, and weak local technical and coordination capacity (Scott and Tarazona 2011).

The principles of participation and *responsiveness* are also closely related, even though responsiveness bears a greater connotation of the state being responsive to the expressed needs of the population. While this may imply proactiveness on behalf of the state towards its people, it is now increasingly documented that this is rarely happening without significant social demand for DRM that is communicated via civic mobilization (United Nations Secretariat of the ISDR 2011 and 2012; Twigg and Bottomley 2011). Civic mobilization around disaster issues, however, has been nominal to date and there is hardly any activism around disaster risk issues, with some exceptions. Examples include the Lower Lempa Valley in El Salvador, where citizens affected by flooding from Hurricane Mitch in 1998 regularly demanded and eventually received more support for disaster risk reduction from the national government (Lavell 2008). In addition, in Turkey during the 1990s, repeated earthquakes led to a wave of public anger and media outcry at widespread corruption (Williams 2011).

In most cases, the engagement of civil society is limited to supporting the implementation of community-based DRM programs, while influencing public policy or legislative reform processes on disaster risk reduction has remained out of reach in most cases (GNDR n.d.; Pelling and Smith 2008). In the aftermath of the Indian Ocean Tsunami, India, Indonesia, Sri Lanka and Thailand enacted disaster management laws without much public consultation. On the other hand, more recent experiences of DRR law reform in the Philippines demonstrate useful good practice of participatory and consultative processes (National Agency for Disaster Management (BNPB) and UNDP Indonesia 2009).

The need to involve a wide range of stakeholders in DRM accompanies the challenge of mediating a variety of interests that are more often than not in outright opposition to each other. Reaching *consensus-oriented* disaster risk governance thus requires agreement on solutions, policies and legal provisions that are in the best interests of society as a whole. This is, in essence, a political process, albeit one in which DRR has hitherto barely been perceived as a truly political issue (Williams 2011). On the contrary, DRM has been praised for being largely politically neutral, as opposed to issues like climate change or environment, thus facilitating collaboration and joint action (UNDP 2013b). Its humanitarian origins may also have contributed to this approach, since relief and disaster response were to be provided without the intent of furthering any political agenda. In reality, however, not having a political space for disaster risk issues is increasingly becoming a liability as other policy priorities are constantly being favored when it comes to the allocation of resources. Here again, the issue of how social demand could be strengthened comes to the fore as a means of generating political will and promoting accountability and responsiveness. Greater sensitivity is needed to the realities faced by those most vulnerable to disasters in public and private institutions at national, subnational and local levels. Any attempt to achieve a greater traction for DRR in the public policy arena needs to result in better access to information, which is critical also for generating awareness of risks, as well as for changing behaviors and reducing vulnerability. Clearly, there is a need for the DRM community to eventually step out of its comfort zone and confront some of the more sensitive issues such as the political economy of disaster risk.

This leads us to the concluding pair of governance principles this section will deal with, again ones that is often sidestepped in DRR because of apparent sensitivities: pursuing *equitable and inclusive* approaches. Much has been written about how inequalities make some communities more vulnerable than others (Wisner *et al.* 2004; Thomas *et al.* 2010). Social exclusion and unequal access to resources and services due to established power dynamics expose some parts of the population to greater risk, such as the poor living in informal settlements or otherwise fragile environments like river banks or steep slopes. Despite this issue not being new to DRM, there are many examples of development and DRM interventions that have worsened the living conditions of marginalized and voiceless populations who may not even have had a place at the negotiating table, while benefitting the establishment and the elites who were able to successfully push for their interests (Williams 2011). Since such practice ultimately results in increased risk, more needs to be done to counterbalance it with careful analysis of the differential impacts of DRM measures on various population groups to ensure that equal opportunities are provided for all. A rights-based approach to DRM may provide a useful avenue for addressing inequalities. The basic human rights that are relevant in the context of disaster risk reduction include non-discrimination (of gender, age, ethnicity, disability), equality, legal protection, the right to security, access to health services, shelter and housing, clean water, education, and compensation. However, while human rights are widely acknowledged as a crucial element of humanitarian response to disasters, the definition and promotion of a longer term, human rights-based approach to disaster risk reduction is still limited.

Conclusion

There is compelling evidence that a considerable portion of disaster risk is shaped by complex decision-making processes and power relations across various population groups (UNDP 2013b). The at-risk population who bear the brunt of disaster losses is seldom the main contributor to existing risk patterns. Addressing this complex set of problems goes far beyond the strictly technical level at which assistance to reduce disaster risk is typically provided; for example, by setting up an early warning system or conducting a risk assessment. While this type of support is and will remain important, especially in low-income countries with limited capacities, it must be coupled with more process-oriented support mechanisms that place governance and political processes right at the center. The governance principles presented above offer useful guidance on how to shape these processes, so that DRM support comes to its full fruition.

It is therefore recommended that, when a DRM intervention is implemented, equal emphasis be placed on the process as well as the outputs to be achieved. For example, any assistance provided on devising a legal provision for DRM – whether a building code or DRM Act – also needs to address the related rule of law which will determine whether a law or regulation ultimately succeeds in reducing disaster risk.

Disaster risk governance and disaster resilience go hand in hand. A society that puts in place the institutional, policy and budgetary means to effectively mitigate the impacts of disasters *as inherent components of development* will be more resilient the next time a calamity occurs. Hence, it is not enough to only prioritize disaster risk reduction on a case-by-case basis. DRR needs to become an expected and pervasive aspect of all development, from building a new bridge to undertaking education reform. This means that nations and communities have the capacities to identify risk and to take meaningful steps to identify and implement risk-reducing and preparedness measures. Should a hazard, or shock, occur, a resilient society should have the capacity to withstand and persevere, bouncing back quickly without incurring massive losses or damage.

Due to the multidimensional nature of risk, governance arrangements for DRM can no longer be perceived as stand-alone or separate from the larger governance context. With the evolution of the concept of disaster risk governance, a good first stride in this direction has been taken. In terms of looking at the next steps, more emphasis needs to be placed on devising a truly "systems approach" to DRM that is able to span multiple disciplines and stakeholders, constantly re-evaluating itself, and renegotiating among various stakeholders to continually strive for improved risk reduction outcomes. The opportunity to do so has never been timelier than during this period of intensive dialogue on the future directions of the sustainable development frameworks, the universal climate agreement and the Hyogo Framework for Action, which will all culminate in 2015.

Recommendation

A society that can draw upon the institutional, policy and budgetary means to reduce the impacts of disasters as an inherent component of development will be more resilient to future shocks. For this to happen, a truly "systems approach" to DRM is required that recognizes the multidimensional, multidisciplinary and multi-stakeholder nature of risk, and builds on process-oriented support mechanisms that place governance principles and the political economy of disasters at the center.

Audiences of the recommendation: NGOs, national governments, donors, international agencies and the United Nations secretariat of the ISDR.

Note

1 Meta laws comprise national constitutions and human rights law.

References

Benson, Charlotte and Twigg, John. 2004. *Measuring Mitigation – Methodologies for Assessing Natural Hazard Risks and the Net Benefits of Mitigation – A Scoping Study.* Geneva: ProVention Consortium.

Gero, A., Méheux, K. and Dominey-Howes, D. 2011. "Integrating Community Based Disaster Risk Reduction and Climate Change Adaptation: Examples from the Pacific." *Natural Hazards Earth System Science* 11, 101–113.

GNDR. n.d. Policy Formulation. www.globalnetwork-dr.org/images/documents/Papers/Policy_Formulation_doc.pdf.

—— 2011. *If We Do Not Join Hands: Summary Report. May 2011.* Teddington: Global Network of Civil Society Organizations for Disaster Reduction. www.globalnetwork-dr.org/views-from-the-frontline/voices-from-the-frontline-2011.html.

Grindle, Merilee. 2004. "Good Enough Governance: Poverty Reduction and Reform in Developing Countries." *Governance* 17(4), 525–548.

—— 2007. "Good Enough Governance Revisited." *Development Policy Review* 25(5), 553–574.

IFRC and UNDP. 2014. *Effective Law and Regulation for Disaster Risk Reduction: A Multi-Country Study.* New York: International Federation of the Red Cross and Red Crescent Societies and United Nations Development Programme. www.drr-law.org.

IPCC. 2012. *Managing the Risks of Extreme Events and Disasters to Advance Climate Change Adaptation.* Special Report of the IPCC. New York: IPCC.

Israely, Jeff. 2009. "Why Do Italian Disasters Kill so Many People?" *Time*, October 6. http://content.time.com/time/world/article/0,8599,1927865,00.html.

Lassa, J.A. 2010. "Understanding Polycentric Governance of Disaster Risk Reduction: An Introduction to a New Analytical Framework". UNU, Institute for Environment and Human Security, Bonn. www.zef.de/module/register/media/f3d5_Polycentric-DRR-Lassa.pdf.

Lavell, Allan. 2008. "Relationships between Local and Community Disaster Risk Management & Poverty Reduction: A Preliminary Exploration." A Contribution to the 2009 ISDR Global Assessment Report on Disaster Risk Reduction. www.preventionweb.net/english/hyogo/gar/background-papers/documents/Chap6/Lavell-C-DRM-L-DRM-&-Poverty-Reduction.doc.

Maskrey, Andrew. 1989. *Disaster Mitigation: A Community Based Approach.* Oxford: Oxfam.

National Agency for Disaster Management (BNPB), Indonesia and UNDP Indonesia. 2009. *Lessons Learned – Disaster Management Legal Reform, Jakarta, 2009.* Jakarta: SCDRR Project Publications. www.undp.or.id/pubs/docs/Lessons%20Learned%20Disaster%20Management%20Legal%20Reform.pdf.

Pelling, Mark and Smith, Erin Michelle. 2008. "From Grassroots to Global: People Centered Disaster Risk Reduction." The 2008 ProVention Forum, Panama City, April 8–10. ProVention Consortium. www.mtnforum.org/sites/default/files/publication/files/4114.pdf.

Scott, Zoë and Tarazona, Marcela. 2011. "Decentralization and Disaster Risk Reduction: Study on Disaster Risk Reduction, Decentralization and Political Economy." Analysis for UNDP Contribution to the GAR11. UNDP Bureau for Crisis Prevention and Recovery.

Shaw, Rajiv (ed.). 2012. *Community-Based Disaster Risk Reduction.* Community, Environment and Disaster Risk Management, Vol. 10. Bingley, UK: Emerald Insight Publishing.

Thomas, Deborah S.K., Phillips, Brenda D., Fothergill, Alice and Blinn-Pike, Lynn. 2010. *Social Vulnerability to Disasters*, second edition. Boca Raton, FL: Taylor and Francis Publishing.

Transparency Accountability Initiative. 2014. Definitions. www.transparency-initiative.org/about/definitions.

Twigg, John and Bottomley, Helen. 2011. "Making Local Partnerships Work for Disaster Risk Reduction." *Humanitarian Exchange* 50, 21–23.

UNDP. 2004. *Reducing Disaster Risk: A Challenge for Development*. Geneva: Bureau for Crisis Prevention and Recovery, UNDP.

—— 2007. *A Global Review: UNDP Support to Institutional and Legislative Systems for Disaster Risk Management*. Geneva: UNDP.

—— 2010. *A Guide to UNDP Democratic Governance Practice*. New York: UNDP.

—— 2011. *Disaster–Conflict Interface: Comparative Experiences*. New York: UNDP.

—— 2013a. *Issue Brief: Disaster Risk Governance*. Bureau for Crisis Prevention and Recovery. New York: UNDP.

—— 2013b. *Changing with the World: UNDP Strategic Plan 2014–2017*. New York: UNDP.

—— 2014. *Thematic Review on Disaster Risk Governance for the 2015 Global Assessment Report on Disaster Risk Reduction*. Draft version. New York: UNDP.

United Nations secretariat of the International Strategy for Disaster Reduction (ISDR). 2009. *Risk and Poverty in a Changing Climate*. Global Assessment Report on Disaster Risk Reduction: Geneva: United Nations.

—— 2011. *Revealing Risk, Redefining Development*. Global Assessment Report on Disaster Risk Reduction. Geneva: United Nations.

United Nations secretariat of the Inrernational Stategy for Disaster Reduction (ISDR). 2012. *Towards a Post-2015 Framework for Disaster Risk Reduction*. Geneva: United Nations. www.unisdr.org/files/25129_towardsapost2015frameworkfordisaste.pdf.

United Nations secretariat of the Inrernational Stategy for Disaster Reduction (ISDR) and UNDP. 2004. "Disaster Risk Reduction, Governance & Development." *UNISDR Africa Educational Series* 2(4).

Venton, Courtenay C. 2007. "Justifying the Cost of Disaster Risk Reduction: A Summary of Cost–Benefit Analysis." *Humanitarian Exchange* 38, 24–27.

Vivek, Vaidya and Rao, Vijay. 2011. "Thai Floods Impact Auto Industry." Motor Trader, October 28. www.motortrader.com.my/news/thai-floods-impact-auto-industry/.

Williams, G. 2011. *Study on Disaster Risk Reduction, Decentralization and Political Economy: The Political Economy of Disaster Risk Reduction*. Background Report for the Global Assessment Report on Disaster Risk Reduction. Geneva: United Nations.

Wisner, Ben, Blaikie, Piers, Cannon, Terry and Davis, Ian (eds). 2004. *At Risk – Natural Hazards, People's Vulnerability, and Disasters*, second edition. London: Routledge.

World Bank and United Nations. 2010. *Natural Hazards, Unnatural Disasters: The Economics of Effective Prevention*. Washington, DC: World Bank.

World Conference on Disaster Reduction. 2005. *Hyogo Framework for Action 2005–2015: Building the Resilience of Nations and Communities to Disasters*. Geneva: United Nations.

Part V

Tools and technologies for disaster risk reduction

12 National disaster databases

An essential foundation for disaster risk reduction policies and disaster-related sustainable development goals and targets

Yuichi Ono and Masafumi Nagaishi

Introduction

Over recent decades a series of dramatic large-scale disasters, as well as the growing economic impacts and losses from these events, have resulted in more systematic global efforts to manage and reduce disaster risks. Disaster risk reduction is increasingly recognized as an important facet of sustainable development. However, while there are several well-established international disaster databases, many countries do not systematically collect and archive data on their own disaster damage and losses, while the much more numerous small events are often neglected. The resulting lack of comprehensive and accurate data impedes research on the real nature of the risks faced by these countries and undermines the development and implementation of sound policy measures. Policymaking action and investment of resources in boosting effective countermeasures should be based on information detailing damage and losses for different hazards, geographical locations and communities. In addition, if measurable goals and targets are to be developed internationally for disaster risk reduction, within the upcoming post-2015, post-Hyogo Framework for Action (HFA) disaster risk reduction agenda, or as part of sustainable development goals (SDG) processes, then national programs for collecting, archiving and statistically analyzing disaster data will be an essential requirement.

This chapter attempts to provide a comprehensive picture of existing initiatives by various organizations at global and regional levels, and to review and evaluate their effectiveness. A number of good practices will be described in terms of developing and operating national and international disaster statistics on damage and losses. This chapter will then outline the benefits of maintaining disaster statistics at the national and international levels, providing examples of the kinds of information management systems that can be produced. These include developing resources such as white books for use as planning tools by policymakers to analyze and reduce disaster risks. It then considers some of the incentives and mechanisms that can sustain systematic long-term programs, extending beyond the achievements of short-term project-based programs. Finally, the chapter will provide a set of conclusions and recommendations on the development of disaster databases and related statistical products. This includes clarifying the linkages with the post-HFA and SDG processes and emphasizing the need to develop regional and global standards for disaster statistics, through regional and global collaboration.

International disaster data

The main international databases on disaster losses and impacts have a particular character of their own, owing to the fact that they were usually developed for a specific purpose, for example, to support humanitarian relief, insurance risk assessment, or for scientific purposes. They have largely been instigated and managed at the international level, reaching down to national and subnational levels for data input. Global archives for disaster data include, among others, the EM-DAT database, the NatCat natural catastrophe database and the multi-agency PREVIEW global risk data platform.

While these databases serve to provide an overall picture of disaster situations around the world, there is now a move to build or strengthen independent national-level databases to reflect country-specific issues and provide more detailed information. Ideally, these should be developed on the basis of appropriate common methodologies and standards. The DesInventar system, which was developed as a common regional system among a number of Latin American countries, is now being used as the basis for the development of national disaster databases in some African and Asian countries.

Data acquisition and archiving for disaster impacts is a complex task, and faces significant methodological problems of collection and standardization. There may be considerable differences in datasets between the different archives. In addition, disaster risk management depends not only on loss and impact data but also on information on hazards, exposure and vulnerability, risk factors and risk management practices. This means that national databases of disaster losses and impacts need to be developed with an awareness of other relevant databases including, for example, information on population, economic development, weather and seismological hazards. Much can be learned from such efforts. For example, national and international scientific agencies have long maintained extensive databases on heavy rainfall, high winds, floods, earthquakes, volcanic eruption, wildfires, etc. and routinely publish statistical summaries for policy-makers and managers. Formal arrangements for exchanges of historical and real-time data on hazards between countries are in place under the auspices of the United Nations as well as some international and national scientific agencies.

The CRED international disaster database

The international OFDA/EM-DAT disaster database contains data records on the occurrence and impacts of over 18,000 mass disasters throughout the world from the year 1900 to the present (the description of this section is based on the OFDA/EM-DAT website and UNESCAP 2011). The main objective of the database is to serve the purposes of humanitarian action at national and international levels. It is an initiative aimed to rationalize decision-making for disaster preparedness, as well as providing an objective base for vulnerability assessment and priority setting. The database is compiled from various sources, including UN agencies, government sources, non-governmental organizations, insurance companies, research institutes and press agencies. Since 1988 the Centre for Research on the Epidemiology of Disasters (CRED), within the School of Public Health of the Université Catholique de Louvain in Brussels, has maintained and developed the database with support from a variety of organizations, including the Office of Foreign Disaster Assistance (OFDA) of the United States Agency for International Development (USAID), the Belgian government and the World Health Organization.

The current EM-DAT data recording system uses a unique identifier for each disaster and attempts to cover all disasters meeting at least one of the following criteria: (1) ten or more people reported killed; (2) 100 or more people reported affected; (3) declaration of a state of emergency; and (4) there is a call for international assistance. In addition to providing information on the human impacts of disasters, such as the number of people killed, injured or affected, EM-DAT provides disaster-related economic damage estimates and disaster-specific international aid contributions. EM-DAT also distinguishes two generic categories for disasters (natural and technological), with the natural disaster category divided into five sub-groups (geophysical, meteorological, hydrological, climatological and biological), which in turn cover 12 disaster types and more than 30 sub-types. Access to the database can be requested and is granted on a case-by-case basis. The CRED and EM-DAT websites (www.cred.be, www.emdat.be) provide a wide range of data summary products, for example, by region and hazard type and for different years.

The DesInventar system

The DesInventar methodology was originally designed in Latin America in 1994 (the description of this section is based on the DesInventar website and UNESCAP 2011). It can be configured and adapted to the needs of the country or province implementing the system, including the ability to run the user interface in local languages and customize the data items to be collected. The databases facilitate the capture and analysis of the occurrence and impact of disasters for 30 different types of hazards and by three levels of administrative regions (e.g. province, district and sub-district).

DesInventar aims to make visible all disasters from the local scale (town or equivalent) to the large scale, and to facilitate a dialogue on risk management among actors, institutions, sectors, provincial and national governments. It is both a conceptual tool and a methodology for the construction of databases, synthesizing disaggregated data on loss, damage, or effects caused by emergencies or disasters. In many countries, data such as population, infrastructure and industries are available and may be used in the context of disaster risk reduction. Analyzing human losses, for example, the DesInventar methodology employs relevant demographic data (e.g., gender, age, households) and socioeconomic factors (e.g., agricultural data, infrastructure data). It includes definitions and help in the management of data, a database with a flexible structure, and software for data input, searching and querying.

The Asia-Pacific Regional Center (APRC) of the United Nations Development Programme (UNDP) has supported the establishment of disaster loss databases using the DesInventar methodology in several countries in Asia. It has been applied in Indonesia, the Islamic Republic of Iran, the Maldives, Nepal and Sri Lanka (providing country-wide coverage) and India (in the states of Tamil Nadu and Orissa). In some countries, DesInventar has gradually been merged into and modified to suit host country governmental administrations. For example, in Indonesia, DesInventar was introduced in 2006 on a project basis and then, in 2007, it was handed over to the National Disaster Management Agency (BNPB), which has continued to develop and strengthen the use of the database. Indonesia has subsequently adapted the methodology for use in the monitoring of poverty. Similar efforts are ongoing in Timor-Leste, Vietnam and the Lao People's Democratic Republic.

Reinsurance company data

Private reinsurance companies operate their own disaster databases for use in the assessment and pricing of disaster risks, and some of these are partially accessible to the public. One of the most well known is the NatCatSERVICE operated by Munich Re (Munich Re 2011). NatCatSERVICE provides key figures (date of loss and time record, type of event, geocoding of main loss areas), loss data (insured losses, overall losses, bodily injuries, infrastructure areas and industries affected), as well as scientific facts and figures (description of events, wind strength, precipitation levels, earthquake magnitude). The data in NatCatSERVICE are obtained as inputs not only from Munich Re offices worldwide and their clients but also from national and international insurance associations. The Sigma database of Swiss Re is also an aggregation of records on natural and man-made catastrophes (Swiss Re 2014). Sigma notes climate change issues in terms of extreme weather and economic losses.

Identifying individual disasters: GLIDE

The Asian Disaster Reduction Center (ADRC) proposed a globally common unique ID code, which was called the GLobal IDEntifier number (GLIDE) for disasters in 2001 (the description of this section is based on the GLIDEnumber website and OFDA/EM-DAT website). This idea has been shared and promoted by a number of organizations, including CRED, the Field Support Coordination Section (FCSS) of the United Nations Office for Coordination of Humanitarian Affairs (OCHA), the United Nations secretariat of the International Strategy for Disaster Reduction (ISDR), UNDP, the World Meteorological Organization (WMO), the International Federation of Red Cross and Red Crescent Societies

(IFRC) OFDAUSAID, the United Nations Food and Agriculture Organization (FAO), the National Catholic Network de Pastoral Juvenil Hispana (La Red) and the World Bank, and in due course was jointly launched as the international "GLIDE" initiative.

GLIDE numbers were issued every week by EM-DAT at CRED for all new disaster events that meet the EM-DAT criteria from 2002 to 2003. From the beginning of 2004, an "Automatic GLIDE Generator" began to generate GLIDE numbers for all new disaster events. The components of a GLIDE number consist of two letters to identify the disaster type (e.g., EQ – earthquake); the year of the disaster; a six-digit, sequential disaster number; and the three-letter ISO code for country of occurrence. Thus, for example, the GLIDE number for the West India Earthquake in India is: EQ-2001-000033-IND. This number is posted by the above organizations on all their documents relating to that particular disaster, and other partners will eventually include it in the various information products they generate.

Regional efforts

The regional and sub-regional scales are well situated for developing initiatives on national databases on disaster losses and impacts, owing to the availability of existing intergovernmental cooperation mechanisms and disaster-related technical and practitioner networks, as well as receiving the advantages of generally closer economic and cultural linkages. The DesInventar system initiated in Latin America stands as a good example of this cooperation in action. Political support may also be mobilized at these levels. For example, in May 2014 the seventieth session of the United Nations Economic and Social Commission for Asia and the Pacific (UNESCAP) agreed on a resolution that a basic range of disaster-related statistics should be developed to help UNESCAP member countries improve and standardize data collection as part of their strategies for dealing with natural disasters. The following sections contain reports on a selection of regional experiences.

Latin America and the Caribbean

According to the official DesInventar web page (www.desinventar.org/en/database) 22 countries currently use the system in Latin America and the Caribbean, namely Argentina, Belize, Bolivia, Chile, Colombia, Costa Rica, Dominican Republic, Ecuador, Guatemala, Guyana, Honduras, Haiti, Jamaica, Mexico, Nicaragua, Panama, Peru, Paraguay, El Salvador, Trinidad and Tobago, Uruguay, and Venezuela. As the records held in the databases are collated using a uniform methodology, it is relatively straightforward to pool the data for regional analyses and to undertake comparative studies between countries. Moreover, the conceptual approach of DesInventar, which seeks to capture all disaster losses however large or small they may be, and to more fully describe the location and character of multiple impacts, allows much better characterization of the ongoing risk profile of communities. Because loss data are disaggregated at local administrative levels, much closer exploration of the spatial factors in the risk becomes possible.

Recent studies of disaster records using DesInventar for countries in Latin America and the Caribbean (the secretariat of the ISDR 2013) have found noticeable differences relative to other databases and studies. Of particular note is the finding that the majority of the loss events were small and localized, with only 1 percent exceeding a threshold of more than 25 lives lost and/or 300 or more houses destroyed in a local political-administrative unit. Some communities had experienced repeated losses from these smaller kinds of events. This presents a picture of disaster risk as a widespread and frequently debilitating condition, related to land use and settlement practice, rather than the conventional picture of a disaster as a low-probability massive event. The data records also show that losses are generally increasing, reflecting both socioeconomic and climatic trends.

It is clear that national databases, coupled with the advanced approaches of the DesInventar system, can provide policymakers of the countries concerned with a rich foundation of information and evidence upon which to design and implement measures to reduce disaster risk. Among the lessons learned, there is a need to strengthen data collection capacity at local levels and to ensure that data collection occurs systematically throughout the year irrespective of seasonal patterns and expectations, such as hurricane seasons and El Niño episodes. The local disaggregation of damage and losses should be emphasized in all disaster events including the major disasters. The comprehensive collection of data requires more active participation of the relevant sectors and their ministries. Better estimations of economic damage and losses in the different sectors are needed.

Europe and the European Commission

The Joint Research Centre of the European Commission is undertaking studies and developing technical recommendations to guide and standardize European Union loss databases (Groeve et al. 2013). A preliminary modelling study is underway to systematically describe loss databases and their applications. Applications may be categorized into three areas of need: loss accounting, forensic risk studies and risk modelling. The study has identified the following characteristics: data are gathered in combination with 12 main sectors (such as health and energy), four principal affected elements and five types of loss owners. Data are recorded in monetary value. The residential sector, for example, is subdivided into four elements comprising (1) buildings, (2) contents/equipment, (3) vehicles, and (4) landscape. The monetary amounts are calculated separately by the loss owners – these being the individuals, businesses, insurers, government entities and non-governmental entities. In addition, the losses are differentiated into direct losses and indirect losses. The data required are designed to be input at municipality, regional, national or international levels.

Asia and the Pacific

The practical management of disaster data has proven to be a formidable challenge for countries in the implementation of the Hyogo Framework for Action 2005–2015 (World Conference on Disaster Reduction 2005) in the Asia-Pacific region. This is partly due to the complex character of disasters and disaster data, and the lack of internationally endorsed methodologies for disaster data management. National disaster management agencies usually gather data on disaster events and may undertake special studies, but typically they do not have specialized expertise in databases and statistical management. National statistical offices, on the other hand, have considerable expertise and experience in socioeconomic data collection, database management and statistical analysis, but do not have specialized knowledge of disaster-related data and generally do not collect such data. Disaster data collection and analysis thus occurs independently from mainstream national statistical efforts. This isolation tends to weaken recognition of the linkages between disaster risk and socioeconomic factors and to reinforce the marginalization of disaster risk reduction in development planning.

An initiative to address these issues has been launched by UNESCAP, as noted above. The ESCAP Committee on Disaster Risk Reduction identified a need to monitor progress towards improved resilience of member states to disasters, including the development of a core set of disaster-related statistics (UNESCAP 2011). This led to the decision to support a regional expert group comprising statisticians and disaster risk reduction experts that would develop a range of disaster-related statistics for approval by the Commission. It also requested that the ESCAP Executive Secretary report on the initiative at the Third United Nations World Conference on Disaster Risk Reduction in 2015 and report on progress at the meeting of the Commission in 2016 (UNESCAP 2013).

With the Hyogo Framework for Action as the backdrop and its successor in the making, the new Expert Group Meeting (EGM) on Improving Disaster Data to Build Resilience in Asia and the Pacific will seek to sharpen the focus on basic principles for disaster data and statistics necessary to achieve evidence-based resilience at national and community levels (UNESCAP 2014). It will discuss a possible roadmap, which entails policy advocacy, gaining technical support, and on-the-field implementation of the minimum standards in disaster data collection and management.

In South Asia, the South Asia Association of Regional Cooperation (SAARC) Disaster Management Centre (SDMC) has a mandate to serve eight member countries: Afghanistan, Bangladesh, Bhutan, India, the Maldives, Nepal, Pakistan and Sri Lanka (SDMC 2014). Set up in October 2006 at the premises of the National Institute of Disaster Management of India in New Delhi, the center is responsible for providing policy advice and facilitating capacity-building services, including strategic learning, research, training, systems development and exchange of information for effective disaster risk reduction and management in South Asia.

Africa

Several African countries are developing DesInventar-based disaster loss databases. Those in Djibouti, Ethiopia, Kenya, Mali, Mozambique, Tunisia and Uganda are now operational while databases in Morocco and Egypt are under construction (DesInventar 2014). The Global Information and Early Warning System (GIEWS), managed by FAO since 1975, is an open forum for the exchange of information on food security, rather than a database (GIEWS 2014). However, the system presents information about drought and other weather conditions and estimates influence on food security. The coverage of data is from 1995 onward. Another resource, the Natural Disaster Database for Central Africa (NDDCA), covers disasters that have occurred in Burundi, the Democratic Republic of Congo (DRC) and Rwanda after 1900 (NDDCA n.d.). Sources of data in NDDCA are gathered from existing databases, such as CRED EM-DAT, Dartmouth Flood Observatory and ReliefWeb.

Japan's experience and cooperation

The White Paper (Bosai Hakusho)

In Japan, a variety of damage statistics of disasters may be found in official reports such as the White Paper on Fire and Disaster Management (published by the Fire and Disaster Management Agency), the annual Flood Damage Statistics Survey (Water and Disaster Management Bureau, Ministry of Land, Infrastructure, Transport and Tourism), the White Paper on Disaster Management (the Cabinet Office), and others. The White Paper on Disaster Management (henceforth referred to as "The White Paper") was originally a set of documents submitted to the Diet. The document of the plan for disaster reduction in the fiscal year 1963 was submitted to the forty-third ordinary session of the Diet and the document of the overview on the measures taken for the disasters that occurred during the fiscal year 1962 was submitted to the following ordinary session of the Diet. From the fiscal year 1977, the White Paper was issued as an official government publication. The White Paper is an obligatory report to the Diet by the Cabinet Office, prepared by its Disaster Management Unit, compiled and published around June each year, and contains an annual overview of disaster occurrences, countermeasures taken during the year and a plan for the following year, based on the Disaster Countermeasures Basic Act.

The Disaster Countermeasures Basic Act is the key law on disaster management, and is true to its name. It was enacted in 1961, in the aftermath of the 1959 Ise-Bay Typhoon,[1] which caused tremendous damage throughout Japan, especially along the coast of Aichi and Mie prefectures. The Ise-Bay Typhoon would now be classified as a Category 5 super-typhoon – the highest category of the WMO classification scheme. The total number of victims reached more than 5,000. It was the most serious event after World War II over the 50 years up until the 1995 Great Hanshin-Awaji Earthquake. In addition, the economic losses were enormous, reaching 505 billion yen in Aichi and Mie prefectures – equivalent to 4.6 percent of the previous year's GDP, more than 40 percent of the General Account Budget at that time. These percentages were close to those of the 2011 Great East Japan Earthquake and Tsunami. In fact the Ise-Bay Typhoon served as a trigger for the publication of the White Paper, one of the principal reviews of disaster management in Japan. The White Paper on Disaster Management has two missions; the first is to keep an accurate record and to report on the situation to the Cabinet. In doing so, the White Paper provides a systematic record and information management system allowing progressive comparison between years and including future events, for example, 5 years and 10 years into the future. This mission is what gives the White Paper its legal status.

The second mission is to present the challenges of disaster management. From the 2004 edition onward, an extra chapter was added to discuss what issues are being considered and tackled as government tasks, thereby providing clear messages to the people. For example, a preventive strategy for earthquake disasters to mitigate damage was presented in the 2004 edition. The following 2005 and 2006 editions urged the necessity of establishing a nationwide popular movement and promoting the development of a wide-ranging movement by showing basic policies to realize mitigation. The 2007 edition urged greater disaster risk awareness and specified needs for actions that needed to be taken by various bodies. The theme of the 2008 edition was to encourage a greater interest in disasters and to link personal actions for disaster prevention through "self-help" and "mutual-assistance" approaches. The catchphrase of the 2009 edition was "Recognize changing disaster risks and mitigate damage."

The White Paper enhances the people's understanding of the outline of disaster countermeasures by the government and their collection of various information that serves as the trigger for future actions for disaster prevention. The White Paper is structured in three parts:

- Part 1: Summary of the latest situation and countermeasures on disaster
- Part 2: Overview of measures taken for the disasters of the most recent fiscal year
- Part 3: Plan for disaster prevention in the coming fiscal year.

In Part 1, the major disasters that occurred in the year are described, along with details of the countermeasures taken by the government. In the latest version for the fiscal year 2013, Part 1 of the White Paper summarizes the work on recovery and reconstruction from the serious damage of the Great East Japan Earthquake. Parts 2 and 3 usually comprise chapters on key topics such as recovery and rehabilitation, disaster prevention, national conservation, and science and technology. Within each chapter there are sub-chapters; for example, in the chapter on disaster prevention and science and technology, there are sub-chapters on disaster types, including earthquakes, wind and floods, volcanoes, snow, fire, hazardous materials, and nuclear hazards. The chapter on national conservation

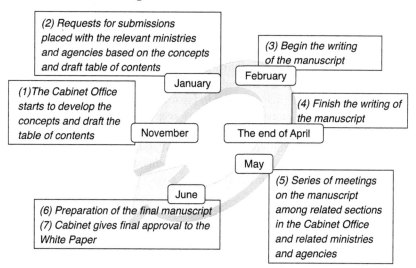

Figure 12.1 Year-round schedule for the White Paper

Source: Authors.

describes disaster issues from the perspectives of water conservation, soil conservation, landslide countermeasures, coastal zone management, etc.

It takes around eight months to prepare the White Paper on Disaster Management. Most ministries and agencies contribute to the process. The officer in charge of the preparation contacts around 100 officers directly, but it is estimated to reach more than 20,000 other staff throughout numerous ministries and agencies that are involved in some way. The White Paper provides an additional valuable foundation of cooperation and coordination among the agencies and organizations that have interests and responsibilities in disaster risk management (see Figure 12.1).

The White Paper on Disaster Reduction plays a key role in tabling disaster reduction on the national agenda, which is one of the intentions of "Mainstreaming Disaster Risk Reduction." This is a way of drawing public attention to disasters not only at the time of disaster events but even in "peacetime," and a way to maintain institutional memories of disaster reduction policies regardless of political changes. Moreover, the compiled disaster database in the White Paper can be used to provide planning tools by policymakers in analyzing and reducing disaster risks, as well as contributing to the establishment of sustainable and measurable disaster-related development goals and targets.

Developing a Thai version of the White Paper

The Indian Ocean Tsunami on December 26, 2004 caused serious damage to Thailand, resulting in about 8,500 people missing or killed. The Government of Thailand had already undertaken disaster countermeasures before the tsunami, including the establishment in 2002 of the Department of Disaster Prevention and Mitigation (DDPM) to assume responsibilities for disaster prevention and response. There are now 12 regional centers and 75 district offices under the DDPM. In 2004 the Disaster Prevention and Mitigation Academy (DPMA) was created with a mandate for human resource development. In addition to these organizations, in the aftermath of the tsunami in 2004 the government established the National Disaster Warning Center (NDWC), which has overall responsibility for integrating forecasts and warnings for disasters across ministries and agencies and has endeavored to establish the framework for cooperation among the related organizations.

The Government of Thailand recognized that the DDPM did not yet fulfill the function of the central administrative body in charge of complete control of disaster management, such as collecting and compiling disaster information, reviewing the various disaster management plans and the implementation of disaster reduction policies based on those plans. To help develop these capacities, the government requested a technical cooperation project with Japan in 2006. It sought to establish a system to collect, accumulate and utilize information on disaster and disaster risk management, as well as enhance relationships and coordination with other relevant organizations.

Accordingly, the DDPM and JICA started a project to build DDPM's capacities for comprehensive disaster management. One of the activities was to publish a Thailand White Paper on disaster prevention and mitigation. The DDPM set up a working group under the National Disaster Policy Division to oversee the White Paper preparation. Drawing on the model of Japan's White Paper, the Thailand White Paper for the year 2550 (Buddhist calendar year, or AD 2007), summarizes information from relevant organizations and was published and distributed at the end of the project. The Thailand White Paper comprises over 300 pages, and a table of contents as shown in Figure 12.2.

In chapter 3 and the appendix, the contents summarized every type of disaster, such as floods, droughts, storms and forest fires. The appendix also included the DDPM's Orders that were issued in the current year.

Indonesia project

Indonesia's National Disaster Management Agency (BNPB) was established in 2008. It supports a disaster data and information portal DIBI (Data dan Informasi Bencana Indonesia) that was launched in July 2008. The objective of DIBI is to provide multi-element disaster information data (e.g., number of deaths, injured, missing, houses destroyed, affected people, evacuees) for risk identification, policy formulation, decision-making and the promotion of disaster risk reduction. Its development was supported by UNDP using DesInventar and DesConsultar software. It can be accessed online at http://dibi.bnpb.go.id.

Via the DIBI system, the public can access disaster data and information from 1815 up until the present. In 2013 BNPB cooperated with the National Statistical

Table of Contents

Foreword
Chapter 1 The Topography and Climate of Thailand
Chapter 2 Organization Structure and Disaster Management in Thailand
- Disaster Management System in Thailand
- Disaster Organization Structure

Chapter 3 Natural Disaster Report
- Disaster Situation during 2002–2006
- Severity Disaster Situation in 2007

Chapter 4 Global Disaster Situation
Chapter 5 Natural Disaster Management in Thailand
- Disaster Management Activities and Budget in 2007
- Large Scale Disaster Cause Analysis, Achievement and Failure and Trend of Disaster in 2007
- Future Operation Plan

Chapter 6 International Cooperation in Disaster Management
Appendix
Bibliography

Figure 12.2 Table of contents of the Thailand White Paper

Source: Thailand White Paper for the year 2550 (Buddhist calendar year, or AD 2007).

Data Agency (BPS) and the UN Population Fund (UNPFA) to expand DIBI's capacity by incorporating socioeconomic data such as the Population Census 2010 and PODES (Village Potential) 2011. DIBI stakeholders and users can now combine disaster data and demographic data to improve risk assessments and decision-making in disaster management.

After the Sumatra Earthquake and Indian Ocean Tsunami occurred in December 2004, the Study on Natural Disaster Management Plan was implemented from 2007 to 2009 with the technical cooperation of JICA. It found that statistical data on disasters gathered at the regency/municipality level were not stored or managed systematically and that there were no unified formats for disaster data reporting. The formats used at the village level were found to be incompatible with the sub-district level, regency/municipality level, and so on. Subsequently in 2011 the BNPB Regulation No. 8 on Standardization of Disaster Data and Information was formulated to guide Regional Agencies on Disaster Management (BPBDs) offices and officials in collecting and reporting disaster data and information. However, much remained to be done to explain in detail the methods of collection and to effectively disseminate and establish the operation of the regulation at local levels.

A subsequent JICA project started in 2011 and is currently under implementation. Entitled "Project for Enhancement of the Disaster Management Capacity of BNPB and BPBD," the project brings together the disaster administration of the central government (BNPB) and the provincial center administration (BPBD) in an effort focused on North Sulawesi and Bali provinces to address the collection of disaster data and information. The Technical Guideline for Disaster Data and Information Collection has been formulated to assist local staff (BPBD Kabupaten/Kota staff) to understand what is required and how to prepare the disaster data and information collection forms. The Technical Guideline chapters include: (1) background and purpose; (2) disaster management cycle and disaster data/information forms; (3) getting to know the disaster data and information form; (4) how to fill out the data and information form; (5) disaster data and information reporting; and (6) closing notes.

The three kinds of BNPB standard formats used in the pre-disaster and emergency response period are described in the Technical Guideline. Among them, the Regional Profile Form and Resource Availability Form are part of the pre-disaster data. These are basic data that provide an overview of the geography, climate, availability of resources, and so forth, to serve as baseline information in disaster management. The Disaster Incident Form is a part of the emergency response data, a recapitulation of the disaster incident starting from the location, the victims and the impact of the disaster. Those three forms are based on the BNPB Regulation No. 8 of 2011 regarding Standardization of Disaster Data. Through workshops and discussions with stakeholders and field trials, the project developed two additional forms to strengthen the reporting capabilities: the Disaster Survey Form and the Daily Report Form.

BNPB is currently in the process of working with selected provinces such as Yogyakarta, Central Java, Bengkulu and Aceh to establish provincial DIBI systems with various training activities. These will make use of the lessons and outputs developed in the above project.

International goals and targets as drivers for enhancing database building

International experience has shown that development targets and goals can be powerful motivators for the achievement of improved development outcomes. Now that the UN Millennium Development Goals are coming to the end of their 15-year implementation period, the United Nations is sponsoring a major international process to develop and agree on a new set of goals and targets, the Sustainable Development Goals (SDGs). Some form of goals or targets for disaster risks or disaster losses would be highly desirable, not only for disaster risk reduction but also for mainstreaming awareness and action on disasters as part of the broader development agenda. However, given the many important goals in development, it is likely that disaster risk issues will be included only at a secondary level in the SDG framework.

A parallel process is also underway to shape a new ten-year agenda for disaster risk reduction that will follow on from the end of the HFA term in 2015. This process is expected to culminate in a new statement at the UN World

Conference on Disaster Risk Reduction in Sendai, Japan on March 14–18, 2015. Consultations to date indicate a general wish to maintain the HFA as the principal roadmap on priorities in disaster risk reduction and to put a new and greater focus on implementation issues, actions and accountabilities, particularly with respect to the HFA Priority 4 (reducing the underlying risk factors), the area where countries have so far achieved the least progress (World Conference on Disaster Reduction 2005).

It is clear that the next decade will see the increased use of goals and targets in disaster risk reduction, especially through the Sustainable Development Goals agenda and the post-2015 Hyogo Framework for Action agenda. Furthermore, it is very likely that goals and targets will not remain only at national level, but will be taken up with enthusiasm at subsidiary levels of government and by non-governmental organizations.

However, the formulation and implementation of goals and targets for disaster risk reduction remains a formidable task. Disaster risk is a complex issue, and data resources are very limited and incomplete. Efforts are ongoing to devise goals and targets that are simple and meaningful, and to consider the requirements for data as well as associated data collection and archiving. For example, a meeting of experts in New York in July 2013 reviewed options for supporting the Sustainable Development Goals process, such as a goal to "build resilience and reduce deaths from natural disasters by x percent." The group reviewed a number of disaster-related indicators, and concluded that a range of indicator types would need to be pursued, including indicators of outcomes, processes and inputs related to disaster risk (the secretariat of the ISDR 2013; IRDR 2014; UNDP 2013).

Conclusion

In summary, this chapter is concerned with the question of how countries document the damage and losses arising from disasters in managing disasters and disaster risks. More specifically, the chapter addresses how to use such databases in formulating evidence-based measures to reduce the risks and losses. The principal conclusions are as follows:

- Most countries do not have systematic mechanisms for collecting disaster damage and loss data under the authority of a national agency such as a disaster management office.
- There are few if any formally agreed common global or regional standards for disaster data collection and reporting.
- Several international disaster databases or data portals exist, mostly with a focus on medium- to large-scale events and on aggregate data. Their data are obtained from varied sources that are usually not part of any formal nationally administered system.
- The DesInventar initiative collects data on all scales and has shown that numerous small-scale disasters contribute a substantial share of losses, particularly at the community level.

- Some countries that maintain data-gathering systems are also being used to undertake annual national reporting on disasters. The annual White Paper produced in Japan, for example, has become a major tool for evaluating and guiding action to reduce disaster losses.
- Regional cooperation has proven to be a successful approach to developing and strengthening the disaster data gathering and archiving of countries.
- Regional approaches capitalize on existing regional political mechanisms and technical networks, and can better address the special characteristics of the region.
- Quantitative goals and targets on disaster risk and loss are being sought in the Sustainable Development Goals process and the post-2015 HFA process.
- A much better basis of disaster data and information will be needed to design and implement the goals and targets at international and national levels.
- The quality of national policies and measures to reduce disaster risk and disaster losses will depend on the quality of the data resources on which the policy and measures are based.
- Some countries are actively fostering cooperation and data sharing between disaster management authorities and the national statistical offices.

Addressing the shortcomings and shortfalls in capacity will require sustained effort at the international, national and local levels. The potential for collaboration is high and has already been well demonstrated, as shown by the examples described above. However, it will need to be more systematically organized and better supported, in particular through intergovernmental agreement and action, development assistance programs, the long-term involvement of scientific institutes, and the active participation of policymakers, client sectors and communities.

Specific recommendations are as follows:

- Systematic efforts to design and implement goals and targets in disaster risk reduction should be undertaken and strongly supported at global and regional levels. These should include mechanisms to monitor progress.
- Systematic approaches to gathering and archiving disaster-related data and preparation of disaster statistics should be rapidly developed, in order to monitor international goals and targets and to support national objectives in disaster risk management.
- The post-2015 HFA agreement at the Third World Conference on Disaster Risk Reduction in Sendai, Japan should contain specific quantitative goals and targets and monitoring mechanisms, and should establish an agreement on the minimum requirements for supporting data and statistics capability for all countries.
- At this early stage of development, flexible approaches to setting goals and targets are needed, covering risk reduction outcomes, processes and inputs.
- The post-2015 initiative on disaster statistics should be part of a package to strengthen national disaster management offices and national platforms

for disaster risk reduction and to enhance linkages with national statistical authorities.

- All disaster data-gathering programs should be accompanied by a publication program that produces as a minimum: (1) periodic studies and summaries of key factors of the country's disaster risks; and (2) an annual report (White Paper) on the year's disasters and on current policies and measures to reduce risk and loss.
- Within the Asia-Pacific region, a roadmap for action on data and statistics should be produced, based on the ESCAP Resolution of May 23, 2014.
- Development assistance agencies should continue to support and prioritize the development of national capacities for disaster data collection and statistics.

Further progress in disaster risk reduction will require much better data capabilities, covering hazards, exposure, damage and losses, vulnerability and resilience. The starting point needs to be the gathering of data on damage and losses, since these are the ultimate manifestations of the disaster problem. As is shown in the country examples outlined above, the damage and loss databases, once established, can be enhanced with the addition of related data that help describe risks, such as information on geography, hazards, population and the inclusion of relevant socioeconomic data.

Recommendation

Systematic approaches to gathering disaster-related data, especially on disaggregated damage and loss, should be developed. This would help develop and monitor international goals and targets for disaster risk reduction and empower governments' efforts in this area at the national level. Based on accurate and dependable disaster statistics, pinpointed evidence-based policy may be produced to reduce disaster risks more effectively. Japan's 'white book' on disaster management provides a good example.

Audiences of the recommendation: City governments, national governments, donors and the United Nations secretariat of the ISDR.

Acknowledgment

The authors would like to acknowledge Mr Zhen Gyi Zhe, a graduate student of the school of engineering at Tohoku University, for his assistance in collecting information and providing analysis for this chapter. Assistant Professors Dr Erick Mas and Dr Jibiki Yasuhito at the International Research Institute of Disaster Science at Tohoku University provided substantial contributions to the chapter. Dr Reid Basher, a formal advisor to the UN Secretary-General's Special Representative for Disaster Risk Reduction, reviewed the draft text, offering useful comments for consideration, and thanks are due to Mr Shiro Katsumata, Cabinet Office (Disaster Management) and Mr Ryoji Takahashi, Oriental Consultants Global Co., Ltd, for providing valuable information.

Note

1   Also referred to as Typhoon Vera.

References

Bousaijyoho Shinbun. www.bosaijoho.jp/.

Cabinet Office. 2013. *Bousai Hakusho (Heisei 25 nendo-ban)*. [White Paper on Disaster Management 2013]. Tokyo: Cabinet Office.

—— www.bousai.go.jp/kyoiku/kyokun/kyoukunnokeishou/rep/1959--isewanTYPHOON/index.html.

De Groeve, Tom, Poljansek, Karmen and Ehrlich, Daniele. 2013. "Recording Disaster Loss: Recommendations for a European Approach." European Commission Joint Research Centre. Luxemburg: Publications Office of the European Union. http://publications.jrc.ec.europa.eu/repository/bitstream/111111111/29296/1/lbna26111enn.pdf.

Department of Disaster Prevention and Mitigation (DDPM). 2007. *White Paper 2007* (Thai Version). Bangkok: DDPM.

DesInventar. 2014. "Background." Accessed May 10, 2014. www.desinventar.net/whatis-desinventar.html.

Fire and Disaster Management Agency. n.d. *Shoubou Hakusho*. [White Paper on Fire and Disaster Management]. Tokyo; Fire Disaster and Management Agency.

GIEWS. n.d. "About GIEWS." Accessed May 6, 2014. www.fao.org/giews/english/about.htm.

GLIDEnumber. n.d. "About GLIDE." Accessed May 6, 2014. www.glidenumber.net/glide/public/about.jsp.

Hayashi, Toshihiko. 2011. *Daisaigai no Keizaigaku* [Economics of Major Catastrophes]. Tokyo. PHP Shinsho.

IRDR. 2014. "Issue Brief: Disaster Risk Reduction and Sustainable Development." Prepared for the Seventh Session of the UN General Assembly Open Working Group on Sustainable Development Goals, New York, January 6–10. www.preventionweb.net/files/35831_35831irdricsubriefdrrsd5b15d1.pdf.

JICA. 2006. *Bousai Nouryoku Koujou Purojekuto Jizen Chousa Houkokusho* [The Preliminary Study Report for the Project on Capacity Development in Disaster Management in Thailand]. Tokyo; JICA.

—— 2008. *Summary of Evaluation Result, Bousai Nouryoku Koujou Purojekuto Shuryouji Hyouka Chousa Houkokusho* [The Terminal Evaluation Report for the Project on Capacity Development in Disaster Management in Thailand]. Tokyo: JICA.

Ministry of Land, Infrastructure, Transport and Tourism (MLIT). n.d. *Suigai Toukei* [Flood Damage Statistics Survey]. www.mlit.go.jp/river/toukei_chousa/kasen/suigaitoukei/.

Munich Re. 2011. "NatCatSERVICE: Natural Catastrophe Know-How for Risk Management and Research." Munich: Münchener Rückversicherungs-Gesellschaft. www.munichre.com/site/corporate/get/documents/mr/assetpool.shared/Documents/0_Corporate%20Website/_Publications/302-06733_en.pdf.

National Disaster Management Agency (BNPB). 2014. Disaster Data and Information Portal DIBI (Data dan Informasi Bencana Indonesia). http://dibi.bnpb.go.id.

—— n.d. "Technical Guidelines for Acquiring and Accumulating Disaster Data/Information for Regencies/Municipalities."

NDDCA. n.d. "About the Database." Accessed May 6, 2014. www.africamuseum.be/collections/browsecollections/naturalsciences/earth/hazard/about.

OFDA/EM-DAT. 2009. "About." Accessed May 10, 2014. www.emdat.be/.

SDMC. 2014. "GENESIS." New Delhi: SAARC Disaster Management Centre. http://saarc-sdmc.nic.in/index.asp.

Swiss Re, Sigma. 2014. "Natural Catastrophes and Man-Made Disasters in 2013, 2014." http://media.swissre.com/documents/sigma1_2014_en.pdf.

UNDP. 2013. "Targets and Indicators for Addressing Disaster Risk Management in the Post 2015 Development Agenda." Meeting of Experts, New York, July 18–19. Meeting Report (Draft August 26, 2013). New York: UNDP.

UNESCAP. 2011. "Addressing Disaster Risk Reduction and Development through Improved Data on Disasters." Economic and Social Commission for Asia and the Pacific Committee on Disaster Risk Reduction (E/ESCAP/CDR(2)/INF/5), 2011. www.unescap.org/sites/default/files/CDR2-INF5_1.pdf.

——— 2013. Expert Group Meeting on Improving Disaster Data in Asia and the Pacific. http://enea.unescap.org/meeting/2013/EGM.html.

——— 2014. "Disaster-Related Statistics in Asia and the Pacific." Draft Resolution Sponsored by Philippines and Co-sponsored by Islamic Republic of Iran, Maldives, and Pakistan. Economic and Social Commission for Asia and the Pacific, Seventieth Session, Bangkok, May 23, 2014. Document E/ESCAP/70/L.5.

United Nations General Assembly. 2014. "Suggested Elements for the Post-2015 Framework for Disaster Risk Reduction." June 16. www.preventionweb.net/posthfa/.

United Nations secretariat of International Strategy for Disaster Reduction (ISDR). 2013. *Global Assessment Report on Disaster Risk Reduction 2013: From Shared Risk to Shared Value: The Business Case for Disaster Risk Reduction.* Geneva: United Nations.

World Conference on Disaster Reduction. 2005. *Hyogo Framework for Action 2005–2015: Building the Resilience of Nations and Communities to Disasters.* Geneva: United Nations.

13 Disaster intelligence

Using geospatial technology to improve resilience in developing countries

Ryosuke Shibasaki and Sho Takano

Introduction

There are currently more than six billion cellular phones in use around the world. This indicates the remarkable development and popularization of ICT (information and communication technology). Data on the positions of extremely large numbers of cellular phones and vehicles may now be collected in real time with satellite-based positioning systems like GPS. Furthermore, digital maps covering the whole world, such as Google Maps, are freely available. This means that information is now directly linked to the real world and, by making full use of ICT, we have the ability to access real-time information about various events and situations around the world quickly. These technologies may also be applied to reducing disaster risks and the minimization of damage. We are now entering a new era of "disaster intelligence."

Data and information on real-world phenomena and events are known as geospatial information. This chapter focuses on geospatial technologies, including acquisition, analysis, integration, visualization and sharing of real-world data, as these can provide the major building blocks of disaster intelligence. Furthermore, this chapter will explore and provide examples of the possible contributions that these emerging technologies can make towards improving local resilience to disasters in developing countries. With proper applications of geospatial technologies, it may be possible to bring about a dynamic change in developing countries, just as those countries have in some cases leapfrogged the landline phone stage to becoming cellular phone societies. This chapter will provide a summary of the current applications, opportunities and challenges as well as proposing new ways of applying geospatial technology effectively to work towards the goal of disaster intelligence.

Utilization of geospatial information technology in developing countries

Geospatial information technology is a field of technology that enables us to acquire digital information indicating what exists when and where, and in what situations. It then also allows us to visualize and analyze that information. This technology can be effectively applied to various situations in disaster risk management, such as development of master plans, project proposals and management of projects, as well as emergency responses. Developing countries have started to apply geospatial information technologies in a variety of domains. For example, geographical information (e.g., topography, road networks, local flood risk maps, etc.) generated from satellite imagery, along with demographic statistics and disaster simulation results (e.g., flood and tsunami simulations), are overlaid onto geographic information systems (GIS) to produce hazard maps and to make disaster risk assessments.

One of the most remarkable examples of this is a recovery plan developed after Typhoon Yolanda hit the Philippines in November 2013. In this recovery plan, supported by JICA (Japan International Cooperation Agency), a damage map was produced using satellite images and an airborne LIDAR (Laser Imaging Detection and Ranging) survey. In the course of planning, flood risk was analyzed, a flood model was developed through simulation and hazard maps were generated. Recovery plans such as this cannot be made without geospatial technologies.

Another example is an information infrastructure reinforcement project with GIS funded by ADB (Asian Development Bank) to support and manage vulnerable local or city administrations in Nepal. In this project, a map-based information infrastructure for building and land property management has been developed and used for taxation. Moreover, GIS and a core information infrastructure have been utilized for city planning and management such as the development of a project proposal (Asian Development Bank (ADB) 2009).

Geospatial information is frequently applied at the individual project level; however, there are also barriers to its further advancement. For example, geospatial information may not always be shared among related organizations. In countries where survey and mapping are traditionally managed by military departments especially, there may be greater difficulties in promoting the sharing of information due to issues of national security.

On the other hand, Indonesia has already started using a large-scale National Spatial Data Infrastructure (NSDI) system to legally promote data sharing and data quality control by the government. NSDI is a relatively new policy implemented by developed countries in recent years, and it means that developing countries are rapidly catching up with developed countries in terms of geospatial information sharing. By way of example, to promote such data sharing in Japan, the Basic Act on the Advancement of Utilizing Geospatial Information was passed in 2007. According to the Act, in Japan data sharing is simply a recommended goal. In the Indonesian case, by contrast, the enforcement of data sharing is stronger and more concrete.

The utilization of cellular phones in disaster-related applications has also increased. The growing popularity of smart phones has greatly accelerated the spread and effectiveness of such applications recently. One example is a pilot project aimed at disseminating direct early warning messages of disasters through cellular phones. The PDC (Pacific Disaster Center) developed a smart phone application, namely "DisasterAWARE," with which users are able to receive disaster early warning messages from the Pacific Disaster Center (PDC 2014). The American Red Cross also provides a similar application, namely "Red Cross Mobile Apps." However, this latter warning service is only available in the United States. Furthermore, only smart phones can access these services, so users in developing countries, where a majority still use GSM (Global System for Mobile communications) cellular phones, would have limited access to such services.

Since it may be used with ordinary cellular phones, SMS has a high potential in developing countries. For example, "Frontline SMS" is free software with which users can easily send short messages to many users from a PC (Frontline SMS Cloud 2014). This service has been utilized in information exchange not only for disaster management but also for humanitarian support and epidemic prevention projects. In addition, in the Philippines, legislation for promoting disaster information distribution by free SMS is under consideration following Typhoon Yolanda (CRS Newswire 2014).

Thus, the popularization of cellular phones and evolution into smart phones enables emergency services to send disaster warning messages and various related information to individuals very efficiently. In the next stage of development, methods for promptly creating and distributing highly reliable information at the most appropriate time will become increasingly important.

One good example of this is a flood-warning project in Bangladesh supported by ADB. It aims at providing an end-to-end warning service proceeding from information generation to dissemination. This project is unique in terms of the use of satellite observations for information generation and acquisition of cellular phone location data through the information dissemination process. In particular, this project aims at strengthening flood predictions for the Flood Forecasting and Warning Centre under the BWDB (Bangladesh Water Development Board). First, a DSM (digital surface model) is generated from ALOS (Advanced Land Observing Satellite) and GSMaP (Global Satellite Mapping of Precipitation) or unique global semi-real-time precipitation data are provided to the project. With these data, the project can perform a simulation of flood prediction that expands the flood prediction lead time from a few days to one week. Warning messages resulting from the prediction have been directly sent to local people or experts through SMS. In this case, more appropriate warning messages may be generated by knowing the distribution of local people in a targeted evacuation area when the flood risk reaches a warning level.

Snapshot data like satellite imagery have up until now been utilized to understand the real-time situation of a region. Recently, however, as an ever-larger proportion of the population is using cellular phones, the movement of people and the distribution changes can be estimated with data from cellular mobile phone systems. The value of this dynamic situational information is very high because it is updated in real time. Thus, geospatial information could potentially reach a completely new level of utility through cellular phones.

During disasters, people are targeted for evacuation and rescue. On the other hand, people create demand for transportation services. In situations where people's residential areas have shifted, new urban development will be required along with new energy demands. Furthermore, in places where people gather, infectious diseases are more likely to occur and special considerations for public health such as waste, sewage treatment and control of vectors like mosquitoes may be required. In this way, people are a key driving force of development projects. Information on population distribution and movement is a common and important basis for various societal benefit services. A social system that periodically collects information on people, through tools such as a census, is usually well managed in developed countries, while the equivalent system in developing countries may be very poor. Even in developed countries, insufficient updating of information has become a major issue. Thus, the use of cellular phones could present a breakthrough in solving these problems.

On the other hand, due to the popularization of cellular phones, more diverse local information other than the position data of a handset may be collected. There are many examples of disaster situations where a large amount of information may be acquired from volunteers and citizens through short messages and Twitter. Moreover, open-source platform software that supports data collection and management can be distributed (Ushahidi 2014). Ushahidi, for example, was originally developed as a platform to receive reports on violence and injustice associated with the vote in the presidential election in Kenya. The reports were received in the form of emails and text messages, and then finally visualized as a map. Such a platform is currently being used in a systematic manner for large-scale disaster responses. Open platforms were also used in the Great East Japan Earthquake in 2011, to facilitate information distribution. In practice, information provided through Twitter, including news, shelter and relief supplies information, was mapped and used by support volunteers (e.g., the Sinsai. info maps).

Opportunities and challenges of using geospatial information technology for disaster intelligence

Geospatial information technology enables us to monitor, analyze and visualize the situation of cities or regions and people. Through sharing and visualizing data, the technology can very effectively encourage stakeholders to coordinate their actions to solve social issues. Especially in disaster response and recovery/reconstruction from disaster damage, geospatial information is expected to play a vital role. In addition, more than six billion cellular phone handsets are now widely used across every country and region. GNSS (Global Navigation Satellite System) provides a basis for determining the location of cell phone handsets, while satellite remote sensing, an indispensable tool for mapping, is available everywhere. It suggests systems or solutions based on cell phone systems and space-based technologies such as GNSS, and remote sensing can be easily transferred from one country to others.

On the other hand, the technologies still have a lot of room for further improvement. Continuous efforts such as social experiments and projects are essential in accumulating and sharing experiences and know-how. Three challenges were identified for the successful application of geospatial technology.

Continuous improvements to increase the speed, accuracy and reliability of situational information

It is important to accumulate knowledge and build on previous experiences for more successful applications within society. Two types of situational information are important in this endeavor.

The first type of situational information is related to the physical changes in cities and regions that occur as a consequence of flooding, landslides, building collapse or damage to the infrastructure. This form of situational information may be described as dynamic spatio-temporal information. Sources of information include high-resolution satellite images (e.g., for the mapping of disaster damage) and satellite-borne sensors (e.g., for measuring weather and water-cycle data). High-resolution optical satellite images are now widely used for topographic mapping. High-resolution radar satellites such as ALOS-2 will become available very soon (the satellite was launched in May 2014), making it possible for us to monitor changes in land and sea surfaces, such as flood inundation and crop growth, regardless of weather conditions or cloud cover. An example of applying satellite-monitoring capability to disaster risk management and agricultural monitoring is SAFE or Space Application for Environment by JAXA (Japan Aerospace Exploration Agency).

Precise measurements for earthquakes, such as long-term precise monitoring of crust movements for earthquake risk evaluation and tsunami real-time warning systems, are based on a high-precision real-time positioning system with GNSS (as shown in Figures 13.1 and 13.2). The system is very effective for construction work and land surveys for recovery and reconstruction.

In non-disaster situations, a high-precision positioning system can drastically improve the efficiency and accuracy of surveying, allowing even less experienced operators to operate construction machinery with better accuracy. To implement the high-precision positioning system, it is necessary to set up a network of ground base stations for GNSS to generate correction information for positioning. Another bottleneck in using geospatial information was availability of cheap and reliable data communication. Nowadays, cell phone systems provide a universal solution to collect digital data easily and efficiently – even from remote areas.

A second type of situational information comprises dynamic information on people and vehicle distribution coupled with movement acquired from the position information provided by cellular phone systems. Some developed countries like the US, Japan and France have recently started to use such dynamic information for disaster responses and traffic management (examples of this are shown in Figures 13.3 and 13.4).

In developing countries, dynamic information derived from cell phone systems has great potential. Although there is a lot of room for further improvement, the

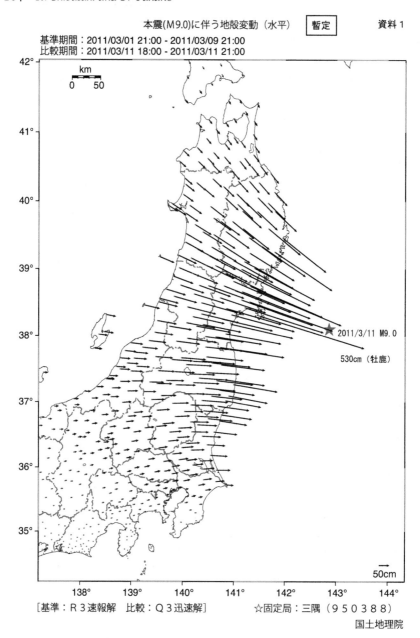

本震(M9.0)に伴う地殻変動 （水平）   暫定   資料 1
基準期間：2011/03/01 21:00 - 2011/03/09 21:00
比較期間：2011/03/11 18:00 - 2011/03/11 21:00

2011/3/11 M9.0

530cm （牡鹿）

50cm

[基準：R3速報解　比較：Q3迅速解]　　　☆固定局：三隅（950388）

国土地理院

Figure 13.1 Horizontal crust movement in Great East Japan Earthquake measured by GSI of Japan.

A high-precision positioning system provides a very reliable basis for land surveys for reconstruction purposes by tracking the changes in ground control points (GSI-Japan 2014).

Source: The Geospatial Information Authority of Japan.

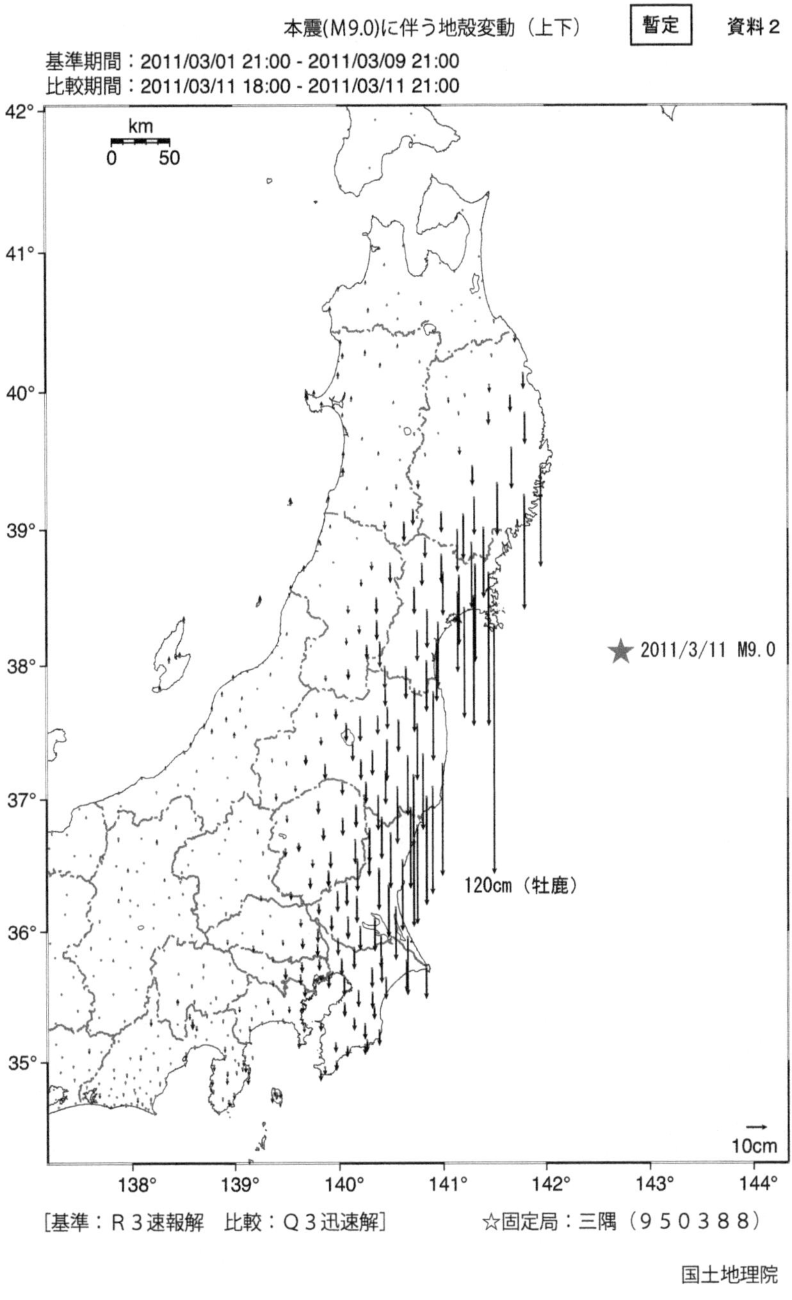

Figure 13.2 Vertical crust movement in Great East Japan Earthquake measured by GSI of Japan (GSI-Japan, 2014)

Source: The Geospatial Information Authority of Japan.

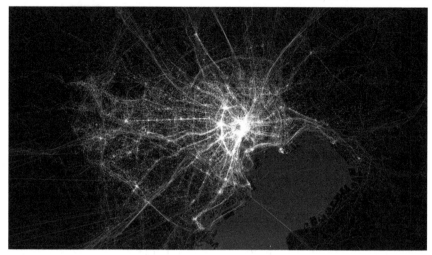

Figure 13.3 Population movement in Tokyo following the Great East Japan Earthquake
        at 14:50

(In Japan, changes in population movement were monitored using data collected
through navigation services. The information will help improve evacuation guidance).

Source: *Disaster Big Data*, edited by Hiroshi Abe and the Production Team of NHK Special
"Disaster Big Data" 2014, NHK Publishing, Inc.

Figure 13.4 Population movement in Tokyo following the Great East Japan Earthquake
        at 15.25

Source: *Disaster Big Data*, edited by Hiroshi Abe and the Production Team of NHK Special
"Disaster Big Data" 2014, NHK Publishing, Inc.

application of data from cell phone systems may be spread in an extremely rapid manner, because there are currently no equivalent data collection systems and very strong demand for such information. The data could have many applications in terms of providing social benefits other than disaster responses. To guide and promote successful applications, social experiments have to be made while ensuring privacy protection and an institutional/legal framework in handling the data.

Accelerate efforts towards data sharing among organizations

As long as data are kept fragmented and used without integration, the values obtained are quite limited. If the data are properly integrated, it could potentially have very large benefits and the information may become increasingly valuable. There has been a lot of progress in the development of technologies to facilitate data sharing, such as network technology and web technology. Comprehensive use of data through data sharing, however, is still rather difficult, mainly because institutional frameworks are not sufficiently well designed to allow solutions to issues such as ways of allocating benefits and costs from data sharing, and of establishing trust among data holders and users. Even within the public sector, data sharing may not be adequate among departments such as the disaster response department, infrastructure department and welfare department. This could result in uncoordinated actions in disaster response and recovery/reconstruction.

The first step is to develop a technical platform to increase the chances for different departments to experience the possible benefits that may be gained through data sharing. They can then gain better recognition of the importance of data sharing and will start to develop an institutional framework. In addition to the NSDI example from Indonesia, successful efforts towards data sharing may be found in the Senegal topographic mapping project supported by JICA. The project aimed at generating digital topographic maps of 1:50,000 to cover the northern part of Senegal (Senegal River basin; about 30,000 square kilometers). In addition to map creation, the project team developed a web-based system to disseminate digital maps, with the goal of increasing the exposure of the maps to public users. It triggered a discussion on the development of NSDI based on open data. These experiences imply that the progress of geospatial information technology can facilitate data sharing among different organizations.

In the case of disasters, data sharing among the public sector, industrial sector and NPOs can also be very important. If the industrial sector and NPOs have very limited access to the information that the public sector has, trust between each sector could be damaged and may accelerate self-oriented actions. In addition, industries like cell phone operators have access to a lot more information than ever before. Thus collaboration among public and industry sectors becomes the key to enriching geospatial information.

Nurture a social framework of collaboration among public agencies, industries, NPOs and citizen communities for disaster risk management, including data sharing and integrated uses

Solving social issues usually requires collaboration among stakeholders. Collaboration should be based on information sharing. However, those who previously collected and managed the information may fear a loss of their monopoly over the information, even though they may subsequently benefit through collaboration. In addition, in the case of personal information, information sharing may threaten privacy. We have to design a fruitful collaboration and information-sharing scheme so that the participating stakeholders can garner sufficient benefits to compensate them for the temporary loss of their power and the risk of privacy violations.

Especially following disasters, communities and individuals may have to cope with situations they have never experienced before and to do so in a very flexible manner. Response to a disaster may require collaboration among organizations and people who are not familiar with each other. We need to anticipate what kinds of collaborations may be necessary to establish a framework for collaboration. This should include defining the roles of each participant, agreement on protocols for information exchange and the development of systems to support information exchange. Such a framework should facilitate the sharing and visualization of information on disaster damage, activities, and the achievements and challenges of each organization, as well as their possible options. Finally, it should encourage them to work as a team in solving common problems.

This framework of collaboration and information sharing can contribute to team capacity building and improvement in the long run as well as supporting teamwork. By recording activities and the consequences for each of the

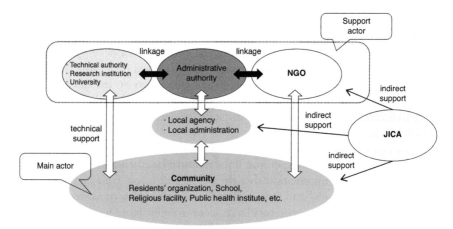

Figure 13.5 Conceptual diagram of community-based disaster risk management actors
Source: JICA (2008).

participating organizations and learning lessons for better actions, team capacity can be improved continuously. By expanding the learning and capacity-building process of society, society will have better disaster intelligence and resilience will be improved. In promoting such ideas, a framework for collaboration is necessary. JICA, for example, has defined the roles and responsibilities of stakeholders, including central government, local government, communities, NGOs, research institutions and universities in promoting disaster risk management (as shown in Figure 13.5). While self-help and the mutual support of community members is at the core of the resilient society, other actors should provide administrative, technical and financial support for such efforts. The goal of this approach is to build the capacity of all actors concerned.

Conclusion

Geospatial information is very closely linked with real-world situations. Through such information, we can monitor what is happening, where, when, how and why. By combining bi-directional communication, we can even guide or control the real world in the same way that we control traffic with traffic signal systems and guide people in evacuations through evacuation information services. The technology has great potential, although there is still a lot of room for further improvements, such as developing methods to more accurately assess situations by integrating large amounts of fragmentary data, and finding ways to minimize the risk of privacy violations without sacrificing the performance of services. It may seem, therefore, that technological advances drive the process of change in society. Nevertheless, the will of people or society should ultimately determine the direction and speed of the implementation of new technologies, because implementation will require some level of social consensus on how the technology should or should not be applied, for what purpose by whom, and how much data and information are to be shared among which parties. Developing numerous successful applications while learning the lessons obtained through the development process should guide healthy development of the technology as well as social wisdom on how to use the technology in a smarter manner.

Recommendation

Geospatial technology based on the data from cellular phones and satellite-based positioning has great potential to improve resilience to disasters. Utilized for the monitoring, analysis and visualization of situations, geospatial information adds significant value in disaster response and recovery. Continuous improvement of the technology is necessary to increase the speed, accuracy and reliability of information. Mechanisms to share information among different organizations should be developed to maximize the effects of such technology.

Audiences of the recommendation: Communities/citizens, NGOs, national governments and donors.

References

Asian Development Bank (ADB). 2009. "Nepal: Institutional Strengthening of Municipalities." Technical Assistance Report, Project Number 42162, Capacity Development Technical Assistance (CDTA). Manila: ADB.

Badan Informasi Geospasial (BIG). 2014. National Spatial Data Infrastructure of Indonesia. http://tanahair.indonesia.go.id/home/, August 22, 2014.

CRS Newswire. 2014. "Early Warning SMS Alerts Coming to Philippines," March 10, 2014. http://newswire.crs.org/early-warning-sms-alerts-coming-philippines/.

Frontline SMS Cloud. 2014. www.frontlinesms.com/, August 22, 2014.

Geospatial Authority of Japan (GSI of Japan). "Crust Movement in Great East Japan Earthquake" (in Japanese). August 22, 2014. www.gsi.go.jp/chibankansi/chikakukansi40005.html.

International Research Institute of Disaster Science (IRIDeS). 2014. Tohoku University, Initial Report of IRIDeS Fact-finding mission to Philippines, May 17, 2014, p. 15. http://irides.tohoku.ac.jp/media/files/IRIDeS_Report_Haiyan_20140527.pdf.

Japan International Cooperation Agency (JICA). 2008. Community Based Disaster Risk Management from the Standpoint of Capacity Development.

Japan International Cooperation Agency (JICA), Aero Asahi Corporation, Asia Air Survey (AAS) Co. Ltd. 2013. "The Study on the Digital Topographic Mapping Project for Northern Senegal." Final Report, March.

Pacific Disaster Center. 2014. "DisasterAWARE Early Warning and Decision Support Platform." August 22, 2014. www.pdc.org/solutions/products/disasteraware/.

Ushahidi. 2014. http://ushahidi.com, August 22, 2014.

Summary

Ian Davis and Kae Yanagisawa

Audiences

Each chapter concludes with recommendations, and the identification of likely intended audiences by the respective chapter authors. We bring these together in the following table and summary. The table below indicates the primary intended audience of each chapter's recommendations; however, it is recognized that other groups may find the advice that is offered useful in their own work.

Table 14.1 makes it clear that the unanimous focus of all the recommendations, as well as the chapters, are of interest to national governments and donors, but it is also apparent that a broad range of groups are being addressed, ranging from local citizens to international agencies and public to private bodies.

Certain concerns may be drawn to the readers' attention with regard to the selection of audiences:

- Only two of the chapters address the private sector, despite its strategic importance at every level. This mirrors the widespread neglect of the private sector as a key element as a cause of vulnerability as well as a key player in risk reduction during the 15 years of the Hyogo Framework for Action (United Nations secretariat of the ISDR 2013).
- While the NGO sector plays an increasingly important role in international disaster risk management, only half the chapters seek to involve the sector in their proposals.
- While all disasters are "local" in their impact, only 5 of the 13 chapter authors focus their recommendations on needs and opportunities at this primary level.

However, these limitations may be explained by the specific nature of the various chapters, where authors have concentrated their attention on their own subject matter in this wide-ranging subject that cuts across all levels of governance, disciplines and hazards.

These varied audiences share in common key roles, unique opportunities, well-defined responsibilities (alas, not in all cases) and a potential concern to reduce the deadly impact of disasters.

Table 14.1 Audiences of Recommendations

Chapters (abbreviated chapter titles)	Communities/citizens	NGOs	Private sector	City governments	National governments	Donors	International agencies	UN secretariat of the ISDR
1. Urbanization and DRR	X			X	X	X	X	
2. Climate change and DRR					X	X	X	X
3. Drought and resilience	X	X			X	X	X	X
4. Effective planning				X	X	X	X	
5. Economic analysis			X		X	X	X	X
6. Culture of DRR	X	X		X	X	X	X	X
7. Recovery and reconstruction		X			X	X	X	X
8. "Build back better" Aceh case study					X	X		
9. Community-driven DRR and governance	X	X		X	X	X	X	X
10. Private sector in DRR			X		X	X		X
11. Disaster risk and governance		X			X	X	X	X
12. Data management	X			X	X	X		
13. Geospatial information	X	X			X	X		X

Recommendations (reproduced from the concluding paragraph of each chapter)

Part I Resilience for sustainable development in a changing environment

Chapter 1 Building resilience to disasters and climate change in the age of urbanization

Cities can increase their resilience if they integrate preventive measures into their urban development processes. Fundamental principles to forge stronger and safer communities include openly sharing risk information for better decisions in urban planning, integrating risk management measures into all sectors, and prioritizing multi-purpose approaches. Balancing and integrating structural and non-structural solutions is a key priority, since improved institutional arrangements, land use planning and ecosystem management are as important as engineered infrastructure solutions.

Chapter 2 Climate change and disaster risk reduction: adaptation to uncertainties of changing climate

In an era of changing climate, adaptation should be pursued with new approaches to respond flexibly to growing and uncertain climate-related disaster risks. A resilient approach will minimize casualties and damage and avoid catastrophic situations even when hazards exceed anticipated levels of severity. A phased approach will entail a flexible response by modifying plans according to new projections and other changes. To facilitate CCA, especially in developing countries, practical guidelines should be prepared by the international community.

Chapter 3 From drought to resilience

ECHO recommends a "people-first" approach to address patterns of chronic vulnerability to avoid recurrent and predictable crisis situations. This calls for longer term and comprehensive development strategies to build household capacities and livelihoods. A broad holistic approach is needed within hazard-prone and fragile contexts by incorporating disaster risk management with ways to reduce poverty and promote sustainable development. This requires the following:

- placing communities and their main duty bearers, such as local governments, at the center of development and humanitarian efforts;
- recognizing and responding to the various needs, capabilities and aspirations of different individuals, households and communities;
- understanding and focusing on social and ecological systems, rather than on individual components of those systems;
- promoting integrated multi-sectoral approaches;
- placing emphasis on longer term investments to tackle the underlying causes of vulnerability.

Part II Building awareness for disaster risk reduction

Chapter 4 Effective planning for disaster risk reduction

Pre-disaster investment in the reduction of risks should be recognized as a critical priority for sustainable development. To make such recognition common, continuous efforts have to be exerted to clearly show the powerful benefits of DRR. Therefore, a strategic and programmatic approach to DRR is crucial to ensure that *ex ante* investment is effective and beneficial with greater attention being paid to the planning stage in the project cycle of DRR.

Chapter 5 Economic analysis of investment in DRR measures

Damage from disasters, both direct and indirect, affects populations and communities, and hinders economic growth and sustainable development. The economic benefits of DRR, expressed in the form of decreased damage, can support governments, strengthen societies and promote stakeholders' understanding of the effectiveness of DRR investment. The international community should join forces in developing datasets, tools and models to clarify relations between economies and disasters to encourage increased investment in DRR.

Chapter 6 Institutionalizing and sharing the culture of prevention: the Japanese experience

Recording the bitter experiences of disasters and the positive effects of countermeasures is the basis of fostering a preventive culture. These experiences, when systematically shared over the generations and across geographical borders, turn into a powerful tool to reduce disasters. The development of national mechanisms for such institutionalization is a necessity, and securing its sustainability and progress over the decades is essential. Furthermore, global action is needed to build international cooperation frameworks to share expertise and transfer a country's experience to others.

Part III Achieving Build Back Better in recovery and reconstruction

Chapter 7 Recovery and reconstruction: an opportunity for sustainable growth through "Build Back Better"

Reconstruction from disasters should be implemented with a clear strategy of reducing the vulnerability of disaster-affected areas and communities. The "Build Back Better" approach has to include a "build back safer" approach, as the essential keys to breaking the negative spiral of disaster and poverty and achieving sustainable development. Competing needs such as the speed in the recovery of livelihoods need to be addressed in a balanced manner so that safety is not compromised.

Chapter 8 Lessons from promoting "Build Back Better" in the post-tsunami recovery of Aceh

To guarantee "building back better" as a priority for reconstruction, there should be an initial focus on ensuring that the governing arrangements for the reconstruction program are founded on high levels of integrity, accountability, transparency and responsiveness. Furthermore, clarity is needed in recovery management to resolve conflicts of interests. This includes an empowered state agency, capable of making informed decisions on reconstruction. This environment enables technical decisions on specifications to be made that produce better reconstruction results.

Part IV Increasing the roles of stakeholders

Chapter 9 Community empowerment and good governance: the way forward for DRM in developing countries

Poor communities in the developing world are trapped in the vicious cycle of poverty and disaster. As such, any effort aiming at sustained community resilience must address the root causes of poverty through a combination of bottom-up and top-down approaches. The disadvantaged communities must be empowered to have access to and control over the public resources to change their life for the better. The service-providing agencies must adhere to the principles of good governance in delivering their services to the people in need.

Chapter 10 The role of the private sector in disaster risk management following catastrophic events

Area-wide disaster management with the significant participation of both private and public sectors is an essential DRM framework to promote economic resilience. This approach will support the continuation of business following a disaster and the early regeneration of local industry. It should include the coordination of all stakeholders in understanding risks, formulating strategies, implementing measures and continually improving the cyclical process of area-wide DRM. To achieve this objective, it is proposed that Area Based Business Continuity Management and Planning (BCM/BCP) be scaled up into a cross-sector coordination framework of disaster risk management to ensure the continuity of area-wide businesses.

Chapter 11 Disaster risk governance and the principles of good governance

A society that can draw on institutional, policy and budgetary means to reduce the impacts of disasters as an inherent component of development will be more resilient to future shocks. For this to happen, a truly "systems approach" to DRM is required that recognizes the multidimensional, multidisciplinary and multi-stakeholder nature of risk, and builds on process-oriented support mechanisms that place governance principles and the political economy of disasters at the center.

Part V Tools and technologies for disaster risk reduction

Chapter 12 National disaster databases: an essential foundation for disaster risk reduction policies and disaster-related sustainable development goals and targets

Systematic approaches to gathering disaster-related data, especially on disaggregated damage and loss, should be developed. This would help develop and monitor international goals and targets for disaster risk reduction and empower governments' efforts in this area at the national level. Based on accurate and dependable disaster statistics, pinpointed evidence-based policy could be produced to reduce disaster risks more effectively. Japan's "white book" on disaster management provides a good example.

Chapter 13 Disaster intelligence: using geospatial technology to improve resilience in developing countries

Geospatial technology based on the data from cellular phones and satellite-based positioning has great potential to improve resilience to disasters. Utilized for the monitoring, analysis and visualization of situations, geospatial information adds significant value in disaster response and recovery. Continuous improvement of the technology is necessary to increase the speed, accuracy and reliability of information. Mechanisms to share information among different organizations should be developed to maximize the effects of such technology.

Key messages

As "content editor" for the book, Ian Davis had the opportunity to read and reread the various chapters, as well as engage with some of the authors as they have developed their chapters. This has been a highly rewarding and informative experience. A number of cross-cutting ideas are expressed and reinforced in the various chapters, but for this final summary a central concern of many authors is selected: the need to integrate disaster risk reduction into all sectors. Following this discussion, the summary will close by considering the goal of the various recommendations.

Integrating or mainstreaming DRR and CCA into planning, policies and structures

One of the three strategic goals of the Hyogo Framework for Action (HFA) was "The integration of disaster risk reduction into sustainable development policies and planning." This is easily stated and clearly understood, but its application has proved to be a challenge to all parties (Lebel *et al.* 2012).

In the chapters, the following forms of integration have been recommended:

- In chapter 1 the authors propose "integrating risk management measures into all sectors" (of urban management).
- In chapter 2 the authors propose that "Strategies to assist developing countries should focus on mainstreaming climate change adaptation measures within other development strategies, incorporating both 'soft' institutional approaches in conjunction with 'hard' structural approaches to reduce vulnerability and exposure."
- In chapter 3 the authors regard "incorporating disaster risk management with ways to reduce poverty and promote sustainable development" as crucial in dealing with situations of chronic vulnerability.
- In chapter 11 a proposal is made that "DRR needs to become an expected and pervasive aspect of all development, giving nations and communities the capacities to identify risk and to take meaningful steps to identify and implement risk reducing and preparedness measures."

Further examples calling for integration or mainstreaming may be extracted from the other chapters, but these examples are sufficient to reveal the variety of forms of integration of risk reduction that are being proposed. Integration of DRR and CCA is needed in "all sectors," "development strategies," "poverty reduction measures" and in "sustainable development."

This poses a pair of questions: Why is the mainstreaming of DRR encountering so many difficulties (Benson 2009)? What advice can this book offer to the new phase of disaster risk reduction following the WCDRR in Sendai?

In 2005, Stephen Lewis, who was the United Nations Secretary-General's special envoy for HIV/AIDS in Africa, wrote about the problem of mainstreaming in relation to incorporating the needs of women into the UN and governmental programs to address the HIV/AIDS crisis. He wrote:

> Instead of bona fide, specializing programs, women get "gender mainstreaming," and gender mainstreaming is a pox for women. The worst thing you can do women is fold their concerns into the mandates of UN agencies, or bury them under the activities of government ministries. Once you've mainstreamed gender, it's everybody's business and no one's business. Everyone's accountable and no one's accountable. I don't know who thought up this mainstreaming guff, but I often wonder what the motives were. And even if the motives were well meaning, surely experience has proved how damaging to women mainstreaming truly is. We've mainstreamed women's needs into some kind of shibboleth, and can someone tell me how those needs have been better served by doing so?

(Lewis 2005, 125–126)

Lewis was writing about gender concerns, not about mainstreaming DRR, but his critique needs to be carefully digested and applied. He observes that there is a pervasive problem whenever you seek to integrate some cause, need or mandate into broad, well-established policies or operational practice. He claimed that there is the inherent risk that in so doing the intended cause inevitably becomes buried as "everybody's business and no one's business. Everyone's accountable and no one's accountable."

Ian Davis recalls a difficult assignment he was given in 1997 that grew out of the International Decade for Natural Disaster Reduction (IDNDR). This involved a visit by the key geographical desk officers in the UK government's Department for International Development (DFID) which were in areas subject to high hazard threats. The task was to discuss with the leaders of each regional cooperation program how disaster risk reduction strategies and measures could be integrated or mainstreamed into their planning processes. The result was a totally depressing experience as each hard-pressed and impatient official virtually showed me the door, since they claimed that they were saturated with the demands of various activists, pressure groups and officials in other relevant government departments who demanded that their particular causes should also be mainstreamed. These causes, all lining up for full integration into project planning and implementation, included such matters as gender concerns, human rights, environmental biodiversity protection, democratization, participatory decision making, etc.

Thus, mainstreaming of DRR always has to compete with other agendas, with pressure groups and advocates behind them, to persuade governments to build, and fund, their particular cause into their policies and structures. As a result, "saturation points" may be reached and may be one explanation why "mainstreaming" has been so sluggish. In the past there has been inadequate recognition that "mainstreaming" cannot just be added according to some official diktat. Rather, the process inevitably requires additional tasks and responsibilities on the part of planning authorities, etc. and that requires significant additional funding for staffing and administration.

There is, of course, no doubting the importance of our author's demands for integration, since that battle has been soundly won during the IDNDR and the HFA, and nobody would now doubt the need for a ministry of education to have the responsibility to ensure that their schools are safe and that children are taught about ways to protect themselves when an earthquake occurs. But the concern remains, as Stephen Lewis has expressed it so vividly, that mainstreaming DRR must never remove responsibility and accountability. Thus, in the forthcoming HFA2, detailed attention is needed by ISDR, governments and donors to ensure that, *in addition to mainstreaming*, effective task forces or bodies are created within each hazard-prone country that will nurture and protect DRR and CCA from neglect, ensuring that it is always somebody's business and specific responsibility.

This concept of national focal points is particularly complex, given the diversity of structural, non-structural and environmental ways to reduce risks. For example, in the building sector alone, this diversity embraces safety by-law enforcement, land use planning controls, training of designers/builders/enforcement officers and building occupants, quality control, selection of materials, structural and detailed design, maintenance requirements, etc. But despite this demanding challenge, creative ways may still be found to ensure that safe and good building occurs. David Oakley, an international consultant, put his finger on the issue when he wisely stated that "every good idea, every important cause needs a secure home."

Thus, all hazard-prone countries need integration in order to institutionalize DRR and build a preventive culture, as described so effectively in chapter 6. But to avoid the risk of DRR and CCA being lost without trace or suffering neglect in the maze of other pressing governmental priorities, there is also the need for "homes," "focal points," "coordinating bodies," etc. to ensure that disaster protection is kept in the forefront of concern by all the audiences of this study. The nature and anatomy of these bodies requires careful study. Will they be public or private bodies? Will they be best positioned inside or outside governments – or perhaps in universities? Will they have budgets and enabling powers, and what will be their responsibility in relation to the powerful relevant government departments and local governments with responsibility for the implementation and hazard protection of housing, health, education, etc. through mainstreamed delegation?

The goal of the recommendations

The ultimate goal of DRR is to achieve sustainable development through building resilience against natural disasters. To reach this goal, the international community should join forces in promoting investment in disaster risk reduction, especially in the pre-disaster stage. In particular, there is ample room for donors and international organizations to support developing countries to cope with disasters. The following opportunities exist:

- First, donors and international organizations can play a pivotal role in knowledge sharing. Through their rich experiences on the ground, donors and international organizations have built knowledge base and lessons learned from a wide range of countries and regions. These lessons should be adequately packed and presented to the world so that developing countries can save the time of learning. In addition, donors and international organizations can contribute to the development of internationally agreed guiding principles such as the post-2015 DRR framework, based on their practical experience around the world.
- Second, donors and international organizations can facilitate partnership among actors with broader backgrounds. Communities and businesses are not just victims of disasters or passive beneficiaries of DRR measures; rather, they should be main actors in promoting DRR. National and local governments should work together with communities and businesses so that more effective DRR may be promoted. Moreover, science and technology can play an active role in DRR. Academics and researchers should be welcomed into

the DRR community to provide innovative and easily available technologies. The broader partnership will also promote participation in decision-making and provide mutual accountability.

- Third, capacity development of DRR-related actors needs to be enhanced. Governments both at national and local levels should develop their capacities in evidence-based policymaking and planning. Communities and businesses should enhance risk awareness and strengthen their coping capacity. Donors and international organizations should further strengthen support for these efforts. In doing so, guidelines and principles developed in other parts of the world should be shared through effective reference material and local guidance.

- Finally, it should be noted that DRR is in fact a continual learning process. In the era of rapid economic growth, urbanization and climate change, it is not realistic to rely on principles and methodologies in a static manner. While applying them on the ground, their effectiveness should always be monitored and changes should follow continuously. In this sense, donors and international organizations should also keep learning and continually improve their practices.

This book has covered much ground, raised many issues and proposed a series of policies and practical actions. It is the hope of all the contributors to this book that our various ideas, findings and recommendations will be both useful and usable to a wide range of readers. We share together in the urgent global need to reduce the escalating impact of hazards upon people, property and our fragile natural environment. Such progress is essential to ensure a sustainable future.

References

Benson, C. 2009. *Mainstreaming DRR into Development. Challenges and Experience in the Philippines*. Geneva: ProVention Consortium.

Lebel, L., Li, L. and Krittasudthacheewa, L. 2012. *Mainstreaming Climate Change Adaptation into Development Planning*. Bangkok: Adaptation Knowledge Platform and Stockholm Environment Institute.

Lewis, S. 2005. *Race Against Time*. Toronto: House of Ansai Press Inc. and HarperCollins.

United Nations secretariat of the International Strategy for Disaster Reduction (ISDR). 2013. *From Shared Risk to Shared Value: The Business Case for Disaster Risk Reduction*. Global Assessment Report. Geneva: United Nations.

Index

Figures and Tables are indicated by *italic page numbers*: Boxes by **bold numbers**; notes by suffix 'n' (e.g. "62n[16]" means "page 62, note 16"). Abbreviations: CCA = climate change adaptation; DRM = disaster risk management; DRR = disaster risk reduction.

For Product Safety Concerns and Information please contact our
EU representative GPSR@taylorandfrancis.com Taylor & Francis
Verlag GmbH, Kaufingerstraße 24, 80331 München, Germany